What Gender Is, What Gender Does

What Gender Is, What Gender Does

Judith Roof

University of Minnesota Press
Minneapolis • London

Portions of chapter 1 were previously published as "Working Gender/ Fading Taxonomy," *Genders* 44 (December 2006): 1–33; reprinted with permission. Portions of chapter 4 were previously published as "Living the James Bond Lifestyle," in *Ian Fleming and James Bond: The Cultural Politics of 007*, ed. Edward P. Comentale, Stephen Vatt, and Skip Willman, 71–86 (Bloomington: Indiana University Press, 2005); reprinted courtesy of Indiana University Press; all rights reserved.

Published by the University of Minnesota Press
111 Third Avenue South, Suite 290
Minneapolis, MN 55401-2520
http://www.upress.umn.edu

Printed in the United States of America on acid-free paper

The University of Minnesota is an equal-opportunity educator and employer.

21 20 19 18 17 16   10 9 8 7 6 5 4 3 2 1

Library of Congress Cataloging-in-Publication Data
Roof, Judith.
What gender is, what gender does / Judith Roof.
Minneapolis : University of Minnesota Press, 2016. |
Includes bibliographical references and index.
Identifiers: LCCN 2015019387 | ISBN 978-0-8166-9857-8 (hc) |
    ISBN 978-0-8166-9858-5 (pb)
Subjects: LCSH: Gender identity. | Sex role. | Sex differences (Psychology).
Classification: LCC BF692.2 .R66 2015 | DDC 155.3/3—dc23
LC record available at http://lccn.loc.gov/2015019387

Contents

Preface

Genders are neither binary nor essential. Nor are they singular, unchanging, invariable, inherent, or flatly definitive. Genders are not names, labels, or identities; they are neither nouns nor adjectives. Gender is a verb, a process. Genderings constantly change. Individuals are always more than one gender. These multiple genderings are culturally intelligible.

To gender is to signal, mask, obscure, suggest, mislead, misrecognize, and simplify the uncontainable, uncategorizable chaos of desires and incommensurabilities characteristic of subjects, but energetically contained by society. Gender's job is always to make the subject fit.

Insofar as one of two binary gender distinctions tends to stand in for and obscure the complex negotiations genders represent, "to gender" is always to reduce, locate, and simplify processes that extend through history from the psychical terrain of the subject to the sociocultural manifestations, ramifications, imperatives, and possibilities attached to genders' binary resolutions.

Acknowledgments

This book comes from the insights and help of many friends whom I thank for their willingness to read and discuss. These include Brian Holcomb, Michelle Parke, Kristina Quynn, Melissa Fore, Lance Norman, Jaime Hovey, Crandall, Fedwa Malti-Douglas, renée hoogland, Jackie Stacey, Jonathan Eburne, Seth Morton, Alex Adkins, Laura K. Richardson, Robin Blyn, David Baulch, Etienne Lambert, Atia Sattar, Colleen Lamos, and Joe Campana. I thank especially Dennis Allen, Cary Wolfe, Alanna Beroiza, Karen Jacobs, Magen Eisenstadt, and Melissa Bailar. And Hannah Biggs, without whom I could never have prepared the final manuscript.

Introduction

Genders are neither binary nor essential. Nor are they singular, unchanging, invariable, inherent, or flatly definitive. Genders are not names, labels, or identities; they are neither nouns nor adjectives. Gender is a verb, a process. Genderings constantly change. Individuals are always more than one gender. These multiple genderings are culturally intelligible.

To gender is to signal, mask, obscure, suggest, mislead, misrecognize, and simplify the uncontainable, uncategorizable chaos of desires and incommensurabilities characteristic of subjects, but energetically contained by society. Gender's job is always to make the subject fit.

Insofar as one of two binary gender distinctions tends to stand in for and obscure the complex negotiations genders represent, "to gender" is always to reduce, locate, and simplify processes that extend through history from the psychical terrain of the subject to the sociocultural manifestations, ramifications, imperatives, and possibilities attached to genders' binary resolutions.

Most of the examples of genders in this book come from popular cultural texts, a changing terrain if ever there was one. Popular culture texts most unwittingly provide examples of gendering trends and styles. The benefit of these examples is that most people will recognize them. The detriment is that such examples become out-of-date rapidly. Hence this book will seem always to be behind the times, but then genders, too, are always changing.

How to Use This Book

Genders are dynamics, persistent sets of operations that link individual desires to multiple, shifting manifestations of sociocultural positioning and self-presentation. These manifestations include narratives of cultural and familial roles, sexual desires (both of the subject and of those for whom the subject is a potential object), economic and political interpellations (i.e., questionnaires), commodified styles, peer mimeticism, imaginaries of identity and the body, and occasional performances. Genders' operations are both conscious and unconscious. They are simultaneously conventional and idiosyncratic. More than one gender dynamic operates at a time in any individual, and these dynamics constantly morph depending on broad context; sociocultural environments such as race, class, religion, education, ethnic tradition, and relative wealth; other cooperating dynamics (social and peer groups, family and local tradition, available popular cultural models); age; idiosyncratic circumstances; and an individual's own history and psychical structurations, desires, and responses. Gender is multiple, chatoyant, messy, and very, very provisional, yet at the same time, seemingly binary.

Because gender is unfixable, much cultural energy goes into to trying to "fix" it. Even apparently countercultural discourses such as "queer" are concepts that find a place for this unfixable gender to stay fixed in the binary normative/queer, even if as an "unfixed" portion of the equation. But if gender, as it operates in and through the subject and culture, is not reducible to any standard, structurally useful binary—male/female, feminine/masculine, normative/queer—what then? What happens to the systems—family, capitalism, reproduction, religion, economics—that genders subtend (and which in turn binarize genders) if we rethink genders as something other than the stylistic and/or identitarian correlative to biological sex? Although, as always, one cannot simply recast a part to change a larger set of apparently inert formations (such as sexual difference or heteronormativity), what if this nonbinary gender multiplicity has been functioning as an intrinsic element in sex/gender organizations all along? If we understand genders as multiple and changing instead of complementary, as a process instead of an ontology, as a flux instead of a stable identification or interpellation, then this binarizing impetus is only one mode of gendering, among others. One function of gendering is to process the messy back into structure's dualistic protocols. How might thinking of gendering as effecting multiple, morphing, and chatoyant presentations alter the ways we think about gender categories, desires, sexualities, and subjectivity? Could admitting what we already know—that there are more than two genders and that these genders are culturally intelligible and operant—change conceptions of the structural "truths"— reproduction, sex, "God's plan"—that gender binaries appear to front? What social and psychical gains might there be should this shift come about?

Genders' apparent binary consistency is the effect of a defensive, taxonomic gender process (one among many) that perpetually re-sorts (and reinterprets) all complex gender operations, manifestations, and presentations back into comprehensible dual alignments of bodies, cultural structures—such as the imaginary of reproduction—and conventional gender displays.[1] This taxonomic dynamic (or "regime") operates both culturally and intrapsychically. Binary gender appears as natural, preexistent, and necessary—as a cultural given that enables the orderly playing out of various meta-narratives (e.g., reproduction, family, capitalism) that both depend on and produce gender as a set of complementary opposites. Although this taxonomic impetus perpetually reasserts gender binaries, it is no more central or dispositive than other regimes of intelligible, cooperative genderings. Despite the apparent comforts of binary organizations, we also constantly recognize and interpret a plethora of other modes of gendering as well as understand the complex subjectivities, desires, and positions they present. Why do we know what "gym teacher" means? How do we understand the beauty queen or the "mean girl"? Who was Paul Lynde or James Bond? How do we understand Jane Lynch, Lady Gaga, or Hillary Clinton? Or the genders of Sheldon Cooper, Howard Wolowitz, and Raj Koothrappali on *The Big Bang Theory*? Or Tyler Perry's self-transformational capacities?

As the continuously revising effect of complex cultural and psychical operations, gendering is a constantly evolving amalgamation of systems, regimes, and structures loaded with shifting dynamics, registers, vectors, and variables. Just as genders do not comply with genomes or hormones, so they are not merely the products of kinship taboos, reproductive scenarios, or religious strictures. These latter formations, understood structurally, supply a part of the symbolic material in relation to which individuals might understand gender possibilities, but they do not define or delimit the genderings that ensue.[2] Instead, these symbolic categories are necessary because genders are rarely compliant; the insistence of ideological formations is an effect of the degree to which subjects do not easily align with, submit to, or emerge from the simplified, binary, regulatory roles of such imperative systems. Genders afford the broad terrain through which an individual's interpretations, both conscious and unconscious, of the relation between mind and body, self and other, and subject and socius manifest as provisional positionings and protocols of desire. Genders enable and signal individual desires, affinities, and sociocultural locations.

As complex dynamics that negotiate the subject's relations to itself and to the larger culture, genders operate through and are generated in relation to all available sociocultural matrices. Genderings manifest through images, narratives, categories, divisions, acts, styles, fantasies, imperatives, and symbolic structures. They are simultaneously unconscious and conscious; subjects perpetually generate them anew from intra-psychic material and imitate cultural possibilities. While on the one hand, genders constitute the very terms through which representation—and especially narrative as an epistemology of meaning—might seem to function, on the other hand, they appear to subtend sociocultural intelligibility while distracting from the impossibility of compliance. Genderings hide the fact that they never organize what they seem to organize— that the reproductive binary that genders front is as much a fiction as the binary types necessary to the tidy dualisms of the sex/gender narrative. In seeming to do what they do, genders never do what we think they are doing. Insofar as genders express a subject's positionings and desires within the range of possible expressions, they also never succeed in this expression. Insofar as genders' appearances signal everything from a subject's sociocultural position to its biological reality, genders are always mis-taken, operating on the objective plane of the fantasies of others.[3] Although subjects express through appearance and behaviors, their demeanors are never what they think they are. In short, genders are not only noncompliant and disparate; they are also approximations, open to perpetual adjustment. This approximate quality makes it difficult to define genders, as we never think we are defining what we think we are defining. Genders and subjects slip out. In the end we guess, we categorize; hence the comforts of a clean binary certainty that seems to line up everything.

Nor do genders constitute a closed system that would enable some outside perspective, some capability of enlisting genders' possibilities and operations.[4] No one can stand outside of gender and describe it, since there is no outside and there is no one (given that our very concept of the subject as always already gendered) who could occupy a vantage that is not already a part of genders' systems. Even if subjects define themselves as Tiresian, as the subject who "has looked at life from both sides now," this perspective is only one regime among genders' many. Although this Tiresian regime seems to stand outside, observing genders' various manifestations—its categorical masquerades, its performance of the provisional securities of identity fictions, the delusively clear terrain of genders' oppositions that sustains so many of our sense-making projects (narrative, epistemology, subjectivity), this chimeric perspective is a gender regime like all the others and, hence, is not outside genders' systems at all.

Genders beyond Structuralism

But how to lay out the complexities of genders without inadvertently returning to a binary habit? How to describe the various regimes by which genders organize themselves without making these appear as an extended taxonomy of equally definitive typologies or categories? And how to do this without making the possibilities seem more definitive—more leading, more expressive, more a matter of choice—than they are? Perhaps models of dynamic processes will serve better than the structuralisms of narrative, anthropology, performance, psychological formulations—such as melancholia or narcissism, or even the processual ossifications of popularized science (genes, for example), all of which thinkers have deployed in one way or another to account for and describe the acquisition of gender.[5] Rethinking genders requires at least two endeavors: (1) reconsidering gender as a process, what genders do, and how they do it; and (2) rethinking the concepts and assumptions by which we understand the intersections of the social, the psychical, cultural imaginaries, and subjectivities. This is necessary insofar as we understand binary gender itself as a structure intrinsic to most structuralist understandings of meaning and subjectivity. If we are to see genders outside of their autopoiesis (i.e., outside of their persistent binary homeostasis via narrative and structuralism in general), we need to deploy modes of thinking that are no longer binary and structuralist, and that allow for the coexistence of multiple, inter-inflective dynamics. This invites the appropriation of concepts from the work of Gilles Deleuze and Félix Guattari, principles from systems theory, and insights from Jacques Lacan's formulations of the subject, its sexuation, and the systemic character of the links between individual psychical systems, available symbolic materials, and the social. These approaches share an attention to post-structural complexity and an understanding of phenomena as multiple, inseparable, inter-inflective, and difficult to delineate.

Just as genders are complex and without beginning or end, the following chapters might be read in any order, especially to avoid the tendency to return genders' multiple regimes to a binary taxonomy, sets of accruing categories, or a series of descriptors like ice cream flavors. Keeping the following set of precepts in mind will help keep genders' dynamic, systemic, complex, and changing character in play:

1. The chapters in this book can be read in any order, after this first one.
2. The book is organized according to some of the grounding dynamics or "regimes" of gender, which, though defined and discussed separately, are entangled, inter-constitutive, nonexclusive, and multiply inflective—that is, rarely isolated or crystal clear, and changing their manifestations as one reads. Although various gender regimes have provisional thematic names, remember that regimes are dynamics, slants, and/or filters organized

around actions, vectors, attitudes (in the aeronautical sense), and motifs, and thus do not constitute the categories of anything like a finished "product" or status.

3. No subject participates in only one gender regime.

4. An individual's genderings change through time. Gender regimes change through time.

5. An individual's genderings change from context to context. Gender regimes morph from context to context.

6. The intersections of gender regimes produce infinite gender variation. Gender variation produces infinite manifestations of any given regime.

7. Individuals accede to genderings in multiple and often contradictory unconscious and conscious ways, including unconscious intra-psychic processes such as sexuation, social pressures, (apparently) conscious choice, unwitting (and hence paradoxical) performative gestures, strategic deployments, irony, and resistance. How individuals participate in this gender system is a part of the organizing dynamics themselves. The primary dynamic of any regime defines its enregisterment—the perceptual order around which the regime organizes (i.e., the scopic is visual, metamorphosis is temporal, etc.).

8. No one ever completely fits a gender regime; no gender regime ever completely fits a binary taxonomy. There is always a remainder. There is always a mis-take.

9. Any notion of regime will always be slightly out of date, as regimes change constantly. We only apprehend a regime as such once it has shifted to something else.

What Gender Is

When we talk about "gender," we seem to know what we are talking about. No one questions what gender itself might be. The word "gender" derives from the Latin root, *genus*, meaning "kind." *Genus* is also the root of the verb "engender," referring to reproduction. Gender is, thus, both effect and process, the hallmark of autopoiesis, or the self-reproduction of systems.[6] In Western cultures, "gender" seems to have a standard meaning, referring to whether someone is a girl or a boy, a man or a woman. Or is that feminine or masculine? Or female or male? We use the term "gender" to refer to these various categorical distinctions without making much of a distinction, but each of the three groupings refers to a different phenomenon with significant social, material, and psychical stakes and effects. "Girl, boy, woman, man" constitute social categories produced as the oppositions that moor systems ranging from kinship to commodity culture, reproduction, and law. These terms are naturalized as imaginary correlatives of the biological categories of "male and female" sex, which are defined as such on the basis of a particular reproductive scenario involving two kinds of synecdochizing gametes (discovered much later in the history of concepts about reproduction), which themselves are usually, but not always, produced by two slightly different versions of the same organism. We imagine that this reproductive scenario subtends social formations that reflect it, such as the patriarchal nuclear family. Masculine and feminine represent the two categories of a binary, taxonomic gender, which may or may not align with "male" and "female." Of all of the terms above, only these two refer to gender; the rest refer to sex. The term "sexual difference" refers to a binary sexual distinction between bodies that underwrites the sets of sexual genderings that seem to follow. Slippages between sex and gender enable the cultural imperative that binary genders reflect ineffable biological conditions; such confusions also subtend such formations as transgender and transsexuality.[7]

We treat biological sex as more materially based than the sociocultural categories of gender, and, thus, it seems to offer definitive somatic correlatives to social categories, from which we then imagine the social categories arise. We assume a causal line from a genotype (XX or XY), to bodies' hormonal and physiological reflection of that genotype, to sets of culturally defined predilections and stereotypes (the ever-present insistence on pink and blue), to reproductive roles, physical and emotional capabilities, rules of deportment, intelligence, and social support systems. We go from the molecular to the cultural as if seamlessly, male/female subtending masculine/feminine.

Different cultures have differing understandings of the relation between sex and gender. The United States, for example, tends to see the relation between biological sex and gender as causal and naturalized, while in some parts of western Europe the sex/gender link may be more displaced from biology. In almost every culture there are exceptions that prove the rule. Any alignment of these binaries—any appeal to "nature" or "God's plan"—requires that we ignore the spectrum of less oppositional biological possibilities such as hermaphroditism and intersex, opportunistic sex (one changes sex depending on the environment), or no sex at all linked to a wide variety of reproductive mechanisms (from cell fission to the development of unfertilized eggs). Only by ignoring biology's alternatives to binary sexual difference can we use biology as a foundation for other conceptions of binary gender.[8] Although, as far as we know, humans reproduce only via sexual reproduction, the nuclear family, imagined as support and correlative for this process (as well as rationalized by it), takes many forms that do not reflect any strictly heteronormative reproductive structure—extended families, matriarchal families, adoptive families, gay and lesbian families, single parents, et cetera.

As "femininity and masculinity," binary gender also refers to culturally available interpretations of individual positionings in relation to desire and sexual difference, both through various social interpellations and "sexuation," an intra-psychical process outlined by Jacques Lacan, through which individuals link mind and body in relation to sexual difference as both a social structure and the scaffold for possible desires.[9] Sexuation's interpretations provide some of the feeling of coherence among the fictions of individual identity, social roles, bodies, and desires. These fictions are organized by and apparently unified, redundant institutional formations aligned with one another around a single axis of oppositional (read sexual) difference (male/female, masculine/feminine, capital/labor). Even though the broad taxonomies of masculinity and femininity exist as a range of expressions displayed through an elaborate lexicon of styles and behaviors, the binary character of this gender epistemology defines and delimits the terrain of individual sexual desires. Culturally, the narratives of desire encoded through binary

interpretations of sex/gender push toward the union of fantasmatically complementary opposites premised on an imaginary of reproductive function.

Individuals, however, interpret their own relation to desires and
fantasies in multiple and conflicting ways, so that even if cultures
tend to be rigidly heteronormative, a wide range of sexual desires
and identities still operate. The alignment of binary concepts of sex/
gender with sociocultural meta-narratives provisionally recontains
this range of desires. An obvious example of this recontainment
occurs when same-sex desires are defined as sexual "inversions,"
or when same-sex partners interpret their own roles within a relationship as male/female or masculine/feminine.[10] "Which one is
the boy?" Individuals may indeed consciously interpret their positions, relations, and identities via the cultural effects of binary
genderings. But even if binary positionings represent the psychical
interpretations of individuals, these interpretations result from and
are enabled by what is available at any given time within cultures
as parts of symbolic and imaginary formations. Hence turn-of-the-
century lesbians might have perceived themselves as inverts, while
'70s lesbians rejected all aspects of patriarchy. The point is that such
interpretations derive precisely from binary organizations of sexual
difference, whether they pervert, reinterpret, appropriate, liberate,
or travesty them.

Cultural meta-narratives—reproduction, capitalist production,
and the structure of narrative itself—transform complex and multifarious phenomena into generic categories whose interrelation
makes sense only within a model of opposition/joinder/product.[11]
Gender is already inflected by a logic that assumes the complementary contribution of "opposites" premised on the interaction of
binary "kinds" glossed reproductively. Understanding (re)produc-
tion as the combining of opposites to a productive end characterizes the broad strokes of capitalism (labor and capital = product),
reproduction (male and female = child), and story (protagonist
and antagonist = result). Insofar as a specifically binary notion of
gender is necessary to enable these meta-narratives, so these meta-
narratives produce gender as binary—but only because genders always threaten to escape, exceed, and evade this structural capture.

What Gender Does

Because we assume that human reproduction—and, echoing its imaginary model, romance—requires two sexes, we must understand gender, too, within the same apparently complementary, binary matrix. It is difficult to tell, however, which comes first. Do we understand reproduction the way we do because sexual difference works as a complementary binary, do we gloss reproduction through the gender imperatives of other cultural formations, or are both of these the products of a binary mode of thinking? Just as products differ from the processes of their production, so gender as processual is not the same as reproductive engendering. By confusing and conflating the registers of the biological, sociocultural, and psychical, what we think of as gender stands in place of the transposition of these registers. Gender is the seemingly stable category that masks the impossible process of aligning individual bodies with sociocultural norms. It is also the systemic effect of that misalignment. The gender system works constantly to negotiate and balance the intersections of different orders (body, society, subjectivity), making them appear aligned, commensurate, natural, and productive, helping to produce oppositions out of confusing multiplicities, and organizing disparate bodies to sustain the imaginary binaries of social and cultural organization.

Although we may want to distinguish scrupulously among the biological, the social, and the cultural, the phenomena we refer to as "gender" belong as much to the confusions, intricacies, imaginary lines of causation, and even similarities among these registers as they do to binary, sociocultural notions of masculinity and femininity. The confusions among categories circulate through and help constitute the prerogatives, practices, and styles of masculinity and femininity both as possible interpretations of subjective positioning and, as themselves, the end product of a much more varied, yet intelligible range of kinds. In this way, gender works to suture the social and symbolic processes of culture to the psychical processes of the individual. Gender, then, is one set of processes by which individuals locate themselves both consciously and unconsciously in relation to a plethora of social systems whose reliance on fictions of complementarity require a certain side-taking. The social system, for example, offers ready-made interpretations of sexual difference—pink, blue—that precede (but which do not define) an infant's encounter with its own difference (from others, from itself). The sets of analogies forged among the various binaries that enable, for example, a woman to become a feminine wife, are not in fact rigid or definitive. Rather, the whole dilemma of gender is that these binaries, though pervasive and apparently controlling, only tenuously organize a polymorphousness that always threatens to escape as chaos.

As genders' homeostasis, binarism appears to ground genders' interpretation of sexual difference; but this binarism also provides the state of asymmetrical imbalance toward which gender systems incline insofar as cultures tend to value one gender (read sex) more highly than the other. The interpretation of difference, whether such process is subjective or cultural, is never symmetrical and never arrives at equality or equanimity. Difference's inherent asymmetricality is counterintuitive insofar as dialectical ideologies (yin/yang, for example) seem to perform the complementarity and interdependence that would signal an equilibrium. The problem is that difference is not dialectical. It does not belong to a realm of balance, but, rather, it destroys balance in its advent as a difference that preserves the same. For Gilles Deleuze and Félix Guattari, "oppositional difference is the same, it is the form of the same: it is the most abstract form of expression of society's homogenizing tendencies"[12] For Jacques Lacan, the advent of difference forces the production of a subjective dynamic in relation to a world that was at one point a universe of sameness that is no longer the same.[13] The advent of difference precipitates sexuation, the psychical processes that constitute the mind and link it to the body.

As an articulation of, or perhaps more accurately, a displacement of, difference, gender offers the register through which intrapsychic processes link to social and cultural possibilities. Although parts of a larger system that inflects them, subjects encounter difference as a condition of their being, and depending on whether one is Deleuze and Guattari or Lacan, that difference makes a difference. For Deleuze and Guattari, gender difference is "done unto it by the

socius." "Gendering is the process by which a body is socially determined to be determined by biology: social channelization cast
as destiny by being pinned to anatomical difference."[14] Deleuze and
Guattari would prefer hypersingularity—that every subject is indeed uniquely different—over binary gender classifications. They
laud the "heteroclite" instead of the gendered, envisioning a culture
of "hyperdifferentiation" in which no pre-set value can delimit becoming. In a sense, this hyperdifferentiation already exists but is
moderated precisely by the homeostasis of cultural systems (such as
gender) that pressures the larger classification of individual differences and from which individuals adapt various modes of individual
differentiation. The problem with Deleuze and Guattari's notion of
the heteroclite is a problem of will and timing. At what point can
individuals choose to be completely different from every other classification? Are individual subjects even in conscious control of this?
Is there any possible way subjects can mess with the system without
reiterating it?

Sexuation; or, The Psyche Meets the Social

Lacan would agree there is indeed hyperdifferentiation, insofar as
each individual finds its own relation to difference. In Lacanian psychoanalysis, however, the range of possible dynamics is defined by
a logic of sexuation, which involves a complex negotiation among
orders that cannot be traded for either a wider or more indetermi-
nate range of operations such as Deleuze and Guattari suggest. Individuals cannot escape their social symbolic contexts. As an incipient
event in the individual's coming into being as a subject, there is, according to Lacan, a point at which something interrupts the subject's
imaginary oneness with everything and the subject splits, becoming aware of its difference from the environment and from others.
The holistic imaginary of pre-mirror-stage infants is disturbed at
the moment the infant subject realizes its potential separateness.
The "primordial identification of a child," then, as Lacan interprets
Freud, "is to difference or Otherness whose referents are symbolic-
order signifiers."[15]

　　In systems terms, the primordial psyche, which exists in a state of oneness with its environment, suddenly encounters this environment as a difference that destroys its sense of being one with the world. This forces the psyche to incorporate its relation to the difference of the environment within its psychical system. The difference, introduced as the subject's relation to the environment, comes to define the psychic system itself, which interprets the psyche/environment relation in terms of signifiers representing difference. This difference is interpreted as sexual difference, which is itself defined by its inherent asymmetries. The key signifier of sexual difference's asymmetry is what Lacan calls the "Phallus," a signifier (rather than an organ) that stands in for having it all in cultures whose symbolic order locates wholeness on the side of what can be seen.[16] As the visible manifestation and, hence, signifier of difference itself, the Phallus becomes the signifier of lack and impossible fulfillment that subtends identifications and desire. The ways that subjects position themselves in relation to this phallic signifier, which also links the operations of language to difference, also defines the direction of their desire.[17] This increasingly complex knot of difference (difference from the environment, difference as grounding and inciting language, differences delineated around the phallic signifier) results in logics of desire and individual positioning that occur in relation to the incompleteness represented by the signifier, which perpetually substitutes for something else and at the same time marks a continual differentiation. And as Lacan reminds us, the "cut" made by the introduction of difference can never be repaired; subjects can only ever keep trying, keep desiring.

For Lacan, subjective identity, including gender "identity," is a way to resolve the effects of sexual difference and lack by identifying with what the subject imagines it has lost. Subjects try to patch lack by identifying with a range of possible objects. What these objects are and the position the subject takes in relation to the problem of difference (interpreted as the asymmetries of sexual difference) produces a range of sexuations as solutions to the problem of difference, lack, and the subject's position in relation to difference. Subjects locate themselves as male/all, female/not all, and (but not necessarily in a correlative way) as masculine/active and feminine/passive. As Ellie Ragland summarizes, "Masculine and feminine distinctions are determined not by 'psychic' essence or behavior, nor by any pre-given active or passive behavior(s) or attitude(s), including homosexual or heterosexual 'postures,' but as gender nonspecific identifications as lover (active) or beloved (passive)."[18] "Lover" and "beloved" orient desires and modes of desiring that become drives. Structuring around desire defines the subject's inclination, instead of such inclinations deriving from any "natural" sexed predisposition. Thus, within Lacan's versions of a systemic subject, individual interpretations of sexual difference can result in a large number of positional permutations in relation to drives and the modes and objects of desire. These permutations are obscured by and interpreted through the asymmetries of binary gender, but they suggest a far more varied and distinctive set of individual differences.

Sexuation is, hence, a systemic aspect of the subject's psyche as it incorporates and processes its difference to the environment as a specific relation to available symbolic material in the environment. This symbolic material does not represent a question of value or object choice, but, rather, a question of whether to submit to the law of difference—difference represented by the Phallus as the literal projection of a difference as well as of the impossibility that any signifier is complete in itself. Submission to the fact of difference takes different forms, both in terms of sex (male/female) and of gender (masculinity/femininity), typified by the cultural association of activity with masculinity and passivity with femininity as positions or attitudes rather than essences. If cultural envaluations were different—say, the feminine was perceived as active—the psychical alignments around sexual difference might shift. There is no correlation between sex and gender in Lacan's thinking; rather, individuals develop differing relations to sexual difference itself. As Ragland formulates it, "The male identifies with a logic of accepting to be *all* under the law of the Ur-father, exception to the law, which also grounds it, while the female identifies a part of herself as *not* [being] *all* under the law of a conventional reality one might describe as patriarchal/phallic/symbolic 'law.'"[19] And as we often see, even male and female may not correlate to biological status.

The processes of sexuation align even more. In addition to adopting positions in relation to all or not all, sexuation also locates subjects along one of the four possible differential axes of the Lacanian clinic—the masquerade, the neuroses, the *père-version*, the psychoses—that map structures of mind according to the subject's interpretations of the sexual difference. Subjects might repress sexual difference in the masquerade, foreclose it in psychosis, repudiate it in perversion, and deny it in the neuroses.[20] Subjects' alignments are specific positions about their knowledge of difference: *repression* means knowing but not knowing one knows, *foreclosure* means never having known, *repudiation* means knowing and ignoring, and *denial* means knowing and denying the knowledge.

None of this, however, yet adds up to a subject's genderings as these emerge from the subject's initial interpretation of sexual difference. The "lover" (active) and "beloved" (passive) first-stage "gender" identity is the effect of confusing gender with sexual difference "at the level," Ragland comments, "where primordial repression is not gendered, but is purely and simply, a *relation* to the objects of the world that cause desire."[21] Lover and beloved represent different positions that subjects take up in relation to lack. These positions are also identificatory and epistemological insofar as they condition the ways subjects know.[22] As identificatory positions irreducible to binary gender, the lover identifies with "a complete Other [the fantasmatic one who knows and has all]," while the beloved identifies "with an incomplete Other." As epistemological positions, lover and beloved represent subject positions in which the lover thinks "he or she knows it *all*," and the beloved "does *not [know it] all*."[23] These epistemological positions are neither biological sexes nor genders; instead, they enact a subject's relation to knowledge as a way of linking mind and body to difference. This difference is itself rendered as a question of an identification to a being who either knows everything or does not.

In addition to these identifications, Lacan defines other epistemological means of interpreting desire for both beloved and lover. These epistemological positions structure not only the subject's ways of knowing, but also the subject's modes of desire. The beloved interprets desire as either the *contingent* or the *impossible*, dynamics linked to knowing there is no *all* and to not identifying with the one who has all. The lover interprets desire as the *necessary* and the *possible* related to knowing or believing in an *all* and that someone might *have it all*. The beloved's logic of the *impossible* correlates with the lover's logic of the *necessary*. While the *impossible* is "that which does not stop not being written," the *necessary* is "that which does not stop being written." The *contingent* is that which "stops not being written," while the *possible* is "that which ceases writing itself." The beloved is linked to what Ragland characterizes as the *"not all* based on the fear of castration, a fear that elicits closure."[24] At the least, the feminine logics allow for an undecidable: "The *impossible* pushes a subject to flee the unbearable, while the *contingent* lets in enough love to allow deadly repetitions to be rewritten." The lover is linked to death and castration, to an "illusion of the whole (or *all*) as the beginning and end of knowledge."[25]

These logics of sexuation refer not only to epistemologies but also to unconscious modes of being—to ways of relating to desire and relating drives and desires to objects that produce and reflect the subject's idiosyncratic resolution to the problems of difference, desire, and love. Subjects' manifestations of sociocultural gender categories, even conscious adoptions or refusals to adopt a gendered position, are secondary to the unconscious negotiations of sexuation linking body and mind to the insistence of the drives that operate only because they are neither instinctive nor linked to any imagined reproductive imperative. Lacan's notion of the drive is, as Marie Hélène Brousse explains, "an apparatus by which to bring some sexuality as the real into the field of the imaginary and the symbolic."[26] The drive is the impulsion or libido by which individuals link sexual feelings to particular acts and objects. The drive, which can never be satisfied, "is not organized by sexual polarity," Brousse explains, nor is there any "relation between the drive, drive satisfaction, and the opposition between male and female."[27] "The drive does not originate in a biological source," Brousse comments, but is a montage of differing sources, impeti, objects, and aims. "It is a montage precisely because it is not determined by a momentous force, an innate object, an aim in its finality, or consumption."[28] In fact, as Brousse continues, "there is no sexual or active/passive polarity which organizes the drive."[29] It is not determined by reproduction; it is certainly not instinctive.

Genders/Desires

A Lacanian interpretation aligns intra-psychical positionings with desires and interpretations of knowledge only loosely connected to possibilities defined not by a "truth" of sexual difference, but by an attitude unconsciously adopted in relation to two poles of belief: one can or cannot have all, and one can go after this all or not. These two beliefs do not transpose into binarized object choices, gendered dispositions, or even formulaic roles. Individuals interpret the effects, epistemologies, drives, and desires resulting from sexuation differently in relation to the codes offered culturally as a means by which to exist and desire. This means that what we take as gender is the result of a series of unconscious interpretations and has some relation, albeit illogical and fairly untraceable, to individual solutions to the problem of sexual difference and desire.

Genderings are, thus, the subjective illusion of positioning within multiple cultural orders that correspond with (1) the subject's interpretation of sexual difference (the four axes); (2) identifications with the position of lover or beloved, all or not all; (3) the character of lost objects (identifications, traces, names) the subject is driven to refind; and (4) what the subject understands the Other (the caretaker, the socius) wants the subject to be. While the first two of these elements reflect subjects' interpretations of difference as helping to manage the lack of rapport between bodies, sexes, and language, the second two define the idiosyncratic character of individual drives and the various themes, attitudes, and regimes that locate drive and position within a socially legible system. "One seeks," Ragland explains, "a replica or semblance of something lost in the first place: the (imaginary) phallus, the urinary flow, the feces, the breast, the voice, the gaze, the phoneme, the nothing around which constellations of meaning build up. We 'think' with our lost primary objects. We are ourselves made up of those *identificatory* (symbolic/imaginary) traits, as well as the real of the marks they left behind as indices of their loss."[30]

These lost objects persist not so much in themselves, but as themes or vectors of identification that manifest themselves within and sometimes as constituting the organizational dynamics of gender regimes. These dynamics are loosely linked to the object vectors, not in any one-on-one thematic sort of way, but insofar as the objects themselves suggest or emblemize certain possible—and multiple—dynamics: for example, the phallic signifier of difference produces a quadratic process (asymmetry as produced by the differential relation of all and not all), the dynamic of the urinary flow is temporal, the feces' dynamic is taxonomic, the breast's is metamorphic, the voice exists in the regime of the audial, the gaze operates anamorphically and vertiginously (either skewing or stuttering through a mise en abime), the phoneme is linked to gesture. Although these extimate objects may in some imaginary way ground the dynamics that subjects ultimately adapt as gender regimes, there is no archaeology, no cause and effect that destines individual epistemologies and objects of intra-psychic processes to any specific regime. Instead, the objects, the vectors, and their dynamics shift in relation to the solutions the subject has produced, as individuals encounter different differences throughout their lives.

How Gender Does What It Does

So this is, very briefly, what genders do: they provide the registers through which individuals can resolve the relation between psychical and social systems, finding vectors of desire and identification that persistently resolve lack and difference and by which their drives find purchase. If we accept a Lacanian account, then these primordial objects are neither completely arbitrary, completely predestined, nor conscious. The same is true of the modes by which desires and identifications organize into genders as positions, epistemologies, and displays of desire. Gender's modes of operation are, thus, not merely taxonomic. If we accept a Lacanian account, then subjects position themselves idiosyncratically among the variables that difference introduces. In this context, gender is not an "identity" as much as it is a machine that perpetually reinterprets lack into modes of drive and desire that partially subtend self-presentation, social belonging (or not), and positions within cultural metanarratives. No one *has* a gender; gender is the constant and provisional adjustment an individual makes among objects, desires, and identifications in relation to the primary positions it has taken in relation to the question of all or not all, lover and beloved.

Individuals constantly negotiate among and morph through multiple gender regimes that operate simultaneously in the myriad orders—law, biology, kinship, society, cultures, subcultures— that constitute both the social map and subjects' psychical universe at any given time. These gender regimes, which are the effects of processes rather than stable, preexisting categories, are always in flux, are always approximate, and yet almost always provide the illusion of a stable, intelligible, categorizable kind. In the end, gender provides an analogical wormhole from order to order, from the psychical, to the biological, to the social, to the cultural, to the juridical, which may be binary (as it is on all institutional forms of self-declaration—□ m □ f), or may involve a complex negotiation among a plethora of gender regimes by and through which individuals locate themselves and are located within the multiple orders that constitute a culture.

Systems of Gender Regimes

Gender works to negotiate a conglomerate of organizations: intrapsychical phenomena (which have systemic dimensions as suggested above); Deleuze and Guattarian regimes organized around attitudinal vectors (such as might be defined for aircraft positioning, but articulated around drives); and first-order systems. None of these organizations is fixed or binary, but all provide mechanisms for constant individual repositionings and adjustments catalyzed by changes in environment, physical capability, and even conscious choice (insofar as conscious choice is ever completely conscious). Sometimes gender works in ways analogous to the ways that systems operate, repeatedly incorporating environment and adjusting its system to that incorporation. The slowness of systemic changes, within both psychic and social systems, accounts for gender's apparent binary homeostasis as well as the limited modes through which culture is inclined to interpret presentations and identities, especially in relation to the conservative character of its meta-narratives.

Gender also organizes itself in ways analogous to Deleuze and Guattari's notion of a "regime" as a "specific formalization of expression."[31] This formalization, they declare, "constitutes a semiotic system" which, as they warn, "is always a form of content that is simultaneously inseparable from and independent of the form of expression, and the two forms pertain to assemblages that are not principally linguistic."[32] Regimes are not always regimes of signs, although gender regimes are sign systems insofar as they both unconsciously and consciously signal specific positions in relation to sexual difference and desire. Regimes also link language (broadly construed as semiotic systems) to the pleasures achieved as the temporary payoff of psychical drives. Gender regimes represent dynamic architectures of meaning and jouissance, language and body along lines that respond to and reflect individual interpretations of difference, lack, drive, and desire. Regimes take advantage of the semiotic systems already culturally available even as they might alter them. This accounts for why genders manifest themselves differently in different cultures, while also explaining why cultures have a similar binary urge.

Regimes manage chaotic variety within particular sets of dynamics organized around object vectors or "attitudes." Insofar as the drives organize around dynamics linked to lost objects (temporality, taxonomy, the audial, the self-reflection, the distorted, the vantage), gender regimes organize around "attitudes" linked to drives (the unconscious, persistent impulsion through which individuals link sexual feelings to particular acts and objects). "Attitudes" are modes of approaching and organizing the chaotic intricacies of engendering—literally, positions in relation to the given binary point of reference (the imaginary difference of difference—all/not all, lover/beloved) toward which engendering always homogenizes. In aeronautical terminology, an "attitude" describes the relation of an aircraft to a given point of reference, usually on the ground. Attitude is four-dimensional and dependent on a complex system of controls, vectors, speeds, and other variables, correlating with the ways gender regimes organize themselves in relation to a fantasmatically fixed point of gender difference in culture. Other meanings of the term "attitude" also impart gender regimes' rich connotation. An "attitude" is also "a bodily posture showing or meant to show a mental, state, emotion, or mood"; it is "a manner of acting, feeling, or thinking that shows one's disposition of opinion, etc.," suggesting as well that gender regimes are ways of locating a subject in relation to the desire of the Other in the many vestiges such desire might take.[33] Thus regimes organize the chaotic disposition of subjective interpretations of difference into a semblance of meaning that can operate within larger sociocultural narratives and fantasies, provide sets of culturally meaningful signifiers that suture subjects into sociocultural matrices, and provide a subtle coding of "attitude" that simultaneously addresses individual drives and displays and elicits desire in relation to others.

The attitudes of gender regimes marshal various dynamics and vectors that link psychical drives with cultural possibilities, producing regimes linked to the gaze (being seen, having a distanced perspective or "vantage," anamorphosis, self-reflection); the aural (the voice, language, being heard); the breast (the temporal, the metamorphic); the fantasmatic and mythical (the Chimera); the anal (taxonomy); the phoneme (gesture, behaviors, and ethics); the Phallus (a quadratic social process organized around the phallic signifier [all/not all] of difference as axes); the ethical, comprising a reciprocal behavioral bounce-back; and the narrative (normative, asymptotic), in the forms in which these themes are culturally available at any given time and place. This means that specific gender regimes change through time. It also means gender resonates through multiple psychical, social, cultural, and symbolic systems, operating as a suturing and negotiating mechanism whose constant process hides behind the illusion of a static identity, performed or performative willed option, or structural position. Gender only seems to be an "identity" and functions as such to avoid its constitutional instability. The very category of "identity" is a defensive posture that operates as a reassuring delusion of self-affirmation and belonging in relation to chaotic multiplicity.

The attitudes adapted as gender regimes organize a dynamic psychosocial system that interacts with other psychosocial systems.

Gender regimes exist in tandem with something like Deleuze and Guattari's notion of the "assemblage." The assemblages of genders are those of order and desire, amalgamating drives, desires, significations, interactions, and transient meanings and functionings. As a species of assemblage, a gender regime works as an abstract machine that operates among actions, interactions, and enunciations. In *A Thousand Plateaus*, Deleuze and Guattari map an "assemblage" as existing on two axes. The "horizontal" axis "comprises two segments, one of content, the other of expression."[34] For example, a horizontal gender assemblage may consist of one of many versions we currently identify as masculine, undertaken by a subject sexuated as lover, expressed as peremptory protectiveness. The masculine protector assemblage signifies passion as well as self-conceptualization through protection of an other within the collective conventions of courtly behavior. This axis is both a *"machinic assemblage* of bodies, or actions and passions, an intermingling of bodies reacting to one another," and *"a collective assemblage of enunciation,* of acts and statements, of incorporeal transformations attributed to bodies."[35] The "machinic" refers to the "abstract machine" that constitutes the subject. It is governed by an equation that "maps a procedure" (88). In their thinking, this machine would ideally produce the heteroclite; in Lacan's thinking, this same machine would operate according to its own mode of sexuation. In gender regimes, these machinic equations are the various attitudes—space, time, the scopic, the voice, narrative, ethics—around which regimes organize themselves and that respond to and enable individual drives and desires.

Deleuze and Guattari's "vertical axis" consists of *"territorial sides,* or reterritorialized sides, which stabilize it, and *cutting edges of deterritorialization,* which carry it away."[36] In other words, gender regimes mark both the illusion of stable binaries and constantly shift them in relation to the particular equation or set of inter-influential dynamics that define the machine. Thus, for example, the masculine being who protects occupies a clear territory understood as male/masculine, but which may be deterritorialized by being occupied by a butch woman or by shifting conventions of what protection might mean. Gender regimes are constantly renegotiated (deterritorialized) and stabilized (reterritorialized) through history and cultures as bodies and regimes interact with one another and in relation to the signifiers which come to define and misdefine the bodies.

Although Deleuze and Guattari set their work in contradistinction to their reading of the work of Lacan, both their project and Lacan's understandings of psychical processes map a systemic, decentered understanding of the interrelations among subjects (and their gaps), significations, desiring dynamics, materialities, and ontologies as shifting machines that operate like systems of perpetual becoming. Deleuze, Guattari, and Lacan agree that no human body ever coincides with the masculine or the feminine and that masculinity and femininity, man and woman, are constructs in relation to which subjects, through complex sets of negotiations, adopt positions. They disagree about how central the archaeology of sexuation is. Deleuze and Guattari "argue," as Massumi summarizes, that sexual difference "does not lie at the foundation of subjectivity."[37] For Lacan, sexuation constitutes the terms within which a more fundamental process of subject formation occurs: the particular relation of the subject to difference, desire, jouissance, and law. All insist on the essential complexity of these processes as well as their generally unconscious status.

Signifying Systems

If we understand subjects as systems that fashion constituting dynamics, fantasies, and objects around signifiers, the signifiers themselves derive from cultural systems. Although regimes may thematize basic drives, there is no necessary or prescribed path from any subject's system of drives, desires, and objects to any specific gender regime. Instead, through a combination of the Other—the mother, the father, the caretaker, the teacher—the subject quickly perceives that the other desires a compliance with a particular taxonomy of difference which aligns male/female and masculine/feminine. Subjects (both unconsciously and consciously) accept, reject, provisionally play along, subtly alter, and/or individualize their positions within this taxonomy, depending, of course, on how freely the environment permits their deviation. Within the general but restrictive materialization of gender difference, subjects continue to forge fantasies, try to refind lost objects, find pleasure, and secure an identity that sensibly organizes the collection of drives, interpretations of difference, and epistemologies of the subject with the sign systems of culture. Individual interpretations are idiosyncratic—almost "heteroclite" as Deleuze and Guattari wish—but the sign systems themselves are loosely organized around certain modes of intelligibility—regimes—that themselves reflect, refind, and enable pleasure and meaning in individual interpretations.

As itself a complex mode of negotiation, as a Deleuze and Guattari machine, as sets of differential equations circulating around binary structures, gender elicits the basic systemic/extra-systemic dynamic that underlies the theories of Deleuze and Guattari and Lacan in different ways. Although the concept of the "system" is ultimately too simple a construct to encapsulate either Deleuze and Guattari's or Lacan's ideas, it provides a basic set of assumptions by which we might understand gender regimes as operating among processes of signification, enunciation, desire, stabilization, subject formation, prohibition (law), materiality, and transformation.

Deleuze and Guattari and Lacan all build on and complicate a basic systems model, several elaborations of which were put forth contemporaneously with Lacan's work in the 1960s and '70s. Writing in 1969, Ludwig von Bertalanffy, for example, defines a system as "a set of elements standing in inter-relations."[38] This broad definition is not so much about excluding phenomena as it is about establishing a systemic way of thinking that depends primarily on the complex and multifarious relations among multiple registers of signification and unconscious processes as opposed to a reduction to and analysis of social, cultural, political, and subjective structures defined by binary oppositions. For example, instead of beginning with a binary notion of sexual difference as a structural "truth" that undergirds other social formations, a systems approach understands difference already as differences that are not necessarily binary, oppositional, isolated, or foundational.

A basic "first-order system" consists of an ongoing, roughly circumscribed set of processes (such as may occur in a cell) that exchange with an environment, but where the system has taken the environment into itself as a part of its system.[39] Subjects' genderings are also continuing, roughly circumscribed (i.e., a part of subjects' psychical and social terrains) sets of processes that are produced both by the possibilities offered by their environment and by the ways subjects have unconsciously made elements of that environment (have introjected) the sets of limitations and made possibilities part of their own psychic worlds. First-order systems are not "closed"; that is, they exchange persistently with the environment they have introjected, altering their processes. More important, there is no vantage outside of a first-order system from which that system may be seen as a system. Gender and subjective systems are perpetually open to adjustment and thus unable to exchange with other systems as a system. Any such exchange is already a part of the environment that has already been made a part of the first-order system itself. No subject can see itself as a subject; any such apprehension is already a part of its own system. Nor can subjects see other subjects without their own subjective processes having already introjected these other subjects as a part of their own environment. This is why, for example, psychoanalysis is premised on transference (the relations between subjects) instead of on one subject apprehending another subject as such. In these terms, gender is a first-order "open" system in relation to which there is no point of observation that is not a part of the system itself.

The analogy between gender and system is part of an emerging way of understanding the subject in relation to the multiple forces of its environment, which include systems of material, juridical, and significatory forces and which persist in the unconscious as well as somewhere between will and the unconscious. What we might understand to be the "insides" and "outsides" of subjects is an illusion produced by the effects of systemic interchange. Subjects are organizations at best, empty at worst, formulated around gaps and nothingness. Our ideas of subjective choice and self-determination are alibis for the ways individual dispositions operate as a part of the systemic operation, determining and determined by complex sets of interrelations that flow through and beyond will and consciousness, but where will and consciousness (such as they are) are parts of the system.

Genders' combination of psychical processes (e.g., sexuation), regime and assemblage, and first-order system operations suggests not only the multifronted complexity of genders' dynamics, but also the ways these various dynamics reappear across processes and discourses. Although one may oversimplify to perceive intrapsychical processes as repeated in the relations between subject and culture (and then among gender regimes themselves), that is exactly what happens insofar as each locus must negotiate its relation to the difference represented by the others. This requires the kind of complexity necessary to gender's operations, which includes the insistence of a taxonomic impetus toward binary simplification. None of these processes represents any individual gender position; instead, all point toward the complex mechanisms involved in producing and maintaining genders. Genders, finally, are less material, willed, or "performative" than they persistently reveal; and they obscure the extent to which sociocultural organizations themselves align subjective drives, desires, and fantasies with economic and material processes in myriad possibilities, seeming cohesion, and concomitant disarray.

Finally, gender is the fantasy that negotiates a subject's drives in legible and material ways, echoing lost primary objects, playing out interpretations of difference, glossed by activity or passivity or both. How one thinks one is occupying, operating, choosing, expressing, or rebelling against gender is a part of this fantasy. Gender regimes, then, offer interpretations, practices, positions, and sets of signifiers that enable subjects to find cultural correlations for their drives and desires. These correlative regimes become a part of the subject's system just as the subjects become a part of cultural systems. As a first-order system, gender plays through regimes that constantly change in relation not only to the subjects who align themselves within them, but also in relation to the material, political, ideological, economic, and juridical systems of the culture itself, or of multiple cultures in a transglobal economy. Gender regimes are neither imposed nor chosen, but are constantly produced as a machine: as complex systems that preserve, in one way or another, a culture's own fantasy. In the case of contemporary Western culture, that fantasy is reproduction merged with capitalism in which babies and commodities are offered as lost objects to be refound but that also compensate for the emptiness at the heart of the paternal function.[40] These objects rarely correlate with any specific individual's lost objects, but their role in cultural reproductive fantasies is to serve as substitutes for loss. Commodities are the pacifiers of culture that pose as objects of desire.

Insofar as contemporary Western culture's fantasy is patriarchal repro-capitalism (a narrative that merges heterosexual reproduction with commodity production), one of its anxieties is gender itself, since a specifically binarized and delusively symmetrical version of gender is necessary for the perpetuation of the repro-capitalist fantasy as well as to sustain patriarchy itself. In this context, gender regimes function to translate gender multiplicities into positions that can be understood within a heteroreproductive narrative—a narrative that situates conclusions (fulfillment or satisfaction) as the result of the encounter of binary differences. One of the functions of contemporary gender regimes is, thus, to negotiate between the extrabinary, nonreproductive interpretations of identity and difference and the exigencies of a culture obsessed with the fantasmatic profit (and compensation) imagined to come from the preservation of a fantasy of organized and very asymmetrical difference.

The Object of Gender

This book offers an alternative account of gender as a machinic process that perpetually reorganizes multiple sets of regimes and operations that link the psychic and the social. Genders are neither a binary given nor a chaotic set of styles, but, rather, a complex range of processes, signifiers, and dynamics that do have, albeit distanced and untraceable, some expressive link to subjective drives and desires. The modes by which genders are derived, produced, displayed, and altered are many, just as genders' processes and dynamics are conscious and unconscious, compelled and voluntary, and compliant and perpetually askew. Most important, individual genderings are always multiple, changing, idiosyncratic, and yet generally intelligible within the binary protocols by which sexual difference functions as a prop and deploys the signifiers and materials available culturally.

This theory contrasts with 1990s theories of gender "performativity," including not only Judith Butler's famous formulation of gender performativity ("In imitating gender, drag implicitly reveals the imitative structure of gender itself—as well as its contingency"),[41] but also other versions of travesty, transition, and transgender. Butler's theory of gender addresses the issue of how subjects become gendered, not what gender itself might be. In fact, the mechanics of gendering Butler's work elicits all must assume sets of cultural gender imperatives themselves fronting a series of repressive regimes— and these genders are already inevitably binary. When cultural formations define genders as binary, appeals to the performative are attractive because they appear to give individual subjects at least partial control of this somewhat intransigent set of signifiers.

Although *Gender Trouble: Feminism and the Subversion of Identity*'s approach to the question of how subjects become gendered already requires the enlistment of several different processes (the production of identity through melancholic introjection of the Other), compulsions (heterosexuality), and formations (such as Foucauldian discursive formations that compel compliance in various ways), Butler's own subsequent work continues to restate, redefine, and elaborate her initial thesis about performativity, especially because the term "performative" itself is vexingly ambiguous (and hence attractive in its elasticity).[42] The key term here is "performative." It has two meanings. As an adjective, it refers to the act of performing. We perform—imitate—attributes, and in so doing we acquire the gender identity of the attributes we perform. But how and when are these "attributes" chosen? Why some attributes and not others? How do we know what a gender attribute is? Clearly there is a vast array of these attributes, and people never perform all of these attributes, some people never "perform" at all, and some perform a kind of pastiche of the attributes. Is this then "gender identity?"

"Performative" can also mean a speech act, as defined by J. L. Austin. This is a very specific kind of speech that must comply with a limited set of conventions. Speech acts, which accomplish what they say in so saying (the marital "I do"), must be sincere, conscious, and compliant with the contexts and conventions within which they have meaning.[43] If gender is performative in this sense, then individuals constitute their identities entirely consciously. While this illusion of conscious control may be attractive, do any of us really do this? Another way we might read this is as a kind of analogy—that the taking on of a gender occurs as the effect of its taking on. But this is a tautology that elides whatever it is that constitutes gender. Gender is gender as an effect of gender.

Butler's notion of performativity is dependent on a concept of gender as an "identity." The various gendering processes operate around "identity" instead of in and through subject formation itself (which is the process wherein sexuation takes place as well as links between a subject's drives and extimate objects). Although Butler refers to "identity" as the sense of unified self that faces the world, this notion of identity is a secondary formation that comes after the subject itself has already emerged. Identities, like genders, are multiple, changing fictions of position, desires, and unification. That Butler links identity and gender makes sense, given that her project defines each through the other to some extent. The coproduction of gender and/as identity then links subjects into the delusions of choice, position, and political stakes that have animated the political listing of various sex/sexuality/gender positionings in the contemporary, ever-expanding list; as Butler herself queries, relying on the work of Monique Wittig, "If the multiplication of gender possibilities expose and disrupt the binary reifications of gender, what is the nature of such a subversive enactment?"[44] The answer is that if gender is not an "identity" but a process, such a "multiplication" has always operated, and is not in itself subversive at all.

The basic conceptual problem with the performance/performativity model is that such a mechanism occurs as conscious and secondary. In this analysis, any gender "performance" comes after the subject's primary sexuation, adheres to binary cultural categories (even if these are redistributed among sexes), and appears to be wieldable. Envisioned as an imitative structure, gender (imagined as categories linked to larger discursive formations related to a heterosexual imperative) shifts to sets of attributes. Dissolved into attributes, some other notion of gender takes the stage—a stage which, it turns out, is not a drag performance but something we call "identity." Gender's "attributes" are not expressive but "performative" insofar as gender's imitative structure (persisting somewhere—in the subject, between the subject and culture, as an imperative) constitutes, presumably in subjects, a gender identity that at the same time also becomes a mode that displays "identity."

This complex yet tautological formulation never actually gets to the point, which may be the point in the end. It appears to provide a feminist (Wittig, Kristeva), psychoanalytical (Freudian), and Foucauldian account of gendering (and not of genders), while never really providing one. Its tautological character resists analysis precisely because it is tautological. There is nothing to grasp, and if one grasps any single piece—the idea of "gender attributes," say, or "imitative structure"—the piece recycles back into the tautology itself, which functions finally to obscure gender in appearing to elucidate it. One cannot wish sexual difference away by operating gender against heteronormativity. In addition, the formulation (and abbreviated or misunderstood interpretations of it) has become so ensconced as the truth of gender that one cannot question it. This has stultified much further theorizing about gender. Instead of working from the canny insights of Butler's work—or arguing with them— the notion of a performative gender closes thinking about gender down with its own self-referentiality.

In *Read My Desire: Lacan against the Historicists*, Joan Copjec offers a reasoned Kantian argument against what she sees as the Kantian unreason of Butler's *Gender Trouble*. "The problem, as I [Copjec] see it, with this exemplary book is that its happy voidance of the dogmatic option simply clears a space for the assertion of its binary opposite, if not for the 'despairing skepticism' about which Kant warned us, then for skepticism's sunny slipside: a confident voluntarism."[45] Questioning particularly Butler's assumptions about sexual difference, Copjec halts Butler's tautology by offering a Lacanian reading: "While sex is, for psychoanalysis, never simply a natural fact, it is also never reducible to any discursive construction, to sense, finally. . . . This is not to say that sex is prediscursive;

we have no intention of denying that human sexuality is a product of signification, but we intend, rather, to refine this position by arguing that sex is produced by the internal limit, the failure of signification. It is only where discursive practices falter—and not at all where they succeed in producing meaning—that sex comes to be."[46] Sexuation is where/when subjects relate themselves to these failures of signification. Genders as contemporary, scripted parts of identity are a long way away. As a process of finding modes of interpretation and display, genderings are even further away from sexual difference and sexuality.

Although Butler's "volunteerism" is appealing precisely because the incipient engendering of the subject seems so involuntary, the difficulty performative theories and practices occlude is what the persistent relation is between bodies and genders within the complex psychosocial environment in which genders have multiple functions and dynamics. The appeal to subjective will coupled with declarations of the nonessential character of gender makes performativity seem like a radical politic, welcome at a point of feminist political impasse.[47] Performativity (in its rather hybridized combination of performance and Austin's linguistic "speech act"), however, is itself an effect of a systemic operation of gender, constituting one part of a scopic gender regime at the point in history when visibility politics had been most persuasive and most conservative.[48] In its provision of a mechanism for engendering, the performative hybrid had a way of occupying the entire field, of occulting not only the nuances of Butler's own argument but also the complex systematicity of gender in cultures, of being an answer—which was no answer at all (no answer to what genders are available or how genders change and interact, for example).

Genders, Sexualities, and Desires . . .

Insofar as any gender is a machine regulating the intra-psychic processes of subjects with the cultural mélange of available styles and positions, genders channel desires and are partly produced by them. The infinite possibilities of desires, however, do not ever align with any specific gender regime. Gender regimes represent both the objects desired (insofar as genders' displays consciously or unconsciously signal desired objects) and the drives that push toward one pleasure or another. Although a structural reading, such as Freud accomplishes in *Three Essays on the Theory of Sexuality*, lays out a series of binary relations among sexes, objects, and aims, the complexity of the systemic operations of gender would suggest a far less rigid and predictable scheme.[49] Instead, desires and genders produce one another in a far more complex system of inflections, equivalent possibilities, commensurate objects, and diverse aims. The closest we might come is to suspect that any regime's attitude (its organizational theme) relates to some effect of individual sexuation, though we cannot know how anyone interprets those connections in the unconscious.

Gender's complexity spurs persistent attempts to organize, reduce, and control its polyvalence. Of course, this book is also an instance of this reductive tendency no matter how complex its formulations. Although in the systems environment of the social, symbolic, and intra-psychical processes in which genders are deployed, there is no starting point, no ur-gender, no privileged site, a book must perforce have one. Any choice will inevitably skew the system toward one process or another, especially insofar as the process of trying to envision gender is already a part of a gender regime which is organized around its imaginary outside vantage (an imaginary point from which one might see gender as such). Ideally, presentations of gender's complexity could be read starting at any point, and the chapters read in any order. The necessities of explication annul that possibility, though nothing would suggest that readers cannot undertake such an experiment on their own.

The rest of this book lays out some of the regimes by which genders orient themselves as interpretations of desire and links to the social. None of these regimes is exclusive and unchanging. It would be impossible to treat or perhaps even identify every gender regime; this project can do no more than offer a suggestion of how this complex intra-/extra-psychical, cultural system operates. Nor can this book do more than hint at the infinite permutations and combinations individuals might evince, define the multiple ways such regimes have been produced and/or adopted, or track any specific route from a gender regime to any individual psychical organization. One thing we may already understand in very complex ways is how such genders signal desire and are oriented toward others.

Necessary Obsolescence

The genderscape constantly shifts. Because cultural signifiers, versions of symbolic formations, possible objects of desire, and other modes by which desire is organized culturally constantly change, genderings change as well. Genderings are transient. The goth of today is now the goth of yesterday, as is the hipster. These spurious genders morph constantly, suggesting that somewhere a metamorphic gender regime (a regime organized around change through time) is always operating. At the same time, throughout history, gender regimes have tended to organize around the same attitudes and processes linked to desire: the scopic (genderings defined by being seen, seeing oneself seeing oneself being seen, vantage as an imaginary second-order systems site [sight], anamorphosis, et cetera), temporality (metamorphosis), the quadratic relation of biaxial positionings (social gender, taxonomic genders), excess (fluidity, travesty, mixed species), ethics (chivalry, generosity), and narrative (schematic compliance, asymptosis). The differences in gender display and manifestation exist because of differences in the environmental material available through which such genderings might organize themselves. For these reasons, we can understand multiple genderings through history even as regimes continue to alter the signifiers with which they operate. Finally, gender regimes rarely operate separately, but, rather, they combine as processes producing positions that are contextually intelligible. And we are all able to read these positions without even thinking about it.

The mappings that follow, relying as they do on popular cultural examples, will, thus, always be both obsolete and recognizable. The dynamics around which these materials organize continue to operate, despite changes in the cultural landscape. Each mapping begins in the first decade of the twenty-first century and ends with the ways even those manifestations have already shifted. Although we cannot predict a shift or find any one-to-one correlation between gender

Regime	Attitude	Dynamic
Vantage	As if detached from above; chimeric	Looking; discerning; apparently fluid
Metamorphosis	Change through time	Temporality, historical
Schematic	Aligning with narrative roles	Narrative
Asymptotic	Secondary narrative positions	Reaching toward but never achieving
Anamorphic	Mistaken apperception	Decoding
Social (quadratic)	The squared manifestation of binary ideals	Working toward failure (feminine); falling from the ideal (masculine)
Vertiginous	Self-reflective	Seeing oneself being seen; seeing oneself as a gender
Taxonomic	Binary reduction	Sorting and classifying; digestive
Ethical	Gesture	Rebound; cybernetic

Figure 1. Some of the nearly infinite permutations of genders.

regimes, desires, et cetera, we can see gender as always a metamorphic process. Thus the book begins with the metamorphic regime.

What follows are sets of cooperating regimes, their constituting attitudes, and analyses of their functions that begin to map gender as a dynamic inter-, intra-, and impersonal machine. Here are the gender regimes the book will examine, defined by the dominant attitude by which they are organized. This by no means represents an exhaustive list of all of the existing, multifarious, chatoyant gender regimes. MOST IMPORTANT, THIS IS NOT SIMPLY AN EXTENDED LIST OF CATEGORIES, NOR IS IT AN EXPANDED TAXONOMY.

1 Making Over

Metamorphosis, Taxonomy, Vantage

The first decade of the twenty-first century hosted an obsession with makeovers. Although versions of the Cinderella story—in which undiscovered beauty and virtue find recognition—have existed since antiquity, the makeovers of the 2000s have focused on the cosmetic mechanics of transformation from dull and homely to gleaming and pretty. Such films as *Miss Congeniality* and *My Big Fat Greek Wedding*, as well as a bevy of reality television series (*Queer Eye for the Straight Guy*, *The Swan*, *The Biggest Loser*) focused on metamorphoses, establishing the makeover as a cultural preoccupation. Unlike film versions of Cinderella (Disney's animated movie was released in 1950, and the Kenneth Branagh version came out in 2015) or even the movie *Pygmalion* in 1938 and *My Fair Lady* in 1964, which tracked transformations from one social class to another, these twenty-first-century alterations took those whose appearances were woefully noncompliant with traditional notions of binary gender conventions and renormalized them. Twenty-first-century makeovers were orthopedic and disciplinary, triumphantly "correcting" nontraditional presentations of an "underlying" true femininity or masculinity to match a character's biological sex. This coming together of sex and gender is a version of a repro-narrative that seeks true meaning in a true match; in the case of the makeover, a match of inner and outer acts as precursor and antecedent to another properly complementary heterosexual match to come.

And unlike the transformation narratives that preceded them, such as the two versions of *The Nutty Professor* (1963 and 1996), where imbibing a formula produced a sudden shift from a nerd to a traditionally coherent version of obnoxiously macho masculinity, these first-decade narratives focused on the processes of transformation themselves. They are about gender both as it changes through time and as something that does (and must) change through time. This metamorphic regime organizes itself around the temporal insofar as it elicits and tracks the processes through which an incomprehensibly (or nonnormatively) gendered subject gradually conforms to normative versions of a social gender whose style guarantees the imaginary of biological sex. This temporal regime is operated by its charmless characters as a way of taking control of their lives, their circumstances, and their stories. It offers the transformative processes of gendering as a way into the starring role of a story that would otherwise leave them behind. As a reward for compliance, this centralizing is an illusion insofar as the haplessly and incomprehensibly gendered character is already, from the start, the narrative's center so that only by coming into gender "focus" can the narrative wrap its reformist and romantic lines into the kind of marital knot that counts. These narratives of transformation anatomize gender itself as a constant production—as sets of processes by which a taxonomic imperative (the impetus to sort into coherent aligned binaries) persistently organizes multiple regimes into the socially recognizable.

In the last few years of the first decade of the twenty-first century, this metamorphic regime gradually shifted its operation from conformative gender processes to a chimeric regime peopled by vampires, werewolves, and zombies whose unquestioned gender presentations conform entirely—even spectacularly in the case of vampires—with conventional social genders, but whose personae are understood to hide a metamorphic power that reveals a hidden species or kind. Signaled by the early twenty-first-century emergence of the Shrek series (2001, 2004, 2007, 2010), which featured comic versions of chimeric metamorphoses, these undead transformers enact concerns with personal empowerment and immortality—with the ability to transform death into a kind of persistent existence.

Oranges and Apples Are Not the Only Fruits

Some of us are oranges and some of us are apples, but we all fruits.

"All fruits," Mr. Portokalos (Michael Constantine) proclaims as the capstone to his congratulatory speech at his daughter's wedding. "All fruits," meaning in this case, all people, Greek and Anglo, a conclusion derived from Mr. Portokalos's favorite hobby of specious etymology. The metaphor meets with a roar of laughter from the wedding guests, not only because it is so typical of the domineering, misguided, but sweet, old patriarch, but also because it connotes so much more. We are all fruits, all the result of someone else's life cycle, waiting ourselves to burst forth in another promising generation, ripe, succulent, juicy, glowing, irresistible, potential seduction and potential sin, expressed from the womb and the loom, good for you and slightly gratuitous, a healthy treat instead of a virtuous snack, exotic rather than mundane, et cetera. And we are all different and a little nutty perhaps, to snatch another trite but equally reproductive agricultural metaphor. And maybe even a little strange.

Mr. Portokalos's clever turn on ethnic diversity, deployed to dismiss the difference between his Greek daughter and her Anglo groom, derives from his penchant for his Greek heritage, a pride expressed by his claiming a Greek derivation for all words. His gambit, simultaneously a social icebreaker and a proud advertisement for the preemptive importance of Greek culture, seeks linguistic roots as a mode of appropriation and explanation. According to his often-clever etymologies, Greek is the origin of all words (including, in one instance, "kimono"), which assumes, among other things, that Greek is a species of linguistic progenitor. Tripping lithely through syllables linked by phonetic similarity, ("Miller," the groom's patronym, comes from "milos," Greek for apple) Mr. Portokalos deploys a logic of similarity and affinity as a mechanism of generation, substituting an imaginary origin for both lexical meaning and processes of linguistic production and change. For Mr. Portokalos, origins equal categories, source defines belonging, and the derivations of signifiers provide great insight into the essence of objects. Language reflects and sustains a taxonomy derived from origins.

Mr. Portokalos's etymological zeal is cleverly allegorical in a film whose simplicity of plot and character belies its canny intervention in cultural anxieties about gender and kind—about taxonomy itself as a process of binary sorting. Focused on the romance of an ugly duckling turned swan, *My Big Fat Greek Wedding* traces the basic shape of a heteronarrative—the paradigm in which "opposite" sexes/genders clash, attract, get together, and produce something, in this case a child. Displacing issues about sexual difference into a question of disparate ethnicities, the film anatomizes the dynamics of binary joinder and categorical certainty that characterize our assumptions about the shape of almost any story in Western culture. Through its obsessive focus on the rituals of dating and matrimony, *My Big Fat Greek Wedding* is itself a ritual of reaffirmation, affording the hard-won certainties of a clearly binary gender, the satisfactions of self-made conformity, the value of sustaining myths of patriarchal power, and romantic love's ability to overcome any difference as long as the involved parties can be reduced to a sexual binary.

Even as the film reassures us that all is well in patriarchy, it is also arguably feminist in its revelation of the means by which subversive female wiles can bend and soften paternal privilege. The relation between males and females in the film shows not only that patriarchy is merely a paper tiger, but also that when women understand patriarchy, they, too, can have power. As Mrs. Portokalos (Lani Kazan) explains to her daughter, "The man may be the head of the household, but the wife is the neck and she can turn his head any way she wants." Insightful women engineer their own solutions by making the patriarch believe that all decisions are his own. The family of strong women overcomes quieter, less striving families like that of Toula's (Nia Vardalos) fiancé. The young couple follows the wife's family instead of the husband's, becoming decidedly Greek, as the Anglo suitor converts to Greek Orthodoxy, the couple ends up living next door to her parents, and their daughter attends Greek school.

Or we can read this film as the drama of the symptomatic relation between sexes in a patriarchy that is clearly fictive and yet still enjoys the delusion of power. The only way women can exert any force or influence, for example, is by carefully maintaining and even nurturing the myth of patriarchal power, a care that pays off in the liberation of the family's son, who wishes to be an artist.

All of the sexual strategizing and all of the elements of romantic narrative and cultural difference provide easily recognizable modes of organizing the complex, self-contradictory environment of the American family. This organization occurs, however, around neither sex nor genes, but around gender and self-presentation. Part of the pleasure in this film is the way the chaos of this environment seems to be so easily ordered through one simple process—the metamorphic feminization of Toula, who begins the film as a being who is monstrously at odds with conventional versions of femininity. In the film's predawn opening sequence, the father's complaint, "You better get married soon. You starting to look old," seems to spur the chimeric Toula toward traditional femininity. The ugly duckling then shows how will, self-help, and night classes can turn a homely geek into an attractive, marriageable woman. With normative femininity situated as an apparently necessary condition for the unwinding of the romance narrative, we might think that Toula's feminization is a voluntary act. After all, its adjustment toward conformity, intelligibility, and cultural perpetuation results in a series of advantages, making it seem as if gender conformity is both enabled by and enables desire, and thus propels the film's narrative toward its fruitful culmination. Toula's reward for complying with normative femininity is the satisfaction of her secret desire, which is both to please and to rebel against her father. In marrying the Anglo Ian, she does both.

But what if something other than desire and the narrative exigency of sex/gender intelligibility spur Toula's makeover? What if her gender conformity is an effect of the environment rather than the cause and pretext of romance? What if the narrative just makes Toula's gender appear to be increasingly normative? And what if her feminization, demonstrated in the film as neither the discovery of a preexisting essence nor performance (or the performative), is instead a gender regime comprising a perpetuated *making* through time, moving backward and forward around normative binary (i.e., social, taxonomic) gender regimes?

The film demonstrates how gendering is a machine, a set of operations and work in relation to complexity and incommensurability. The romance narrative glosses over and frantically organizes this ongoing gendering process that floats as one perspective—and as one regime—among many, equally operant others, including a regime of vantage organized around perspective itself (as the attitude from which genders can be perceived as such). By situating Toula's gender transformation and ensuing wedding as the end of a meaningful ritual, by distancing the viewer cynically from the binary "sex" roles subtending patriarchy, and by drawing attention to the role of linguistic subversion, *My Big Fat Greek Wedding* makes Toula's gender metamorphosis visible precisely as a gender regime emblemized by temporal processes, merging toward and yet avoiding the compliance both narrative (and its desire) seem to demand. The film also demonstrates that Toula's metamorphic process, however it may seem to cooperate in this narrative as organizer, as mode of intelligibility, or as truth, consists of open-ended change instead of a static, binary certainty, instead of an arrival at successful and static compliance. What the film plays out is (1) the drama of how, when, and why multiple disparate genders seem to become binary; (2) what conditions—the exigencies of narrative, kinship, patriarchy, the axioms of desire, the needs of biology—produce the distillation of many into the appearance of two; and (3) how a gender regime is intelligible as a temporal dynamic—as change through time. In addition, *My Big Fat Greek Wedding* enacts the relations among at least three gender regimes: the temporal dynamic of metamorphosis, the sorting impetus of binary taxonomy, and "vantage" as a gender regime through which we imagine we apprehend gender as such as if from outside it. All three are affected by narrative as a set of ideologies (romance, oppositional joinder, product) and by the perspectives that reveal them and put them into play.

Toula before Her Makeover

For a large portion of *My Big Fat Greek Wedding*, Toula is in the process of becoming something, by the end seeming to become intelligibly feminine. But if she does not begin the film as feminine, what is she? Before and after, cause/effect, Toula's gender constantly changes through time. But what if there is really no before and after? What if narrative's apparently linear cause and effect is itself part of the illusion of structure, merely feigning linear chronology? The exigencies of the story may shape Toula's metamorphosis as much as or more than Toula's metamorphosis pushes the story. Toula is always changing; the narrative merely appears to organize and track the change, providing meaning for certain manifestations at certain narrative points. Narrative invites us to believe that such change has motivation and leads toward a neat alignment that permits closure. But what if Ian is attracted to Toula because she is not conventionally feminine, because she displays some gender other than a taxonomically compliant femininity? How much of Toula's apparent gender alignment represents conformist stasis and how much of it is an effect of the story's gloss? Does she ever stop morphing?

My Big Fat Greek Wedding begins with father and daughter driving through the rainy predawn streets of Chicago to open the family's restaurant. Gentle thunder accompanies a series of slow aerial panning shots of wet, lamp-lit, deserted streets, finally craning and tilting slowly down to the family car as it glides to a stop under a red light. Through the driving rain and screeding windshield wipers we see Toula in the passenger seat, garbed in oversized glasses and earmuffs, yawning audibly. Father, behind the wheel with a look of patient disgust on his face, asks Toula when she is going to get married, says she is getting old, and advises his daughter about the urgency of her next step. The comment casts Toula's oddly androgynous appearance as an effect of age rather than any uncertainty about gender, even though in this first appearance in the film her gender does not conform to the clean binary exigencies of gender taxonomy. Her response to her father, presented as a voice-over interior monologue, turns Dad's comment into a ritual: "My father has been saying that to me ever since I was fifteen. . . . 'Cause nice Greek girls are supposed to do three things in life: marry Greek boys, make Greek babies, and feed everyone until the day we die." The connection between marriage and appearance is less about her age than about the proper shape of the story.

The camera continues to scan the cityscape as the stacked words of the title—"Big, Fat, Greek"—insert themselves vertically between the words "My" and "Wedding." Father and daughter run through the rain to their restaurant, "Dancing Zorba's," and we watch Toula remove her earmuffs and oversized sweater to reveal not a svelter hidden beauty, but a bespectacled, bedraggled, practically clad person whom we see through the slats of a venetian blind as she looks out through the window. As she gazes, she occasions a flashback, recalling her childhood during which she enjoyed the same out-of-joint condition: "When I was growing up, I knew I was different. The other girls were blonde and delicate and I was a swarthy six-year-old with sideburns." While the other girls are eating sandwiches, she is eating leftover moussaka (which the other girls call "moose caca"). When the other girls go to after-school Brownies, our heroine attends Greek school. Toula's monologue implies, then, that her odd or unintelligible gendering is really an effect of her ethnicity, an effect apparently centered on language, as her flashback girlhood sequence cuts to the large face and Hellenic syllables of her Greek school teacher and the Greek cultural message that all facts and relations have meaning only within the context of marriage. If enculturation is the problem, however, why is not Toula already compliant?

A large part of Toula's ethnic alibi is an insistent appeal to a marital narrative as the rationale for almost everything (Why should she go to Greek school? So she can write her future Greek in-laws). The gloss of ethnic connubial imperative, however, works only to situate our protagonist as odd, as somehow not aligned with the program in the way her successful elder, "perfect," married sister Athena is. In the restaurant, her father talks to his relatives about how Toula refuses to go to Greece to find a husband. "It's almost," he says, "as if she no want to get married." Father, aunt, and uncle all cross themselves superstitiously. Toula slumps around the restaurant, definable only as an incipient, suspiciously gazing functionary until she describes herself as "thirty and way past my expiration date." Confessing that she "has no life," Toula watches the parade of normative binary genders perform around her from her sister's maternal busyness to her cousins' spectacular arguments about hairstyles and "big-assed girlfriends."

The film's elaborate introduction to Toula's changing self-presentations also maps the conditions that seem to require her transformation. Her constant metamorphoses, however, never seem to go anywhere or produce any kind of binary intelligibility. Years of indoctrination into the desirability of marriage have not yet inspired Toula to normative femininity. With oversized glasses and a haunting stare, the vigilant Toula constitutes the vantage of the nonparticipant, distanced and commenting, eccentric and aware—the one whose perspective makes visible the narrative and ideological investments of the others. Her wry observations derive from and constitute an exile, a condition conveyed both by her spatial alienation from her riotous family and by an introspective moment in the alley behind the restaurant, as she wishes for a "better life" in which she is prettier and happy. But just as she decides that dreams are useless "because nothing ever changes," she catches her first glimpse of Ian Miller (John Corbin) as he enters the restaurant to meet a friend. Ian's friend (Ian Gomez) is busy trying to set the bachelor Ian up with dates, but Ian objects, observing that "they are all the same." Then he catches sight of Toula, hovering catatonically with a coffeepot. Suddenly nervous, Toula begins to babble that her brain has stopped and that she has become their "own private Greek statue." As the men leave the restaurant, Toula sinks down behind the cash register, all awkwardness as Ian's friend pays the bill to a spinster dwarf. Throughout the scene Toula persistently morphs, changing height, posture, persona, and general appearance.

As observer, Toula has also been the observed, her lack of conventional narrative direction a problem for a family bent on understanding what her proper function should be. But has she no apparent direction because her gender is insufficiently normative, or vice versa? As it is, her aunt proclaims, she will be the devoted daughter who never leaves her parents. The position of daughter, however, is what seems to cause the problem for Toula. Daughterness inspires questioning and timid rebellion that manifests itself in her unconscious refusal to conform. Her gender, then, is precisely about cynicism, distanciation, and unintelligibility, scanning and morphing through a range of apparently "unintelligible" positions, which add up only to a regime of constant change. Toula is an enigma, a stalling yet morphing statue, who functions to highlight the marital normalcy of the rest but whose unintelligibility also portends a necessary transition from the Greek to the American, from tradition to an updated version of gender relations.

So what gender regime marks Toula at the beginning of the film? Is her big-eyed, aquarium-lensed, unruly-haired, makeup-less eccentricity simply a vision of failed or as-yet-undeveloped femininity, or is it something else altogether? Is our push to define gender itself the problem, as gender categories do not really align with the possibilities? Part of the problem is certainly taxonomic thinking, or our need to identify and marshal individuals into binary categories that operate within a narrative scheme subtended by the structural regulation of kinship and motivated by a narrowly directed desire for product and closure. Part of the dilemma is the self-contradictory fictional delimitations of the categories available. In other words, that I need to pose the question of her gender at all suggests both the imperative of categorical intelligibility and the stakes of gender inquiry itself. But how I pose the question may make a difference.

A Big Fat Deal out of a Big Fat Wedding

Instead of asking how Toula might herself come to acquire or relate to these regimes, let us ask what these regimes do and when they do it. At the beginning of the film, Toula persists as unintelligibly gendered, and because altering her genderings seems to produce a series of consequences, Toula's gendering has an organizing function. It accrues the effects of change instead of persisting as originary (always there to be uncovered) and/or ontological (the truth of identity). Whether Toula's gender shifts or her gender regimes are by character intrinsically shifting makes little difference to the film's narrative. This metamorphic regime organizes and contains everything that may go out of control both in the telling of her story and in the life the film constructs as the subject of that story.

In the film, Toula's gender metamorphosis regulates an environment of multiple, intersecting, and conflicting perspectives, temporal multidirectionality, and a psychic urge toward the homely, the familiar, and the organized that exists only in contrast to some other, coexisting *un-heimlich* chaos. The film enacts Toula's metamorphosis not only through her shifting appearance but also as an effect of perspective. As a regime operating through time, the metamorphic not only participates in multiple perspectives simultaneously, it also retains perspectives as they seem to change. Its metamorphic quality is temporal and conservative, depending on change through time and visibly archiving its own history. At the same time, the metamorphic tends to be uncanny in that it enables the coexistence of primitive and repressed states of being, while simultaneously appearing to be progressive as it seems to enable narrative closure by ceding to taxonomy.

Putting aside for a moment the paradoxes of taxonomic processes (categories produce divisions as they name them, categories are produced by structures instead of subtending them), the film inscribes a metamorphic regime as the condition of its consumption. The question of Toula's gender, which is a question the film raises as temporal—as a problem of Toula being somehow out of time—registers also as a problem and effect of perspective. From the opening scene of the film, Toula has functioned as a point of view, a way of drawing the viewer into the story, as Toula is situated as eccentric observer, voice-over narrator (and origin of this story), and as object of the look. Her decentered first-person point of view, defined here as a narrative rather than a literal perspective, draws the audience into the terms of the story—ethnic patriarchy, marital imperative, reproductive duty—as the lens through which to understand the motives of relatives and the predicament of the protagonist. Because the terms of the story are so familiar, we readily accept the film's incipient imbalances, reading them as the problems that the film's romance narrative will resolve, anticipating the happy ending the film's comic codes promise. The film's discombobulated landscape of Cadillac-ensconced geek and markedly paternalistic Greek anticipate pleasurable mastery in the film's coming reorganization and revised intelligibility. Toula is a problem; Dad wants her to get married, so we know she will.

Through this lens of narrative convention, Toula's lack of gender conformity presents itself as a curable aberration, the hurdle to overcome in the happy alignment of sex and gender as well as the fulfillment of desires. This narrative perspective poses the whole problem of Toula as a temporal hurdle in relation to the anticipated progress of the romance. Toula is not unfeminine, merely unripened. Her presentation connotes an untimeliness, an individual who has stayed adolescent and daughter-like for too long. Hence her father's understanding of her predicament as one of age.

But just as the story promises a happy ending from the beginning, the image of the insufficiently categorizable Toula remains throughout the film as the benchmark against which we can compare her progressive compliance. If the relative chaos of our first vision of her through the pelting rain and windshield wipers anticipates her eventual jubilant mastery of intelligible femininity, our pleasure in her apparently triumphant reformation depends on our memory of her in the opening portrait. If, however, multiple times and perspectives are perpetuated as coexisting—if temporality is not unidirectional, and perspectives are multiple instead of serial—is the source of pleasure in this film really about conformity and closure? When two dynamics—narrative and morphing multiplicity—overlap, which dynamic produces pleasure? Is pleasure a product of narrative mastery and compliance, of the resolution of chaos and anxiety into an intelligible, socially acceptable form with a hint—a mere soupçon—of joyful rebellion attached (after all, she marries a kind, gentle, loving non-Greek)? Or does pleasure come from the sustained coexistence of multiple possibilities, from the polymorphousness that permits many directions at once? Or both, as they seem to seam together interdependently? If this last option is the case, how can we understand such polymorphousness in the face of what seem to be definitive and exigent taxonomic and narrative drives?

There are three presuppositions about narrative that might urge us toward a pleasure in the conformity and mastery narrative affords: (1) an assumption of gender as a binary, regulatory category; (2) a belief in temporal unidirectionality; and (3) our blindness to (or willful discounting or even disavowal of) the multiple, coexisting perspectives already offered as a pretext for narrative in this film. If gender consists of a complementary binary, then Toula's original version is indeed out of joint and in need of repair. If we insist that time and cause and effect move only in one direction, then Toula's changes represent a movement toward intelligibility. The problem this film itself presents comes in the co-presence of a system of surprisingly complex, contradictory, and inapposite perspectives whose polymorphousness unravels the relative security and certainty of the film's very conventional narrative, as well as the linearity of any movement in time.

The film initially offers three kinds of perspectives: the unlocated skyscape view of the panning, craning aerial camera; the local and immediate patriarchal perspective offered by the father; and the more historical, contemplative view of Toula's voice-over. The cityscape is environmental and universalist. Toula's father's complaint is ideological. Toula's own commentary is individual and idiosyncratic, but we easily understand their nested interrelation as a movement toward the breakage focused on Toula. These perspectives, which are defined by their narrative vantage, contrast with any literal use of point of view (camera shots understood to come from the specific site of a particular character), a strategy this film uses sparingly. Once the opening aerial shots float to the ground and disappear into the image of the stop light, the two perspectives that continue to battle are the familial gaze at Toula (one we share by a default alignment with the camera) and Toula's gaze at herself (a doubled view we share by virtue of camera's image of Toula and Toula's voice-over). These perspectives fragment as Toula's ruminations flash back to the past, providing a presumed cause for her current predicament (her Greekness) and an inevitable contrast between the young Toula and her current manifestation. Toula's perspective fragments again when the film returns to the present and Toula looks away from herself to the future, mulling vague desires and dreams rather than looking self-consciously at herself. Instead of trading off, these perspectives accrue like flowers in a bouquet, providing multiple intersecting and conflicting lenses which render Toula herself rather confusingly multifaceted. And interesting.

The same multiple perspectives accrue, too, for the family members—mother, father, brother, aunts, uncles, et cetera—who, though stereotypes, gain complexity in the multiple perspectives through which they might be consumed. These multiple perspectives often consist of narrative vectors presented as character revelations—Mom is neither as nagging nor as subservient as we thought; Dad is loving in the midst of his imperatives; Grandma was once young and beautiful; macho Brother is an artist at heart. If we understand the introduction of perspectives as a linear trajectory toward knowledge and insight, we tend to see these revelations as the progressive acquisition of deeper truths, new insights replacing our previous superficial, stereotyped ideas. Linearity and revision, however, are illusions produced by the dynamics of the narrative itself, which create the fantasy of progressive organization and depth as the payoff of consuming the successive layers of narrative's illusion of unidirectional cause and effect.

The persistent shifting and splitting of visual and narrative perspectives provides the film's enunciative structure, highlighting clashes of opinion and conflict. The constant change of perspective, however, is less a linear grammar of successive positionality than a systemic shifting in the process of regulating and balancing a stalemate focused on Toula as the site of familial imbalance. The many perspectives coexist, each perspective the effect and product of those that precede and follow. This means that the presentation of any given perspective, say, that of Toula's family huddled in consternation over her apparent lack of connubial ambition, both elaborates and revises the problem with Toula. The first image of Toula in the car ("past my expiration date") revises itself in the image of a de-cloaked Toula in the restaurant, where she is introspective and perceptive. The family's discussion introduces an additional gloss on the opening patriarchal perspective—Toula's out-of-placeness is a familial rather than merely a paternal concern. The perspective of the huddled family is itself retroactively re-signified by a return to Toula's self-conscious perspective, which relocates the family group within a history of marital obsession that makes this particular huddle less a crisis than a convention. These perspectives can form an argument or discourse only if they interact with one another through the accruing history of the film, and to do that, they must remain in play even if no longer in sight.

The familial perspective, which fans out like Toula's, begins to make it clear that there is another glitch in the smooth operation of family: the father whose ideological rigidity is a problem must be managed by his wife. That Dad is as out-of-date as Toula seems to provide a balance to Toula's developmental stall. The bait-and-switch quality of his wife's subversions seems to offer a maternal alternative to patriarchy as the real governing order of the family. But if Toula is unintelligibly gendered, the family is not unintelligibly patriarchal despite the performance of Pop as a problem (which may in the end be what "patriarchy" has always been about). What the film quickly makes evident is that familial ideologies exceed individuals or genders. Mother is as good (even better) at policing patriarchy than Dad is, because her subversion in its service provides simultaneously the illusion of rebellion and choice. The very act of manipulating egos and desire is about making the story right, about adjusting ideological rigidity into a realistic but elastic compliance. The mother's gendering as, well, a mother, though never in question, already functions as a masquerade (of her real power) and indirection through her complex management of the multiple elements of the familial system.

Understanding perspectives as part of a systemic, interdependent discourse ultimately suggests not only that no perspective ever disappears, but also that, rather than merely accruing or building, which presupposes the unidirectional aegis of a narrative drive toward ending and resolution, all perspectives coexist from the beginning—that the "universal" camera-eye view with which the film begins is one enacting the chaotic, directionless multiplicity of perspectives that populate the film and subtend the narrative. The film's opening sequence of aerial shots establishes the narrative in an urban area, Chicago, in the dark and in the rain, on a vista of empty streets, hence very early or very late. But although the series is formally linked by a right-to-left panning of the camera in each shot, each shot also comes from very different perspective on Chicago, the first looking in one direction, the second in another, the third in yet another, then a shot that begins to descend into the heart of the city. The opening is multiply perspectival.

Although we often understand aerial establishment sequences as a filmic convention, when considered as something other than a perspectival funnel they establish a broad range of perspectives that the film actually perpetuates rather than narrows. Aerial shots, by definition, have both attitude—a specific relation to a fixed point such as a building or the ground—and an elastic point of view as the camera swoops, pans, tilts, helicopters, and cranes its way through the networked city. As these shots are edited, additional and conflicting attitudes and perspectives accrue, producing, if we think the point is the establishment of environment, an impression, but also a model of flexive and coexisting directions—different ways of relating to the same space. The concurrence of similar camera direction and different vector and attitudes of view at the film's commencement enacts the layering and splitting of differential perspectives throughout the film: Toula's, the father's, the mother's, Ian's, and, of course, the camera's, which often functions in this film as an ironic perspective that self-consciously splits scenes into their conflicting components. These aerial views also reflect the coexisting temporalities of Toula's present, past, and future. And all of these multiple perspectives and temporalities operate in relation to and may well produce the "problem" of Toula's gender nonconformity.

The film's perpetuation of multiplicities is particularly evident in scenes specifically focused on the clash and proliferation of perspectives. After Toula's initial encounter with Ian in the family restaurant, she undergoes a series of self-initiated transformations, which are pragmatically alibied by the familial need for someone to work in her aunt's travel agency. Proposing that she go to night school to learn how to computerize the business, Toula simultaneously undertakes a gradual makeover, getting contact lenses, learning how to do her hair and apply makeup, changing her wardrobe, and finally getting to sit at the lunch table with the other girls.

The madeover Toula takes over her aunt's travel agency. We see her set against the multiple views afforded by a series of travel posters on the wall behind her, as she busily manages multiple phone calls, makes airline reservations, and switches between customers and vendors. From her vantage, though she is not in fact paying any attention, we see Ian purchasing a hot dog from a vendor in front of the travel agency window. Ian turns around toward the window and catches sight of Toula busy at the travel agency desk. Attracted by her, he stops and looks. The next shot frames Toula from desk height in the vector provided by Ian's gaze, but at odds with his actual point of view. This replicates the counter-high point of view performed by Toula in her first encounter with Ian. The next shot images Ian from this same desk-high vantage, as he looks curiously at Toula happily gliding between workstations on her chair. This series of reverse shots continues, with Toula gaily dancing about her workplace and Ian gazing through the window, neither, however, imaged from the point of view of the other. As Toula stops gliding to get a drink from the watercooler, she finally catches sight of the gazing Ian. Her face assumes the characteristic uncertainty of the pre-makeover Toula. Ian smiles and waves. Toula, now in medium close-up, frowns in an even more recognizable reprise of her original self. Ian nods encouragingly at her, and as his attention is distracted by someone on the street asking the time, Toula turns to the side and slides down the wall beside the watercooler, returning to the counter-high vantage of hidden safety she assumed in her first encounter, looking at Ian through the watery glass of the cooler. Ian looks for her through the window; however, he does not see her vaguely visible through the thick cooler glass and so walks away. Toula gets up and looks after him through the sleeker surface of the window glass, though what we see is Toula looking rather than what Toula is looking at. The scene ends as a timid smile lights Toula's face.

This scene, which functions as the second of a set of three encounters between Toula and Ian that lead finally to romance, traces the systemic production and unmaking of Toula's normative social femininity as an effect of a perspective, illustrating how gender functions as the operator and regulator of multiplicity, while at the same time offering a site (sight) for romantic intelligibility. At the beginning of the sequence, Toula, who has effected her vision of a feminine future, operates the multiple intersecting lines of travel— telephone, computer, fax. Her thrumming joy at the center of this network attracts the attention and sustained look of Ian, who recognizes something, whether that something is her joy, some uncanny sense of having seen her somewhere before, or maybe even the coalescence of her metamorphic gender with something more intelligibly taxonomic. His sustained gaze and acknowledgment catalyzes Toula's repetition of her earlier disappearance, this time behind a thick glass water bottle, itself an uncanny return to the blurry and partially repressed image of a chaotic Toula through the streaming car windshield. The system of looks clashes with the literal point of view produced by the camera height of the returning glances; this collision reprises an earlier scene of looking in the restaurant, which has already been the condition of possibility for this second encounter. The network of looks—Ian at Toula, Toula at Ian, the camera at both of them as accomplished through the mediating, filtering intervention of the window and its frame—produces Toula both as a spectacle to be seen and as an object that is simultaneously morphing and recognizably feminine. Her shrinking escape to the desk-high vantage of the series of reverse shots not only retroactively supplies the point of view for the first series of shots, but it also links this sequence to the earlier one, unmaking and blurring her gender intelligibility as an effect of literal perspective. When we see her distorted by glass and water, she becomes invisible, not because she is really hidden, but because the structural effect of her gender conformity disappears. The scene falls apart: Ian, unable to see her, leaves, and Toula reverts to her originary status as the observer.

In its reversions and reprises—in its provision of the uncanny specter of the "before" in its rendition of after—this scene and its third incarnation a bit later in the film also illustrate the way gender intelligibility exists in relation to the temporal disparities of the uncanny. Like the uncanny, genders exist in concert with the out of joint and out of place. Produced systemically in this uncanny economy, genders provide the link between multiple perspectives and flexible temporality. It may seem odd to make this extended case for a different way of understanding the dynamics of gender systems based on a trite conventional film like *My Big Fat Greek Wedding*. But in its utter normalcy and comic predictability, this film is the symptomatic formulation of resurgent political conservatism and anxieties about the loss of both gender and genre abounding at the time of its release (and maybe still) as manifested in the plethora of contemporaneous reality makeover shows—from Tyra Banks's *America's Next Top Model* to *Queer Eye for the Straight Guy*, *Extreme Makeover*, *What Not to Wear*, and the truly down-market, *The Swan*.

One virtue of *My Big Fat Greek Wedding* lies in the beguiling simplicity of its non-horrific enactment of the relation between the uncanny and the normative, the repressed and the comic, as a circulating juncture that recombines temporalities and perspectives into a dynamic of productive uncertainty. This is not to suggest that the uncanny, especially as defined by Sigmund Freud, is a model for a different understanding of gender. Rather, the uncanny is one dynamic within which interlinking gender systems become visible and operative as layered temporalities. The uncanny's frisson temporarily congeals metamorphic processes in the specter of the return of repressed objects, themes, and desires from the past, expanding and enabling multiple, coexisting temporalities and gender regimes. Through the register of the uncanny, one time confronts another, as these coexist within the recognition that no time is ever over. *My Big Fat Greek Wedding* enacts a metamorphosis from a gender largely defined by its distanced and observing regime of vantage and illegible appearance to a regime that seems to comply with normative social expectations, the two linked by a third, metamorphic regime. Toula's metamorphosis and her vantage on gender, together with the exigencies of a heteroreproductive narrative, produce a complex system of constantly shifting coexisting gender regimes that, in their very changeability, elicit a sense of the uncanny. And perhaps vice versa.

Un-heimlich *Maneuvers: The Psyche Meets the Social in Taxonomy's Origin Story*

My Big Fat Greek Wedding musters an uncanny self-doubling as a part of its fascination. Released in 2002, the film is the cinematic rendition of star Nia Vardalos's autobiographical one-woman stage show. Her performance as herself and ten of her Greek family members impressed the actress and producer Rita Wilson, Tom Hanks's wife, who with Hanks bought the screenplay and produced the film independently. With a $3 million budget, no money for advertising, and most of the production in Canada where filming was cheaper, the film caught on through word of mouth and the Internet, ending up as the largest-grossing romantic comedy ever made. Vardalos herself earned a Golden Globe nomination for acting and an Oscar nomination for screenwriting.

The story is essentially Vardalos's own story, the film's success mirroring—in fact producing—her own success as art and life congeal. Vardalos grew up in a large Greek family in Winnipeg. Wanting to be an actress and comedian, she won an acting scholarship to Ryerson University in Toronto and, by means of a wannabe made-good story of box-office girl taking the stage in a pinch, was invited to join Toronto's Second City comedy troupe. She moved from Toronto to Chicago's Second City, where she met her husband, Ian Gomez, whose appearance in the film as Ian Miller's less uxorious buddy enacts its own kind of uncanny doubling.

As the film traces the transformation of its protagonist from an observing vantage point to a normatively gendered binary, its also enacts a recognition of Vardalos's own version of femininity. Dubbed a "comedic girl" by the *AskMen* website, Vardalos enters the pantheon of desirability because, as the Internet commenters of *AskMen* declare, "We like ladies who do their own thing." The website does acknowledge varying versions of femininity, observing that "Hollywood actresses tend to fall into certain molds: the skinny starlet, the tough-as-nails action chick, and the overly dramatic thespian, to name but a few."[1] Clearly intelligible as feminine to the authors of this website (who may or may not actually be men), Vardalos used weight to alter the appearance of gender normativity. Having gained twenty pounds to portray herself in the film, Vardalos underwent a makeover before Oscar night, again reiterating in her life the direction of the film (or vice versa).

The film's critical reception also mirrored the film's uncertainties about gender and genre. Although it finally made $241,250,669 at the box office, its critical reception was more or less indulgent. Most thought it a "fresh," low-key "good ride," as Ebert and Roeper declared, but some critics opined that it had an odd, sitcom-like quality, usually attributed to the hand of director Joel Zwick, a veteran television director.[2] Some, though notably not the Greek community, thought its ethnicity heavy-handed and offensive, but most thought it authentic. Most of all, perhaps, the film was a comforting vision of predictable comic plot, underdog success (within and as a film), and a reassuring reaffirmation that the American Dream still functions after 9/11. The uncanniness of the film's pervasive

Canadian doubles for presumably American institutions echoes the subversiveness of Mom's kindly manipulation of stubborn, self-centered Dad in the film. Without a Canadian film industry, this paean to the American Dream would not have been possible. Perhaps the film's success and its insights about gender lie in its pervasive, yet curiously domesticated, versions of uncanniness, especially in the ways it engages the uncanny to reveal and normalize a repressed polymorphousness as itself a pleasure at a moment in culture when gender seemed to be coming apart. In an era when popular culture mainstreamed transgender and transsexuality—after, for example, the 1999 triumph of *Boys Don't Cry*, the success of *Will & Grace*, the coming out of Rosie O'Donnell and Ellen DeGeneres, and other normalizations of "queer" genders and sexualities (the two often confused and/or overlapping)—the happy narrative through which the unintelligible becomes normative elicits a big sigh of something like relief for many. "It has charm to spare," comments Craig Roush, "and unlike many romantic comedies, it does not alienate either gender in the audience."[3] Or any of the other genders and sexes either. And its uncanny use of the comic, or comic use of the uncanny, is in large part why it can masquerade as a sitcom lightweight, as a film with very little to say.

In any case, the film is a comedy—its moment of most sincere horror comes with the pimple that spontaneously appears on Toula's face on her wedding day. How then might the uncanny and the comic coexist in the same vehicle? What does the uncanny have to do with gender regimes? Taxonomy—the sorting of types into binary classes—is both instigated by and a defense against the uncanny.

We tend to take the uncanny seriously, as an effect or cause of horror, or at least of those odd feelings of creepy recognition. In his study of the uncanny, Freud defines the phenomenon as one of affect, or feeling, and begins his analysis looking for the "common nucleus" that "distinguishes" the uncanny "within the field of the frightening."[4] Working through theories of the uncanny as the previously familiar, intellectual uncertainty, and unintelligibility as well as a long study of its etymology, Freud concludes that the uncanny has some relation to the hidden and secret. Freud looks for the secret of the hidden by recourse to E. T. A. Hoffman's story "The Sandman," beginning with a rejection of E. Jentsch's idea that the uncanny springs from an uncertainty about whether an object is animate or inanimate. This raises a problem of taxonomy—of whether a being is animate or inanimate, a differentiation that also operates in some analyses of comedy. In *Laughter*, Henri Bergson, for example, suggests that comedy is an effect of the animate, or human, behaving, or mistaken as the inanimate or as machinelike.[5] The uncanny as one kind of feeling is linked to a confusion about status; comedy as another kind of feeling is linked to a conflation of the same oppositions. The uncanny and the comic are perhaps, then, two responses to a similar problem of failed taxonomy—of unintelligibility—even as they appear to resolve the problem through different modes of "affect." Both the uncanny and comedy, however, depend on moments of taxonomic failure, of a lack of distinguishability and a confusion that, in the case of the uncanny, represents the return and coexistence of repressed material—of multiple temporalities and operant regimes.

In Freud's analysis in *The Uncanny*, "The Sandman" links questions of animation to issues of a repressed fear of castration. Freud's reading of "The Sandman" focuses on the story's different crises of the eye: the protagonist's early fear of being blinded, the uncanny appearances of the oculist/lawyer Coppelius, the strange telescope that turns the protagonist mad. Freud's conclusion is that the uncanny has two sides. The first, and least traumatic, is that the uncanny is produced by the reappearance of something from the primitive past, in the case of the story, the reappearance of Coppelius and the lawyer's association with threats of blinding. The second, and more substantial, is that the uncanny is evoked by the return of repressed material such as the castration complex. This material and the temporalities with which it is associated also pose a problem of resorting categories produced by the chaos intrinsic to unrepression. What emerges in the uncanny's revival of the castration complex is the first moment of sorting itself—of the emergence of a fantasmatically sexual prop for the interpretation of difference.

The castration complex is the series of events, recognitions, fears, and compensations that come at the point in time when a young child (in Freud's account, a male child) perceives that another (in

Freud's account, the mother) does not have a penis. It is a moment when, in Lacan's terms, difference turns into sexual difference. This incipient moment of organ-based taxonomizing precipitates the individual's fear that he, too, might lose his valued organ at the hands of his father in punishment for his desire for his mother. Mingling a notion of retributive law with a cognizance of sexual (or at least anatomical) difference, the castration complex links the recognition of difference with law and kinship systems. The moment when a different sex is perceived is also the moment when this specific sexual difference bears the entire weight of individual threat and culpability. Of course, the moment itself is a fantasy that already retroactively overdetermines binary anatomical differences as constitutive of a whole series of effects—desire, guilt, acquiescence—making the mythic originary moment of sexual difference the apparent cause and foundation for an entire familial system and life narrative from the limited point of view of a male child and in relation to the imaginary of the possible irrelevance of the losable part that inaugurates and subtends patriarchy.

Even if we dismiss Freud's Oedipal chamber drama and understand castration more figuratively as the moment individuals begin to recognize difference—that they are separable and perpetually separated from their environment and from others around them—castration still signals the point when a polymorphous lack of differentiation gives way to differences and taxonomies. If we understand castration as the process which institutes the lack of connection and satisfaction that inaugurates desire and language, then the castration complex has everything to do with the compensatory meanings endowed by divisions, taxonomies, and intelligibility. These compensations are founded on the incommensurate translation of multiple possibilities into the rigid, ill-fitting templates produced by cultures as the necessary foundation for the divisions of law and power. Appended to desire and basic to language, these divisions substitute for what can never be had again (a lack of differentiation) as well as what may be desired (the Other, whatever that is).

This complex, however, forever hovers around both a fantasmatic threat of punishment and the condition of unintelligibility that haunts and threatens the termination of lack, and hence desire itself. The castration complex is a perpetual process of sorting differences into difference as the symbolic condition for desire. It needs the sustained spectacle of unintelligible polymorphousness to continue its process. Lacan's theory of subjective sexuation, then, provides multiple possibilities for individual positioning in relation to this sorting that interpret this difference through vectors that simultaneously define difference as binary and leave the binaries behind. Sexuation thus results in multiple postures and attitudes in relation to difference, which suggests in the end that whatever binary imperative sexual difference might represent, individual subjects already interpret that difference in a variety of ways. The process of sorting itself, then, is only delusively binary, a binariness that obscures the variety it hosts.

Freud's reading of the uncanny thus merges the individual's "primitive" past with repressed episodes that are precisely about this process of sorting and differentiating. Cast as originary by an Oedipal gloss, this repressed drama is bound up retrospectively with both a narrative of developmental progress and a binary gender taxonomy, itself already confused with reproductive anatomy as its "natural" support—that is, as the product of power systems premised on continued practices of inequitable division. Primitive (pre-Oedipal) material that returns out of its place in the uncanny is the return of this repressed disorganized polymorphous world where there is no distinction between animate and inanimate, human and object, one type or another. Although Freud singles out the female genitals as the uncanny reminder of origins (an example that inscribes castration anxiety at the moment it tries to probe it), what seems to return is always already there as the polymorphousness that is only ever provisionally organized by such fictive "natural" categories as gender and race. The uncanny glimpses a "no difference" that subtends all difference.

Because the castration complex imposes the story of temporal development and causality—of a before and an after, desire and guilt—the primitive also becomes a temporal designation. Coexisting polymorphousness is repressed as the past, although its lack of taxonomy radically disorganizes what might even constitute material for organization. The primitive is reconstituted as retrospectively chaotic, becoming material that has become intelligible through time and civilization. Since this primitive world knows no cause/effect narrative nor understands source and connection, the primitive may equate a look from the mother with the breast, the feces, or even the voice. Freud's attraction to the eye as the center of both Hoffman's story and repressed castration depends on an equation between the eye and the penis, on the symbolic confusion among or interchangeability of objects. Reprising repressed (i.e., unavailable to memory) castration anxiety as the motive for the uncanny is itself a way of keeping the uncanny at bay, or, rather, a way of displacing teeming polymorphousness into a mythical past where its threat comes only in the uncanny's strange affect of its momentary recall. The account of the uncanny is itself a mode of repression as is the narrative of castration by which time, too, is organized as unidirectional.

The uncanny, then, may be understood not so much as the sudden appearance of primitive elements, but as a moment in which the field of primitive polymorphousness is re-catalyzed by an image or event that recalls the dynamic of differentiation—sexuation—itself. This means that this primitive field has never really disappeared, but is always copresent (even if repressed) and provides the ground against which categorical distinctions are in fact continually remade and sustained. Feelings of doubling, also identified by Freud as catalysts for the uncanny, actually constitute a part of the polymorphous field, which, though it seems a reversion or return to another time, is actually more a momentary shift of focus. Meaning may be especially linked to the eye, not as an organ, but as the focal point of a range of perspectives whose variability both threatens and produces the fictive unity of the subject.

What the operations of the uncanny, like those of the comic, suggest, finally, is the coexistence of temporalities, objects, and even causes and effects rather than any necessary linear ordering—the coexistence of multiple systems in and as environments that jostle, intersect, and open and close as the subject's relations to environments become parts of systems (i.e., an individual's relation to sexual difference as a symbolic environment is already a part of the subject's own system). The "primitive" and the "inhuman" persist and are necessary to ground difference and the taxonomies by which subjective and social separations and distinctions are made and preserved. The illusion of order simply (or actually with a lot of anxious work) organizes what then appears to be the polymorphous disorder of a pre-Oedipal existence. Organizing temporalities themselves produces an illusion of before and after, of cause and effect, centered around taxonomic sorting as the act of dividing and distinguishing objects and phenomena according to the binary schemes that subtend the imaginary/symbolic protocols of kinship, law, capital, narrative, politics, and religion.

What this means is that gender, one of whose regimes is taxonomic, functions as a sorting machine always in the process of discerning difference from a coexisting polymorphousness. Both the uncanny and the comic make the two—polymorphousness and categories—visible at the same time. This sudden apperceivability constitutes an overload that takes on the appearance of return, of temporal and ontological disorder in the place of taxonomic disorder. On the one hand, this overload has to do with unintelligibility insofar as such a feeling is manifested as a gender question—Are you a man or a woman?—or as a question of animation—Are you alive or dead? The latter is the basis of both the horror produced by the broad category of narratives about the undead, such as vampire and zombie stories, and the comedy produced by the sudden clash of systems and analogies. The question of sexual difference is *heimlich* not only because cultural institutions depend on it, but also because it is terrifyingly omnipresent and ultimately uncertain insofar as the Phallus (already never the thing it purports to be) is never a guarantee.

On the other hand, the reprise of disorder may take the form of proliferation, of the unmotivated multiplication of beings within categories where quantity itself threatens the system. These narratives, rarely recognized as having the same uncanny affect as vampiric horror, are equally bound up with gender, though not apparently with its potential unintelligibility. Instead, uncanny proliferations dramatize the ways structures such as marriage actually subtend the taxonomizing from which such structures themselves seem to derive. Showing the persistent mismatch of structural position and the genders of its potential occupants, proliferations make multiple genderings visible by offering what appear to be different "versions" of genders in the same structural position. Proliferations expose the sorting impetus of narrative itself as it orthopedizes noncompliant characters into place. Just as Toula's metamorphosis makes her seem to come into focus as a coherently conventional feminine person, the sorting operations of narratives beset by proliferations appear to discipline variety into categories of narrative value—the "good wife" or the "home-wrecker." These narratives transpose different genderings into narrative roles, thereby making sense of the proliferation as a middling, confused, unsorted state of affairs.[6] At the same time, however, we know how to read these different genderings precisely as different genderings, whose positional cues define in advance their ultimate narrative dispositions. Proliferations in popular culture tend to end up as comedy.

But When They Don't

In contrast to the uncanny frisson of the vampiric that lurks on the other side of the metamorphic, proliferations also hint at zombies, whose main feature (apart from an abject lack of bodily coherence) is that they proliferate. Unlike comic proliferations, zombies reveal only minor differences among themselves: shreds of clothing, hints of features, enough that if we have previously seen the "living" versions, we can now recognize them as the walking dead. If comic proliferations expose the operations of multiple gender regimes, zombies front the process by which genders re-sort themselves into sexual binaries. The disintegrating zombies' reduction of gender differentiation to sexual difference calms the confusing furor of a proliferation of inchoate types, of too many genderings. Increasingly in the twenty-first century, the figure of the zombie has occupied this uncanny site of a bodily proliferation of postmortem beings who resolve confusions back into intelligible binary orders— alive, dead, male, female. Zombies resolve the gender problem, as do vampires, by trumping a proliferation of genders and types with a version of life after death. Why might uncertainties about genders be resolved by recourse to perpetuating existence beyond death? Why do makeovers turn into vampire narratives (as another kind of makeover), or why do proliferations of differently gendered characters in the same narrative position transpose into an attacking hoard of hungry, mindless corpses? Is the stake of gender taxonomy a question of life and death?

Too Many Wives; or, How the Folding Up Unfolds

When, for example, as happened in the mid-twentieth century, wives (instead of zombies) proliferate in narratives, the effect of this overloaded structural position on the sorting powers of taxonomy produces a species of causal reversal. With too many wives, narrative's "natural" impetus of marriage momentarily sidetracks, catalyzing the emergence of a variety of gender regimes instead of preserving the normative binary genders necessary for a happy marital conclusion. As in Freud's narrative of the uncanny, organizing these proliferations involves displacing anxieties about gender into problems of temporality. Taxonomizing, like the uncanny, also requires a ground of "unintelligible" genders, as well as the suddenly precarious stability of kinship and other structures that occurs when copresent polymorphousness is unrepressed. Returning dead wife movies are all about this bad timing and gender splintering. *My Favorite Wife* (1940) and its 1963 remake, *Move Over Darling*, both involve an ostensibly widowed husband, Nick Arden (played by Cary Grant and James Garner, respectively), who, at films' beginning, must declare his wife, who was presumably drowned in a shipwreck or plane crash seven (or five) years ago, dead. Both films begin in a courtroom as Mr. Arden, an attorney, brings a petition to declare his wife dead at the same time (or right before) he asks the judge to marry him to another woman, Bianca (Gail Patrick, Polly Bergen). The befuddled, comically Napoleonic judge (Granville Bates, Edgar Buchanan) has difficulty sorting death from marriage, which is not really his difficulty at all, but rather the structural relation and confusion between the two as compelling "proper" endings in narrative. The happy new couple embarks on their honeymoon at the moment the not-so-dead dead wife, Ellen (Irene Dunne, Doris Day), returns. The returnee, clad in sailor's clothes and dropped off unceremoniously at the driveway of her former home, first encounters her mother-in-law (Ann Shoemaker, Thelma Ritter), who, initially shocked at the uncanny appearance of her daughter-in-law (Thelma Ritter faints three times), welcomes her home. The wife then goes to observe her children, who do not recognize her (although the dog does) and are even unsure of her sex/gender. In *My Favorite Wife*, they ask her, "Are you a man or a woman?" In *Move Over Darling*, they ask, "Who are you? Are you a lady or a man?"

The dead wife has uncannily reappeared at the moment—the seam—between law and consummation—between social structure and the "natural" reproductive function that the law sanctions and that also underwrites the law. As the husband and his new bride embark on their honeymoon trip, one crassly taken at the same hotel as the husband's first honeymoon, the "dead" wife follows at the urging of her mother-in-law, determined to intercede between ceremony and deed. Appearing in the hotel lobby and spotted by her husband as the elevator door shuts him in, the "dead" wife gives her husband, who cannot believe his eyes, a big dose of the uncanny. Just in case he takes her as a guilty apparition, she sends a bottle of champagne to the newlyweds' room with a note and her locket. Now believing his eyes, Nick frantically claims he needs a shave and escapes the marital suite in search of her. Finding the real, live thing, the husband's uncanny shifts from being the effect of the return of the dead to the comical affect produced by the wifely proliferation's problems of prevarication and timing. Registering his wife in their former bridal suite, Nick runs between the future and the past. His bride expecting romance, his wife hoping for loyalty, Nick delays satisfying either by running from one place to another. Playing two roles simultaneously, Nick himself becomes a species of comic uncanny, appearing, disappearing, putting off his commitments to either woman way beyond their proper time. He ends up driving home with his new bride without having changed the status quo.

The uncanny itself proliferates in this plot in which the scene of untimely appearance/disappearance is played over and over and in which wives and male partners multiply. Nick finds out that Ellen has spent the last seven (five) years on an island alone with a man named Stephen and that the two have referred to one another as

"Adam" and "Eve." When he challenges her, she tries to reassure him by describing her shipwreck companion as an unmanly man, as essentially a different and unthreatening gender. She goes so far as to locate a substitute, a meek shoe salesman (Chester Clute, Don Knotts) to stand in for her island buddy. Meanwhile Nick seeks the man out on his own and finds not the docile unmanly specimen his wife described, but a hyperbolic he-man (Randolph Scott, Chuck Connors) jumping on a trampoline, flexing his muscles and bouncing goodwill and testosterone, but like the shoe salesman, enacting a gendering different from Nick's gentlemanly and hesitating self.

Uncanny disturbances and splits in what we expect to be a reproductive narrative force and nurture this emergence of polymorphousness. The films now count two wives, each playing through a different gender regime, and three mates for the returned wife, Ellen, each also from a different regime. The two first wives incarnate different combinations of gender regimes. The Gail Patrick/ Polly Bergen fiancée second wife is a specimen of socially conformative gender with a vengeance, who deploys conventional feminine appearance to masquerade ambitions to power and control. The signifiers of these overlapping regimes of "social" gender (see chapter 3) and dominatrix are hints of sharpness and edges that expose sets of phallic signifiers, or dentata, that emerge from the finely tuned feminine veneer. The returned wife (Irene Dunne, Doris Day) not only begins as unintelligibly androgynous, but also belongs to a metamorphic gender regime as she transforms from an apparently nonconforming being to a conventionally feminine partner. The three "husbands" range from Stephen's he-manity, or masculinity squared (he is mistaken at one point for Johnny Weissmuller), to the shoe clerk's meek eunuchness (masculine minus—both positions on the parabola of social gender), to Nick's suave courtliness (a regime of ethical gender; see chapter 8), mixed with a more centered position on the social parabola. The film's marital crisis actually demands not the complementarity of sexual difference and binary order we might expect, but rather the proper matching of temperaments (themselves signaled by variations in the characters' combinations of gender regimes), which both of these films constitute as a shared sense of humor and the desire to manipulate—by the partners' similarities in personality. Although the marital crisis of the film would seem to produce the imperative of a binary gendering that signals complementary oppositional sexual difference, what happens instead is that the uncanniness of proliferations reveals a coextensive lack of gender binariness, an uncanny polymorphousness that will eventually (almost) be re-contained by law, while the various characters in the film paradoxically seek to find someone who is the same.

The remainder of both movies consists in Ellen's attempts to stop the new marriage before the other shoe drops. Most of the time, the three characters—Nick, Bianca, and Ellen—exist in a species of limbo, where the roles of each proliferate into impermissible combinations. Nick is widower, husband, and bigamist. Bianca is virgin, bride, and adulteress. Ellen is dead and wife. After an additional period of delay where Bianca calls in her shrink (Pedro de Cordoba, Elliott Reid) because she is convinced Nick's marital reluctance is psychogenic, Nick's mother finally lowers the boom, having Nick arrested for bigamy. Back in court with the same befuddled judge, Nick's marriage to Bianca is annulled and Ellen is declared undead. In *My Favorite Wife* the law does not clean up the problem, as Ellen refuses to take Nick back, angry with his procrastinations. But as mother and children go to their vacation house in the mountains, Ellen tells Nick that she might reconsider their relationship around Christmas. The film ends as Nick approaches her contritely dressed as Santa Claus.

The differences between the 1940 *My Favorite Wife* and the 1963 remake themselves represent an increasingly proliferated polymorphousness, but at the same time provide more sites of anxious control. The hotel manager in *Move Over Darling* (Fred Clark) plays a much larger part, demanding that Nick comply with a one-wife, one-room rule. Nick's mother is also more prominent, first making excuses for Nick, then suggesting that Ellen take the role of Swedish masseuse when Nick returns from his honeymoon feigning a bad back (which enables a comic romp with Ellen chasing a half-naked Bianca around the bedroom "massaging" her). This second Ellen is more angry and vindictive. The film itself includes more physical comedy—purse-wackings, tumbles, massages, and complications in general. In addition, *Move Over Darling* is more openly framed by

Bianca's fixation on psychoanalysis, which she deploys as a mode of understanding the strange set of complications catalyzed by the return of the dead (but, which, of course, does not account for them at all). The frantic proliferations of this second version suggest an anxiety about structure itself—about the impossibility of containing this polymorphousness—which is why the film deploys multiple levels of authority and accountability. The presence of psychoanalysis is not only a joking jibe at its stylish ineffectuality; rather, the film evokes psychoanalysis precisely because the institutions of law and family cannot seal up the breach of the uncanny return. Lacking the elegant, almost androgynous match of the protagonists of *My Favorite Wife, Move Over Darling* struggles to find a way to tuck its polymorphousness back into structure, a process that involves a more prolonged and somewhat painful court scene in which causes of action and plaintiffs multiply. The law reveals itself as simultaneously the ultimate sorter and the ineffectual taxonomist.

As an uncanny return disturbs the marital narrative, coextensive polymorphousness reveals itself and is reconfigured as the middling proliferation the film needs to end in some sort of resolution. We might understand these proliferations as simply different versions of binary gender, but what these films make evident is that a perception of gender as binary depends on where one is in relation to structure—the structure of kinship, the structure of narrative. At the moment the marriage (or rather both marriages) is (are) disturbed, the two women very clearly present different species, the undead wife almost unintelligibly gendered. The breach in structure makes visible the disorder in category, and the certainty of gender taxonomies dissolves into a series of questions about the categories into which characters fit. These questions of category are produced by the crisis in structure, and the illusion of clarification is a product of appearing to sort the structure out. In the end, the structure of marriage produces the illusion of organized, binary genders. The intrinsic binary character of structure (and hence narrative) produces gender; gender does not undergird narrative's binary structurings. The disturbance of what appears to be narrative's stable structure via an uncanny return exposes an always coextensive polymorphousness. Gender's appearance as an organized set of binary taxonomies dispels the uncanny, while the appearance of the uncanny makes visible the pretense of category.

The differences between these two versions of the uncanny loosing of polymorphousness in films twenty years apart also relate obviously to their historical moments. While 1940 is less threatened altogether by the comic sameness of its couple, 1963 seems far more worried that something is out of place. *Move Over Darling* repeats the James Garner/Doris Day formula of other early 1960's films, most notably *The Thrill of It All*, where the unprepossessing wife (Doris Day) accidentally has a media career that threatens her James Garner husband's masculinity as well as their family (at one point he drives his car into a backyard pool). The comic insecurity of the '60s may be pressured by the increased visibility of feminism, but it is already oddly less playful than the '40s while trying a lot harder to be funny.

Why Use Popular Cultural Texts?

Why look for understandings of gender regimes in cultural texts? If what we think we are dealing with are sociopsychic formations in some relation to a "biological imperative" on the one hand and desire on the other, why would evidence of the complexity of genderings and multiple regimes emerge most clearly in popular culture? It is not simply that films and television programs showcase examples of various gender regimes. Their very structures—narrative, presentation, sound, style, possible roles—play out not only the manifestations and available styles of gender regimes, but also the dynamic quality of the relations among regimes, narratives, social convention, and sexual, familial, and capitalist ideologies. Thus, popular cultural texts are not merely symptomatic evidence of gender regimes: they are the sites where the systemic intermingling of these regimes reveal their manifestations, dynamic interrelations, possibilities, and alterations through history, rehearsing repeatedly the dramas by which the obvious (that genders are multiple, chatoyant, morphing) is folded up into the conventional (that genders represent the binary truth necessary to subtend patriarchal organizations, capitalisms, and the cultural imaginary of righteous asymmetries).

Although gender regimes shift their operation through time, we can also read them through time. Despite the decades that separate the present from 1963, for example, Doris Day's genderings are still coherent and legible, as are James Garner's and Cary Grant's. At the same time, some regimes fade from currency—the virago, for example, exemplified by the Gail Patrick/Polly Bergen characters in these films. Because that version of extreme social femininity has altered its outward manifestations in relation to changes in style, class protocols, and notions of deportment, these characters seem unusually hard and grasping. Because both films still resolve the issue of proliferation by recourse to the marriage of temperamentally matched protagonists, the second woman is still legible, but perhaps less comic as the satire on her presumptions is lost in historical shifts in manifestations of conventional femininity.

Reading popular cultural texts matches the processual character of genderings themselves. These texts—films, television, commercials, popular music—provide a part of the logic by which gender regimes morph, layer, and drop away. But popular cultural texts also trade on issues of desire, where the relations among genderings, individual desires, and the larger environment of the socius constantly renegotiate structures and roles. Although narrative seems to dispose of most anxiety, and although narrative is a pervasive epistemology when it comes to issues of sex and gender, one of the elements that narratives enact is exactly what narratives cannot control: all of that chaotic material that persists as uncontained. If genderings are partly defined by narrative and partly contained by narrative, they also partly evade narrative and yet still show up symptomatically as the "extras" that cannot be tucked in.

Confirming the Pre-Oedipal in Its Joy, Joy, Joy

The multiplication of occupants of a specific structural position in the heteroreproductive narrative is one form of a comic uncanny that is less about affect than effect. Repetitions of plot and circumstance constitute another manifestation of uncanny comic effect, though one with which we are far more familiar. Repetitions set up a version of the uncanny by evoking feelings of déjà vu and producing the tensions of anticipation, which are the tensions produced by the difference between the apparent departure from narrative structure we see in unmotivated repetition and its resolution and retroactive resignification as the narrative winds it in. If we say "the third time is the charm," what we often mean is that if an event is repeated three times, it gains an uncanny magical significance that will result finally in resolving meaning and effect that make the first two tries significant as well. Repetitions of three occur in relation to particularly difficult and stubborn endeavors, situations so intractable that two tries are not enough. Three means the near infinity necessary to resolution as well as the perennial likelihood that all can be resolved.

My Big Fat Greek Wedding's third replay of Toula and Ian's encounter scene is finally the charm, but, like the others, it also verges on the uncanny. In the first scene in the restaurant Toula is an inanimate statue of illegible gender. In the second encounter Toula repeats her slide out of sight into unintelligibility. The third reprises the previous window encounter and occurs just after a single intervening scene of the Portokaloses at home. Toula is seated on the couch between her parents watching television, a scene which inscribes her most definitively as the spinster daughter, but a scene also haunted by the very uncanny black-garbed grandmother who has just been returned home by an irate neighbor, who requests that Mr. Portokalos keep her "out of her basement and off of her roof." Returning to his place on the couch, Toula's father comments to her, "Toula, there are two kinds of people—Greeks and everybody else who wish they was Greek." His ethnic taxonomy produces a frustrated reaction from Toula.

The next sequence reprises Toula as the busy center of the travel network. Ian again walks by the window but does not get far before Toula spots him. Viewed again from her desk-high vantage point— finally her vantage point and physical position align—Ian pretends he does not see her see him and walks tauntingly by. He comes back and waves in recognition and Toula smiles. They exchange looks and smiles and he gestures to her to wait. The phone rings and Toula's attention is diverted as Ian performs a goofing, gradually descending walk in front of the window. As he disappears from sight in a structural parallel to Toula's two descents, his position is occupied by a little old lady. Ian, thus, seems to turn into the old lady Toula resembled at film's beginning. The little old lady begins whacking Ian with her purse as Toula watches. Again diverted by her duties, Toula is distracted as Ian's head reappears at the level of the window, a position that reprises Toula's vantage in the first two encounters. This time, however, Ian enters the travel agency to talk with her; although she registers briefly the same look of panic as in the previous two encounters, Toula, herself at desk level and looking up, musters the courage to greet him and smile. She stands up, asks him if he wants to see brochures, walks toward the table where they are kept, and is suddenly yanked backward to the floor by her headphone cord. As Ian looks over the desk to the now-prostrate Toula, she says, "Found 'em," a homonym of "Found him." The scene continues as the two sit on the floor behind the desk laughing about the encounter they just had, as he finally asks her out on a date.

This third instance both reiterates and seems finally to dispel the anticipations and uncanny feeling of the first two. Working two ways at once, the automatonic and inhuman unintelligibility Toula represents at the beginning transforms to Ian's positional joke by the third encounter. This third encounter, however, also represents the culmination of another kind of transformation—the visible work of making Toula comply with normative "social" femininity. Although the film presents her feminizing process as a series of comic vignettes that mask the real work involved, Toula has to change almost everything about herself. Love and happiness are the reward, of course, as Toula is finally a visible participant in a romantic narrative. But, as in *My Favorite Wife*, proper coupledom in *My Big Fat Greek Wedding* seems to be more a matter of similarity than difference. Toula and Ian resemble each other physically. They both erupt pimples on their wedding day. The only categorical difference seems to be Toula's Greekness, which is itself overcome in large part by Ian's conversion to Greek Orthodoxy and sincere but comic attempts to speak Greek at family gatherings.

With Toula's compliant transformation, the film's anxiety about category finally resides in language itself. The father's trademark etymologies, which convert all semantic difference to the category of the Greek, resonate with Ian's misguided attempts to speak Greek. Asking his future brother-in-law Nick how to say various ceremonial greetings, Ian recites the syllables Nick has fed him, which turn out to be such phrases as "I have three testicles" instead of "Let's eat" or "You have nice boobs" instead of "Thank you." The sexual innuendos of these phrases as well as the repetition of the joke (Ian never seems to learn), play out the film's categorical instabilities on the level of discourse itself as a comic problem of translation. The father, however, does get it. He understands on some deep level that taxonomy is what it is all about. He leaves nothing hanging in claiming the Greek in everything.

2 Prosopopeias

Exceeding Kind

Very well, but just how shall we pose the question? And, to begin with, who are we to propound it at all? Man is at once judge and party to the case; but so is woman. What we need is an angel—neither man nor woman—but where shall we find one?

—Simone de Beauvoir, *The Second Sex*

My Big Fat Greek Wedding's opening sequence offers a model of a "vantage" gender regime as the imaginary site from which gender can be viewed as such. The film offers this site of vantage as a conventional establishment shot, thereby naturalizing such a position of unattached vantage. Because gender is an open system and no one can be outside of it, there is no place outside of gender from which we can view gender as such. All environmental views of gender are only partial, some providing the illusion that in seeing two clear taxonomic genders, we have seen it all. The question *My Big Fat Greek Wedding* raises is who or what operates the array of establishment shots that open the film and why do those shots ultimately settle on the enigma of Toula? This question of vantage—of the imaginary position from whence genders and genderings can be seen as such—is, of course, also an issue in this book. From what vantage can one try to discern the workings of the open gender system?

The Place of the Angel/Chimera

There are many coexisting, cooperating attitudes constituting gender regimes. One gender regime we have glimpsed is the "taxonomic," organized around mechanisms for sorting the binary—masculine, feminine—that are produced in and through and also produce such structures as kinship, narrative, market categories, and the mobile prop of mirroring otherness. At the psychical root of taxonomy is the tendency toward binarism produced in the process of interpreting difference sexually (sexuation). Culturally, we taxonomize our taxonomies, regarding the duo "male/female" as biological and the pair "masculine/feminine" as sociocultural, although more often we conflate these dichotomies with each other. Collapsed into one another, sex/gender binaries sustain the series of divisional inequities (gender roles, patriarchy) that characterize the binary epistemology through which structure constitutes meaning and meaning structure and that accept categorizations as always already determined and determinative. Through its roots in structure, the taxonomic falls prey to its own illusions of linear cause and effect, the meaningfulness of origins, and the essential and/or already (over)determined disposition of its categories. As simultaneously category and process, the taxonomic is both effect and function, a sorting regime that adjusts through contexts, times, and roles to retain the illusion of balancing, yet asymmetrical complementarity, as well as the impression of an ever-readily ordered distribution necessary to and a condition of our making sense of things. But the taxonomic is only one regime among many.

Fronted by the categories themselves in the guise of the ambiguous and pervasive m □, f □, which demands a compliant response from all beings (including animals) and which behaves as if their very existence has already determined all possible interpretations of ontology, the taxonomic is, by definition, intractable, an apparatus that covers over its own tracks so that its operations and mechanisms appear always to have been there. Its sorting operation disguised as a concentrated typology, taxonomy takes the form of a determination, the reductive essence of one of two nouns/adjectives as a given status, an "identity" (with its multifarious assortments), as an imaginary box into which we self-evidently and with the illusion of choice sort ourselves as a return to kind. The taxonomic regime is a Maxwell's demon subject to its own paralyzing and imperializing self-contradiction. The paradox of taxonomic gender and the spur to its perpetual sorting is the intrinsic mismatch between the regulating fiction of its categories and the necessary polymorphousness that must be there for taxonomy to organize. Coupled with our inability to escape its aegis, the taxonomic is the Sisyphean rock we must trundle for the momentary breather of sense.

Although *My Big Fat Greek Wedding*, for example, maps a "metamorphic" regime that operates through time, it also presents the dilemma of a gender regime defined through the illusion of a vantage on gender itself by occupying and organizing subjectivity in relation to a visual attitude. The unintelligible Toula (Is she old? Is she Greek? Is she feminine?) characterizes "herself" ("herself" since she already is, by virtue of being alive, caught up in the taxonomic project) as a Greek statue, but she also occupies a vantage in relation to the visible ideologies of gender and family. At the beginning of the film, Toula's vantage assures other characters' gender and kinship organization as they attempt to taxonomize her, but the intersection of her unusual gender presentation and her function as observer/commentator already produces her as an intelligible gender, albeit one that simultaneously believes in and eschews taxonomies. As a position linked to an attitude of distanced vantage enacted by the film's opening sequence, this vantage regime is organized as the place outside, the position of the observer who is otherwise not intelligible in relation to normative taxonomy. As a regime, the dynamics of "vantage" are already culturally intelligible; we always think we can see gender for what it is. And this sense of being able to see gender qua gender can partially constitute a subject's self-positioning as the subject who thinks it knows. (Any writer of a book on gender would have to participate in this regime.) This observer is, like de Beauvoir's angel, both outside and a gender naïf in a regime produced as an analogy to an environmental outside vantage (a second-order observer in systems terms) from which one can watch the intersection of other gender regimes as they interact. What vantage omits is any relation between gender regimes and the imaginary environment vantage seems to occupy.

But in relation to what is the regime of vantage defined? If it persists in an imaginary environment, is vantage a mere host for other genderings? Clearly not, since any position "outside" emerges in relation to an existing structure, while that structure, even if reacting and evolving, responds to constant observation and re-characterization. The "outside" is already inside. Is vantage, then, merely parasitic, its vantages all inscribed as viewpoints onto a familiar taxonomy? Although we might be insistently drawn back to an idea of vantage as dependent on taxonomy—that framing presumes the existence of the phenomenon being framed—it may just as easily work the other way around, or in a more systemic perspective, both ways at once. Taxonomy is produced and catalyzed by the illusion of an outside vantage. The two modes coexist as necessary stimuli to one another, neither first, neither preeminent. Taxonomy supplies the lure of quiescent order and delusory certainties, while vantage enables and evades our scrutiny, ending up occasionally as the illusion of a superior viewpoint, an epistemology, a metaphysical knowing that knows it knows, but of course can never really know because it, too, has a blind spot.

The vantage regime is polymorphous in that there are an infinite number of vantages one may occupy, from the point of the framing observer, to the "subject supposed to know"—whom we imagine occupies whatever the last frame is—to the unlocated and mobile viewer analogized only by the imaginary flight of birds and angels. Not only is vantage an imaginary framing position, such as the instance of Toula observing her family observing her, it is also the position of the undefined looker such as the camera view (e.g., as manifested in the opening establishment sequence of *My Big Fat Greek Wedding*), which has neither a specific location nor even the oppositional apparatus that may invite the taxonomic to define it within its binaries.

Vantage is angelic, chimeric, and intrinsically multiple. Its mobile, polymorphous quality is an effect of its constantly shifting positions. Figured as extraterrestrial and tertiary, vantage, which seems curiously singular as a suspiciously synthetic, more-or-less judicial point, is, by definition, impossible to pin down. Rendered as an imaginary in- or super-human point of observation, vantage exists on the imaginary border of the polymorphous (that is, of course, within it), providing, on the one hand, the illusory vantage from which the taxonomic can be viewed as taxonomic, and on the other, working as a toggle among the different regimes of gender. Although, like de Beauvoir, we may ascribe a celestial whiff to vantage, the figuration of this observing ilk indeed characterizes the working of this regime. And we do understand vantage as a mode of gendering with attitude, though we do not recognize either that do we do so or that so doing is a necessary enabling vector to our taxonomic sorting. The binary categories to which we so insistently and so intractably ascribe always mean at least three (m/f plus an angel). Vantage is, as its cherubic figurations suggest, neither inside nor outside, but framing, observing, contingent, and uncontained.

Holy Gaze

As a gender regime, vantage is inflected by yet another, even more unlocatable vector that Lacan identifies as the "gaze."[1] This gaze—this sense of being seen—explodes the fictive complementarity of voyeuristic structures (looking and being looked at) by splintering any two-way economy. All lookers are also the object of a gaze with no specific source as a "being stared at" from the outside world.[2] The omnipresence of the gaze multiplies the necessary vectors of being looked at to no fewer than three at any given time—looking, being looked at, and what the subject has that is "given to be seen." This gaze is itself also the object of desire in the drive for a particular look back, even though it always eludes us. The vector from which this being-seenness emanates is unlocatable.[3] Because both the looker and the looked-at are simultaneously subject to and object of the gaze, the look itself circulates among ever-proliferating terms governed by the subject's drives and the cultural modes through which the gazing and gazed constitute privileged sites of desire and the desire for desirability.

Although structure and taxonomy can easily translate even the gaze into the illusion of an oppositional binary—looker and lookee (sorting operations do this to everything all the time)—the disturbing function of the gaze as the site of invisible vantage works in a way analogous to de Beauvoir's figure of the angel or the chimeric observer. Insofar as feeling (the uncanny, pleasure) signals the clash of systems and logics, this extra-worldly jitter produces an affect— not the uncanny's feeling of queasy discomfort nor the pleasure and relief linked to comedy, but the fleeting sense of awe and privilege common both to religious mystery and to the primal scene. Vantage's affect is a frisson of the sacred, a sense of admission to the forbidden, as the obscene yet fascinating witnessing of origins that persist in a different register of existence altogether. This impression is produced by a feeling of extra-corporeality that slides between the gaze and alienation. Envisioning the point of envisioning, this mise en abyme frames the frame potentially infinitely through a regressive hall of consciousness. To see three, we occupy four, we see four from five, and so on. The beatific third fronts both the infinite repetitions of the mise en abyme and the looming polymorphousness of the "heteroclite" differences that linger and threaten just outside the frame. Hence vantage's occasional configuration as angelic or chimeric.

The affect of vantage, however, may also evince uncanniness when the subject's look meets the angel's roving eye. When this occurs, the subject has the sense of seeing itself see itself, eliding the gaze as the sense of being seen. Or as Lacan suggests, this seeing oneself seeing oneself represents "mere sleight of hand. An avoidance of the function of the gaze."[4] The layers of self-reflection proliferate: the subject sees itself seeing itself, then sees itself seeing itself being seen, becoming another site of ambivalent mise en abyme proliferations. The imaginary relation of seeing oneself see oneself see oneself see oneself . . . is infinitely regressive and uncannily doubling, like the framing vantage of the angel who is always one step out, hence the angel figure's amalgamation of superior, mobile vantage and extra-corporeality.

This infinite regression is also fronted by mimicry, by "the stain" as that which offers itself to be seen. The figure of the stain "is valuable," according to Lacan, "in marking the pre-existence to the seen of a given-to-be-seen."[5] "The presence of the gaze," Robert Samuels comments, "causes the inversion of the subject's consciousness and narcissism."[6] This inversion—the subject who is invested in self-contemplation becomes aware of being seen—reorders the relation between vantage and self-regard as the result of a consciousness of one's own objective status. One sees oneself as if one were someone else seeing oneself (in both senses of the phrase—both as if a subject sees itself from the vantage of another and as if the subject sees another subject see itself seeing itself as if from the vantage of another). These mise en abyme processes are also a part of the dynamic by which the relations between positional and taxonomic gender regimes are played out as excess, display, camp, and the impersonation of taxonomic gender itself, resulting in a gender regime organized as a vertiginous, self-conscious redoubling of taxonomies staged for a perpetually redoubling gaze. This "vertiginous" regime operates in relation to notions of gender as "performative" insofar as it elicits a consciousness of convention and of itself as an intrinsic part of the process.

As the unlocatable seen of being seen imagined to emanate from the Other, the gaze threatens the re-evocation of taxonomies insofar as we imagine that the gaze belongs to the order of law and its categorizing imperatives. Who looks but one who potentially judges? As a part of the complex interweaving of gender regimes, the stain as the feigning of something to be seen offered to the gaze, then, appears as a hyperbolically taxonomic gender, as gender with a vengeance, like the femininity assumed by Joan Rivière's example of the overly masculine woman, the camp display of transvestic femininity, or the classed masculinity of drag kings.[7] These gender "stains" eventually tip into an anamorphosis in which taxonomic gender appears as a folded-up, coded, or redoubled version of itself. This constitutes an "anamorphic" regime that continually folds scopic self-consciousness into coded displays. These displays, which play with taxonomic gender signifiers, persist in the realm of interpretation, requiring perpetual decoding and re-encodement. Insofar as its operative dynamic requires a persistent interpretation of mimicry working through enframings, the anamorphic regime's operations are ultimately digestive.

Another manifestation of the stain, however, is the figure of the eye itself, which produces a short circuit in the regressions of framing looking. By standing in for both the gaze and self-regard, the image of the eye halts the proliferation of frames while seeming to occupy the fictional place from which the gaze emanates. The figure of the eye works as a decoy, soliciting the look so that the gaze can persist in its operations. The figure of the eye, thus, combats mimicry by enacting a stain on the horizon of the gaze, a something to be looked at in the imaginary place of the looker, delusively harnessing the gaze (which is by definition unlocated) by providing a representation of and specific point for its function. Thus the all-seeing eye on the American one-dollar bill enacts the democratic drama of "watch the birdie," as the layers of our corporatization proliferate. The eye as the stain of the gaze also enacts the ways the regime of vantage is itself represented as simultaneously invisible, unseeable, and spectacular.

De Beauvoir's evocation of the angel in the introduction to *The Second Sex* plays out the set of contradictions that circulate around vantage and the gaze, but in a way that is curiously resonant with the position Toula occupies at the beginning of *My Big Fat Greek Wedding*. De Beauvoir's use of the figure of the angel enacts the contradictions that seem inherent in the illusory totality of the taxonomic. The nature of the taxonomic is that once there, we cannot see beyond it. Imagining, then, a site from which binary categories can be seen as if from outside, de Beauvoir situates the angel as the front man for a second figuration—the hermaphrodite. The one who sees both genders also incarnates them. Her rhetorical slide from angel to hermaphrodite unwittingly enacts the mise en abyme dynamic the angel already represents, producing the hermaphroditic angel as itself an example of the coexistence of binary categories. "Still," de Beauvoir comments, shifting from the angel, "the angel would be poorly qualified to speak, for an angel is ignorant of all the basic facts involved in the problem. With the hermaphrodite, we should be no better off."[8] The hermaphrodite, it seems, being neither man nor woman, is no more qualified as a vantage than the angel, who is also neither man nor woman. Requiring, then, the very knowledge by which she originally disqualified men and women, de Beauvoir concludes that "after all, certain women . . . are best qualified to elucidate the situation of women. . . . It is not a mysterious essence that compels men and women to act in good or in bad faith, it is their situation that inclines them more or less toward the search for truth."[9] Thus, playing both sides, de Beauvoir produces a truth-seeking vantage, one dependent on the "restoration of privileges pertaining to the estate of the human being" which affords them "the luxury of impartiality."[10]

That impartiality and truth would be located in a vantage that can be occupied even by beings who have otherwise been subject to the operations of the taxonomic reinforces at least the idea of the vantage as a gender epistemology. But considering Toula's example in relation to the hovering angel shows how vantage itself constitutes a logic of gender for which the binary has long been surpassed—the gender which is not one, nor two, nor three . . .

Angels on High

The celestial quality of the angel veils what Michel Foucault identifies as the cultural imperative of taxonomy: the need to discern a "true" sex, which is presumably located beneath the confusions of body and appearance.[11] Foucault is talking about hermaphrodites, and sex functions here as a symbolic guarantor of the taxonomic. Finding a true sex means finding the proper classification; finding the proper classification means finding the permanent truth of the unstable taxonomies that subtend social and juridical structures. The hermaphrodite per se, though a naturally occurring variety, is only intelligible as hermaphrodite within the focused lens of the taxonomic, which always already defines the hermaphrodite as a patchwork, part one category, part another, instead of seeing its mixtures. The problem with the hermaphrodite from the perspective of the taxonomic is, of course, that the hermaphrodite is unintelligible both as sex and as gender. Culture can no longer depend on nature as its support.

Like de Beauvoir, Foucault notes that the possibility of sexual intelligibility has been displaced into an inhuman position—in his analysis a chimera rather than an angel. "Sexual irregularity," he comments, "is seen as belonging more or less to the realm of chimeras."[12] The chimera's impossibility, reflected in its unlikely knitting of inapposite parts, supersedes both gender and genre, evading and suggesting affiliations, while canceling them in its perpetual circulation of taxonomies. Although Foucault observes that displacing the problem of gender/genre into the figure of the chimera evades cultural gender confusions, his introduction to Herculine Barbin's autobiography prefaces Herculine's own evocation of the angelic and extra-worldly as the only possible vantage for gender polymorphousness. Addressing the firmly male of the world, Herculine proclaims, "You are to be pitied more than I, perhaps. I soar above all of your innumerable miseries, partaking of the nature of the angels; for, as you have said, my place is not in your narrow sphere. You have the earth, I have boundless space."[13]

The relation between this regime of vantage and polymorphousness also appears in the accounts of transsexuality collected in Catherine Millot's *Horsexe: Essay on Transsexuality*.[14] Millot performs a Lacanian reading of the phenomenon of transsexuality based on various clinical and autobiographical accounts. In the final chapter of the book, "Gabriel; or, The Sex of the Angels," she recounts how, in an interview, a female-to-male transsexual suggested to her that transsexuality "is something abstract, as if we were spirits, as if we ought not to have bodies at all, as if we were complementary to something somewhere."[15] Millot characterizes this out-of-body vantage as "outsidesex" insofar as the transsexual "personifies the term relative to which both sexes must situate themselves."[16]

Transsexuality, like hermaphroditism, does not in itself constitute a gender regime organized around vantage (around the illusion of seeing genders as if outside of gender), but both possibilities represent the configurations by which vantage is evoked as the by-product of the clash between the taxonomies of biological sex and conventional binary genders. The figure of the angel or evocations of the spirit, for example, remove vantage from a taxonomic arena to a place where the arena itself can be seen and which is exempted from taxonomy because of its inhumanity. Another analogous version of vantage is offered by Jan Morris in her autobiography *Conundrum*. Morris, a male-to-female transsexual, understood her "outsidesex position" as the vantage of the "secret agent." For Morris, this position is itself multiple, both "from without" and "from within." "Sitting there undetected, so to speak," she writes, "I evolved the techniques of analysis and observation that I would later adapt to the writer's craft."[17] "For me," she continues, "it was as if I had permission to listen at doors or to see without being seen, safe behind a two-way mirror."[18] Morris picks up on the secret, forbidden quality of vantage, the feeling of privilege engendered by occupying a vantage from which taxonomic categories can be perceived as such. Although transsexuals evoke vantage as a position that explains their relation to gender, vantage also hides the transsexual shift from gender to sex—to the point where gender is imagined to be guaranteed by the body. The polymorphousness that exceeds any body's sexual conformity is displaced into vantage as the regime that offers both a polymorphous perspective and an epistemology of gender itself.

This open vantage is also reciprocally configured as the chimeric, monstrous, and mutant, especially insofar as chimeras express simultaneously the multiplicity of their patchwork of referents (essentially a combination of different species) and the implied range of vantages such a combination enables. This version of mixed-species creature is chimeric not only because it defies taxonomies and even orders of organization (taxonomy, hierarchy), but also because it affords a form of invisibility insofar as multiplicity camouflages multiplicity itself. The figure of monstrosity slides into the figure of the incorporeal and unlocatable—the infinite of the angel or the invisibility of the secret agent. These two figures are linked by the implied lack of limit on their vantage which, hence, becomes multiple and flexible. The transposition from taxonomic violation into the ubiquitous vantage of the invisible performs the systemic relation between these two gender regimes (taxonomic, vantage). Taxonomy's relation to vantage appears as a metamorphing process; morphing is the mechanism by which being in excess of taxonomy becomes a superhuman vigilance. The spectacle of morphing is the signifier of this multi-vectored vantage. Exceeding kind itself inevitably morphs into the metamorphic.

A Decade of Change

The makeover is a version of a temporal regime in which a subject transforms from the incommensurate or incomprehensible into the taxonomically certain. Makeovers involve human things: people, houses, wardrobes. Their governing dynamic is time, and time is what it takes to see change. Makeover narratives also belong to the genre of the self-help commodity narrative, by which the aid of products can regulate the infelicitous irregularities of presentation—as if the genuine, conforming regime has always lurked within the changing subject/object as its "potential" "true" self.

The first decade of the twenty-first century also hosted the visible polymorphousness of mixed-species (and -genre) films as cultural narratives of taxonomic transformation. Although these transformations also take place through time, the duration of metamorphic processes has diminished, sometimes down to an instant. Transposing temporality into multiple possible embodiments, the metamorphic regime organizes around vantage as the process that envisions multiples. Vantage offers a special ability to envision the range of gender and subjective possibilities. Like the subjects of transformation who are endowed with some perspective on their change, such films as *My Big Fat Greek Wedding* offer soaring perspectives on the range of polymorphous possibility.

While affording some imaginary sense of transformational capacity, this first-decade preoccupation with metamorphosis is simultaneously liberating insofar as it affords a range of possibilities and defensive in that it provides a spectacularly roundabout way to return to clear, conventionally ordered taxonomies. It may be that these taxonomic categories refuse to stay in place and that gender reveals itself as an unstable, mutable thing. But the promise of free-ranging taxonomic choice, though perhaps appealing, is still subject to the imaginary of binary categories, as some chimeras themselves front categorical order.

Teratological Vantage

As an aspect of the clash of taxonomy and vantage, morphing is figured literally in superhuman, mixed-species characters such as Spider-Man, and more figuratively in the rubbery capabilities of animated characters such as Shrek. Linked to cartoons (or the "cartoonic"), figures like Spider-Man and Shrek visibly enact the interweaving of different gender regimes. Even in his moniker, Spider-Man combines mixed species with a distinct sexed taxonomy—"spider" and "man." Shrek defines himself as an ogre, a monster who eats humans: one who, by definition, is situated outside, and one who sports green skin and speaks with a Scottish accent. The films *Spider-Man*, *Spider-Man 2*, and *Spider-Man 3*, and *Shrek*, *Shrek 2*, *Shrek the Third*, and *Shrek Forever After* defy genre in so far as each of them transposes one medium—the cartoon, the realist human film—into the other. The combination of species, genres, and gender dynamics produces superhuman power and, in the case of Spider-Man, the ability to occupy the wheeling aerial vantage of the craning camera.

Spider-Man and the universe represented in the Shrek films provide two versions of the interplay of the gender regimes of vantage and taxonomy (among others), configured as morphing, represented as a celestial perspective, and colliding with and participating in the heteronarrative disposition of beings. The series of first-decade Spider-Man films, a series directed by Sam Raimi and starring Tobey Maguire in the title role, render something from the genre of the cartoon in terms of realist cinema. The term "realist" here refers to both a filmic style and to the physical register denoted for the film's diegesis. Although the effects through which the Spider-Man films were produced were anything but "real" (the photography of extant proto-cinematic beings doing things), the films' combinations of computer-generated imaging (CGI), puppetry, and other special effects technologies with live-actor performances produces "realistic" worlds insofar as phenomena seem to comply with the rules of physics. Where they don't—such as how Spider-Man and his nemeses defy the possibilities of speed, mobility, and gravity—those deviations are accounted for by the narrative details of the film itself, generally by a fictionalized "scientific" explanation. The Spider-Man films are all about exceeding genre—film realizing comic and cartoon, characters as examples of mixed-species or cyborgian beings, film production the merger of computer generation and photography. In relation to the ways the films exceed genre, the realistic style through which their stories are rendered is significant, then, as a way of reining in this excessiveness, of making this polymorphous contribution seem a very normal view.

Spider-Man's rendition as an odd combination of extra-human

and very human is reflected in and produces his vantage as angel/ chimera. Spider-Man is a split being whose two identities correlate with the two parts of his interspecies composition, yet which together produce a being greater than the sum of its parts. Enacting a mobile gender defined and expressed through his flying vantage and deflected by his costume, which acts as a stain (the mimesis of the environmental arachnid that accounts for his capabilities), Spider-Man's webbed spectacle and hidden eyes also function as a stain that deflects regard and decoys the gaze, enabling him to appear to disappear, to see without seeing, and to see without being seen. Literally moving from the taxonomic class of the masculine being sexed male to a mixed-species chimeric vantage, Spider-Man observes and rescues from a place imagined as above, even if in fact Peter Parker is actually observing from street level. The vantage of Spider-Man defines Peter Parker's look while Peter Parker's ethics define Spider-Man's capabilities and behavior.

The film *Spider-Man* literalizes the chimeric in the Spider-Man super-position, which at the same time removes his vantage from this cherubic realm even as it locates it there. Spider-Man's celestial vantage does not perform the angelic impartiality evoked by de Beauvoir, but is instead anatomized as an effect of Peter Parker's cross-species history, of his inability to occupy any single vantage— human male, Spider-Man, or chimera. Mixed species swerving into the hermaphrodite, Spider-Man's gendering is less Tiresian than premised on the perpetuated split between the heteronormative desires of Peter Parker and the limitations imposed by the weight of Spider-Man's public obligations, played out in the layering of clothing: his Spider-Man suit under his street clothes. There is no reason Parker cannot perform as Spider-Man in Peter Parker clothes, except that the layering of costume and the Spider-Man outfit itself signals the complexities of a vantage gender regime that oscillates the look, the gaze, and the stain. In this way, the example of Spider-Man plays out a version of a vantage regime as that regime is literally expressed through vantage but produced—as it is imagined in the angel and the hermaphrodite—as an effect of split or warring desires, of vantage as itself an effect of a disjunction between looking and the gaze, between sexual aim and object.

How is it that the vantage regime, then, becomes an effect of warring desires? Are gender regimes always enactments of particular structures of desire and/or particular manifestations of the drive? What is the relation between subjects' idiosyncratic drives, the objects of their desire, their sexuation, and the gender regimes they inhabit and display? Gender regimes represent both the objects desired (insofar as a gender display consciously or unconsciously attracts the desired object) and the drives that push toward one pleasure or another. Insofar as any gender is both an effect and a regulating machine, genders, from both taxonomic and vantage regimes, channel desires and are partly produced by them. The vantage regime, for example, may be an effect of a lack of correlation between what one wants (to see or be seen) and what one wants to do (see, be seen, or not be seen) and/or an effect of wanting more than one thing at a time, as such warring desires manifest themselves as a positioning outside—a vantage on the dilemma and choices themselves.

The History of an Eye

Although the first decade of the twenty-first century hosts a suspicious number of metamorphic examples, the scopic has long figured in a similar species of reciprocal transformations, such as those in which the one we imagine or which imagines itself as all-seeing becomes the incomprehensible chimera. This seeing is not only the perception of kind, but also the register through which all kinds can be sorted and organized. Even if a "true" gender is hidden, psychoanalysis tells us that symptoms will appear to cue the hidden state of affairs. But what appears: "gender" or desire? Why are these two very different phenomena confused? What might make us think that gender is a subjective "truth"? Or is desire that "truth"? Does gender signal desire? Perhaps in concert with very conventional narrative dispositions of characters, we assume a link between these revealed genders and assumptions about desires. Or perhaps somehow genders signal desires, maybe indirectly, but nonetheless legibly through some unconscious, untraceable process. Does desire constitute some sort of subjective "truth" hinted at by genderings, which are less about coherence than they might be about an entire subjective systemic inscription of positionings, appeals, self-regard, and subjective history by which a subject's desires manifest, shift, adjust, and perpetuate themselves?

From Sigmund Freud's reliance on E. T. A. Hoffman's "The Sandman," organized around issues of sight, seeing, and eyes to define the uncanny feeling of return in *The Uncanny*, to Freud's notions of the "reversal of affect" illustrated by the relation between voyeurism and exhibitionism (the voyeur is the one who wants to be seen, while the exhibitionist is the one who wishes to look), to the uncanny character of the vampire's opening, unseeing eyes in classical film renditions of vampire stories, scopic drives have long been configured as the intersection/resolution of polymorphous kinds and desires.[19] In addition to Freud's and Lacan's situating elements of the scopic as central to subject formation and desire, estimations of the effects of pornography beginning in the nineteenth century, feminist film theories of the 1970s and '80s, and many cultural historical locations of a shift to the visual as a primary feature of industrialization accompany a sense that sex and gender are there to be seen and that the desire to see sex is not only curiosity, but also a desire to discern the differences by which difference is maintained.[20] The specific connection between scopic drives and the clash of gender regimes comes to a frantic head between 2000 and 2010, as metamorphoses speed up to the point where specific sexual desires drop away, leaving only the question of incommensurate genders and kinds to resolve. But the sexual component of the scopic still underlies chimeric assays to harness, delimit, or even escape desire altogether.

The Story of an Eye

The specimen example of the link between vantage and polymorphous desires occurs in Georges Bataille's perverse *Story of the Eye*, which also plays out the drama of the eye as the stain of the gaze.[21] The story, which follows the exploits of a renegade young couple who recognize no sexual limit, produces the eye as the only possible vantage from which the story's activities can be imagined, the vantage itself gaining simultaneously a beatific and diabolical character as an effect of an unrestrained polymorphousness that operates finally on the level of detached and scattered organs. Although the eye does not equal vantage in Bataille's narrative, the position of the eyeball becomes the vantage from which we might perceive a plethora of sexual permutations. Sexual behavior between the protagonist and his girlfriend, Simone, is only possible as an effect of the gaze. Instead of copulating, they indulge in sexual acts that enable them to watch themselves. They prefer to include a third party who occupies the position of the gaze watching them watch themselves. Although taxonomic gender is never at issue in *Story of an Eye*, the complex dynamics of vantage and the eye play out as a version of polymorphous perversion notable for its excess. The narrative of perversity ends with the protagonists killing a priest, removing his eye, and using it as an object of sexual play.

With the stain of the gaze transformed into a literal sexual toy, the vantage regime takes the form of polymorphousness, as a kind of fusion or con-fusion of subject and object that dismantles any foundational notion of the binary even as it pumps out its permutations. Unleashing polymorphousness and multidirectional desire contributes to the production of vantage as both an effect and a cause, a phenomenon seen even in such prosaic texts as *Spider-Man* in the necessary doubling of the mixed-species Spider-Man with a series of enhanced and/or cyborgian nemeses—the Green Goblin and Doctor Octopus (or Doc Ock). *Spider-Man 2* links Doc Ock to the production of fusion energy, as he has been accidentally fused to the handling equipment for his fusion reactor.

Although the Spider-Man persona's positionality is accounted for by Peter Parker having been bitten by a genetically modified spider during a visit to a natural history museum, his mixed-species condition may have been produced as well from Parker's divided desires to be a good nephew, a research scientist, and the boyfriend of the attractive girl next door. Parker, a humble, hesitant geek whose avocation is photography and whose passion is science, registers as male, but not as entirely masculine in his pre-spider existence. He is the object of bullying; he is small, flabby, and bespectacled. He does not know how to woo Mary Jane, the girl next door. He is not even a son, existing instead in the status of nephew. For Peter, mildly thwarted in romance, science is a philanthropy, and duty is the legacy of his hardworking uncle. Unlike other boys, Peter seems unable to overcome ethics for desire, even before the spider bites him. The spider bite gives him an ethical reason to put off sexual desire, to sublimate it to the public service indentured as an obligation of his superpower.

Being bitten by the spider does not necessarily masculinize Peter Parker. Rather, the mixed-species spider morph locates him in another position correlative to his previously unsteady hold on the categories of binary taxonomy and his split and conflicting desires. Although his body takes on the firmer characteristics of normative "social" masculinity—he bulks up, loses the glasses, gains confidence—his persona remains humble and hesitant, restrained by an understanding of the powers of his new vantage. His decision to use his spider powers for the betterment of humanity makes it impossible for him to function as a normal male in a romance narrative because he does not want to risk the object of his affections becoming the target of his enemies' revenge. Spider hybridity enters him into yet another gender regime organized as ethical—as defined by actions in the care of others. Occupying the vantage of the arachnid angel, then, means refusing the romantic structures associated with the taxonomic, but permits the resolution of his ethical dilemmas by giving him the power to effect change.

Spider-Man films love to render the illusory vantage of the angel's point of view in computer-generated sequences that enact the wheeling, swinging, mobile experience of the web-slinging savior. While some of his adversaries are typical street-variety skels—burglars, holdup men, purse-snatchers—his primary nemesis turns out to be the genius entrepreneur/scientist Norman Osborn (Willem Dafoe), who is the father of his best friend, Harry. Osborn, a slightly twisted developer of performance-enhancing drugs for the military, is, like Spider-Man, another mixed-order being. Impatient with his lab's inability to work the kinks out of his performance formula, Osborn tries it himself, becoming, as a result, monstrous and uncontrollable. The formula makes him psychotic, splitting his personality so that he hears his evil other self tempting him with his new powers from the mirror (more scopic incitement). Targeting the executives who kicked him out of his own company, Osborn morphs into his monstrous other, whom the newspaper dubs "The Green Goblin," encounters Spider-Man, who is, of course, trying to save the victims of Osborn's revenge. Osborn eventually endangers Peter's girl next door, taunting Spider-Man to a showdown. The conflict between the mixed-species Spider-Man and goblin-man Osborn resolves when Spider-Man destroys Osborn, saving the city.

The first *Spider-Man* film left Peter Parker in the middle of this dilemma, the climax of the romantic narrative postponed indefinitely as Peter refuses to respond to Mary Jane's interest in him. Two years later, *Spider-Man 2* begins with the romance plot, as Peter encounters Mary Jane and learns that she is dating his best friend. Another cyborg nemesis again involves Spider-Man in a series of battles between the mixed-genre super-beings, this time a well-meaning scientist (Alfred Molina) whose Promethean ambition to provide a controllable fusion-energy source morphs him into the mechanism he designed to handle the fusion reaction. Spider-Man suffers a crisis of confidence in this second film, as his warring de-sires render him impotent in both directions. Jobless, girlfriendless, and even for a time powerless, as his spider powers abandon him (or he abandons them), Peter Parker loses sight of his unifying direction and wallows in self-help therapies (trying for example, to visualize himself as Spider-Man, which does not work). But an attack by the fusion monster remobilizes his angelic vantage as the film moves toward resolving the incommensurability of Peter's desires. Making his identity public when he snatches off the spider mask to save a speeding train, Peter unveils himself to Mary Jane, who assures him that she is willing to risk being endangered to be his girlfriend. Spider-Man has, in the meantime, convinced the fusion monster to destroy itself, although his best friend, son of his late enemy Osborn, appears to have taken his father's place as the Green Goblin, promising another sequel. With the alignment of his desires, Spider-Man is reduced to the taxonomic, the merely human heterosexually engaged male. His chimeric vantage seems domesticated, subordinated to the exigencies of an almost-quiescent romance, a desire fulfilled, at peace with itself, extinct.

Spider-Man 3 resecures the taxonomic normativity necessary to the romance narrative by finally getting rid of mixed species and multiple suitors. Peter Parker must regain his love, Mary Jane, whose affections have been poisoned by his friend Harry, who seems to be carrying on where his Green Goblin father left off. Believing that Spider-Man had killed his father, "New Goblin" Harry woos Mary Jane after failing to defeat Spider-Man in a one-on-one battle. But new forms enter the scene. An alien symbiote takes over Spider-Man and then, when Spider-Man recognizes its toxicity, the symbiote takes over the body of Peter Parker's photography rival, Eddie (turning him into "Venom"). There is also the criminal who really murdered Peter Parker's uncle in the first film, Flint Marko, who is transformed into a silicon monster—"Sandman"—when he accidentally falls into a pit in the middle of a scientific experiment while trying to escape from the police. Able to convince Harry that his father had actually killed himself, Spider-Man calls on Harry to help him vanquish the Sandman. The dire straits of Mary Jane, who is kidnapped in a taxi and then suspended precariously on the top of a high-rise construction site via the concerted action of the two hybrid villains, motivates Spider-Man and Harry to work together to rid the world of these two mixed-species villains and save Mary Jane. In the process, Harry dies and Spider-Man remains, now able to marry his love. Multiples dissolved, proper taxonomy restored, all is righted. Good prevails.

Anamorphosis: Seeing with the Heart

In tandem with his performance of the stain, Spider-Man's angelic vantage is one version of the homeostatic relation between illegible polymorphousness and conventional binaries. The romance narrative negotiates what seems to be the incommensurate positions of polydirectional angelic vantage and the singularity of the taxonomic male. Because narrative itself performs a taxonomic distribution as a part of our very concept of it (it re-sorts the "wrong" into the right categories as a mode of resolution), narrativizing vantage produces an ambivalence about taxonomy often displaced into the mixed-species status of the characters, suggesting a link between a loss of genre and a problem of gender imagined as recurrent taxonomic failure. What does not fit into binary gender categories is transposed into the realm of media itself as the spectacle of "mixed media," which then works as a lure distracting us from the generic and narrative problems of the rest of the vehicle. The Spider-Man films exceed genre (film, cartoon, romance, action) seamlessly, while also mixing media: CGI, live action, and other conventional special effects in the production of an identifiably human universe. Spider-Man films condense all generic (and gender) excess into the outlines of a believable world that adjusts physical laws to account for the abilities of the film's extra-human subjects. The whole point of the films is to exceed genre while remaining entirely within it. The realistic style of *Spider-Man* contains its generic transgressions, which we never even regard as transgressions at all. Just as narrative resolves non-taxonomic genders back into binaries, current digital practices resolve all modes of producing images into a species of "realism" that aspires to appear to be as much as possible the result of analog processes (analog photography of a historically present proto-cinematic scene).

In the context of popular cinema, exceeding genre may mean one of several things: (1) A film combines multiple modes of production to render an effect not typically associated with a particular production method (as photographing live actors is associated with cinematic realism, for example, a genre that is exceeded by generating the illusion of live characters via computer). (2) The literary or tonal genre of a piece becomes mixed (as it might in some of Federico Fellini's or Charlie Kaufman's films, for example). (3) The actual medium in which a work appears (film, photography, sculpture) has been grafted onto another, a practice that has been happening at least since turn-of-the-century avant-garde movements such as Dada. Evoking "mixed media" as a generic practice is a way of containing and often ignoring the very different modes of consumption demanded by particular media. These mixed-media works push our assumptions about the genesis of images, while producing generic ambivalence, which, reflected in the works themselves, is also transposed into the site of viewing as the displaced condition of their being seen. This is part of the way mixed media make apparent our assumptions about consuming art. But they also produce an anxiety about genre deflected into castigations of postmodernity as artless, or fatuous statements about deconstructive meaninglessness. These are defensive postures raised against the loss of taxonomy and its illusion of subjective ordering.

Exceeding genre and media unsettles our view, which, nostalgically clinging to some illusion of perspectival centeredness, resists assuming a vantage other than the centered viewpoint offered by the perspective of the camera and cinema screen. The Spider-Man films let us have it both ways, titillating with the vantage of the angel while reassuring us with conventional heteronarrative. *Shallow Hal*, another film of the same era, engages another gender regime— the "anamorphic"—organized around a skewed image that can be corrected into normalcy if seen from the correct perspective. Just as an anamorphic lens is necessary to render cinemascope in traditional perspective, so *Shallow Hal* plays out how the insightful heart perceives a conventional beauty indiscernible through conventional taxonomies. What the heart can see in *Shallow Hal* is the continuous unfolding of enfolded, encoded, and systematically distorted genderings into clear binary taxonomies, a resistant process that requires not only a different vantage, but also a lensing perspective that matches and "corrects" anamorphic distortions.

Operating as a process of perpetual interpretation, the anamorphic regime is an epistemology rendered as the cause of a romantic mismatch. Instead of generic mixing occurring within an individual (as in Spider-Man) and creating the illusion of a vantage onto all gender regimes, the anamorphic is constituted by the interaction of two perspectives: one conventionally binary, literal, and superficial; the other open-ended, metaphorical, and insightful. Operating together, these differing perspectives focus on a second being whose gendering is the object of perpetual interpretation. In Western culture, this anamorphic regime is evident in couples where one is regarded as handsome and the other homely: "I don't know what she sees in him." Although in the context of a romance the anamorphic appears to be merely a permutation of desire, it is nonetheless also a gender regime organized around a figuratively scopic epistemology in which knowledge always exceeds sight, but which also requires continuous processing.

In *Shallow Hal*, Hal (Jack Black), himself a bit less than conventionally handsome, is initially a superficial taxonomy freak, attracted only to conventionally feminine women. On an elevator ride with self-help guru Tony Robbins, Robbins hypnotizes Hal into seeing the inner beauty of people instead of their compliance with social gender norms. Hal turns from being that loathsome species of beta male with an unjustified demand for compliant female beauty to a discerning individual who can see through it all. Although the film presents this as a question of surface and depth (Hal can see what is "inside"), a better way to understand what Hal sees is to understand the film as juggling the regimes of taxonomy, vantage, anamorphosis, and social gender regimes. The object of Hal's attraction is the three-hundred-pound Rosemary, the daughter of his boss, whom he perceives as someone who looks like the actress Gwyneth Paltrow (mostly because Rosemary is played by Paltrow). In a predictable series of difficulties, Hal woos an unbelieving Rosemary, then, his eyes re-opened (or re-shut), he sees her taxonomic form and rejects her. Returning later to his anamorphic sensibility and superior insight, he regains her affection.

The film has a curious (though perhaps predictable) subtext of interspecies suggestion. No character in the film has a firm purchase on binary gender taxonomy or conventional social genderings; they are all in a perpetual process of interpreting others or their own particular place in an anamorphic register as they shift back and forth. At the same time, the film itself offers a vantage on this anamorphic process as such. This vantage, incarnated by the self-help guru Robbins and enacted by the camera, appears and disappears in the film in relation to whether Rosemary appears as a three-hundred-pound woman or as Gwyneth Paltrow. If she is Gwyneth, then the film's audience sees through Hal's eyes. When she appears as three hundred pounds, we see through the vantage that observes the interplay of the taxonomic and the anamorphic. We do not see the constant interpretive process of Hal's anamorphic vision, but rather its raw materials—the before and after of transformations in perspective. Audience compliance with Hal's anamorphic process, urged by the film's shifting of Paltrow's costume rather than use of an anamorphic lens, is bounded by the phobia of Hal's best friend, Mauritio

(Jason Alexander), about any indication that genre, type, or species is exceeded. He rejects his beautiful girlfriend because her second toe is larger than her big toe, a permutation he sees as bestial. His fear is caused by his own species throwback in the form of a small vestigial tail at the base of his spine.

Morphings

The "metamorphic," as *My Big Fat Greek Wedding* illustrates, represents a history of change as well as its moments. The metamorphic encapsulates a range of possibilities from nonliving molecules, to molecular soup, to DNA, to single-celled organisms, to plants, primeval sea creatures, dinosaurs, birds, mammals, reptiles, blastulae, fetuses, mold, fungus, cyborgs, and extraterrestrials. This list constitutes (in a spotty but representative way) the imaginary of life on earth as seen through time and across possibilities, including the developmental history of individual organisms. We understand the relation of these kinds as historical and interwoven not only within the more temporal notions of phylogeny and evolution, but also within a range of interdependent and constantly morphing choices in a fulgurating biosphere seen simultaneously from all points, from the germ to the extraterrestrial, from the egg to the fossil, all understood as ontological possibilities.

In contrast to a metamorphic gender regime organized temporally, the anamorphic regime decodes sameness from difference and vice versa in both the sudden revelation of the coexistence of forms and regimes and their recoding into normativity. The anamorphic transforms insight into sight, the figuratively "inner" into the manifestly outer.

Shallow Hal is certainly not a radical film, but its very run-of-the-mill normalcy is what is remarkable, as it anatomizes the relations among several regimes in a realist style tied to conventional narrative. The dynamic interplay among the taxonomic, vantage, and the anamorphic presents itself as a question of vision—as a matter of perspective understood both geometrically and metaphorically. A similar dynamic appears in the Shrek films, whose CGI technology transposes the three-dimensional perspective of living beings into two-dimensional re-renderings of three dimensions. The film's contrivances of depth and volume are produced in such a way that they point to their illusion of multiple planes as a manufactured marvel, a triumph of the capabilities of the combination of camera, computer algorithms, models, and live voices. Although live-action photography also presents the illusion of three dimensions in two, the evident marks by which volume is produced in CGI make visible the perspectives they imitate via anamorphoses itself. Unlike more traditional animated cartoons whose two-dimensional drawn quality exists within conventionalized gestures toward the illusion of depth (overlapping, shadows, scale), CGI animations morph the flatness of animation into an illusion of volume and depth, produced by volume shading, the play of light, and algorithmic deformations that represent depth perspectives.

Their illusions, however, are not total; the play of light across surfaces, for example, deployed to create the impression of solidity in CGI animations, sometimes plays too much or too obviously, pointing to the trick of the illusion. The visibility of depth and volume strategies in *Shrek*'s CGI make conscious the films' continuous processes of anamorphosis that subtend the status of their characters not as believable, but precisely as the product of a transposition, the constant interpretation of one code in terms of another. Not all CGI is produced in a way such that it marks its anamorphosis; *Spider-Man*'s deployment of CGI to produce large portions of its cityscape, for example, passes without notice. The marks of anamorphosis appear in *Shrek* for a reason, linked specifically to the Shrek films' dramatization of gender, genre, and species crises.

The Shrek films center gender (and other kinds of) anamorphosis within a range of mixed-species permutations alibied as belonging to the capacious and infinitely expandable order of the "fairy tale," but inscribed simultaneously within multiple kinds, genders, and moments of transformation, all configured around crises in vision. The first *Shrek* (2001) is organized around a romance plot, ostensibly an attempt made by the diminutive and imperious Lord Farquaad (voiced by John Lithgow) to find a suitably royal wife to cement his claim to the throne. Lord Farquaad, whose first appearance in the film consists of an overt anamorphosis as his giant shadow gradually reduces to a three-foot-high midget through CGI illusions of shifts in perspective and camera distance, is selfish, cruel, and narcissistic. He tortures the Gingerbread Man and selects his future mate from a talking mirror (that which reflects him back, as Virginia Woolf would say, at twice his normal size) with the emcee's voice from *The Dating Game.* The film opens as Shrek, an ogre (voiced by Mike Myers), is disturbed in his daily swamp routine by the raid of townsmen who have come to hunt him down for the bounty. Offering a reward for Pinocchio, the Three Bears, the Three Little Pigs, the Witches, Snow White, Tinker Bell, the Fairy Godmother, Three Blind Mice, and a talking donkey (known simply as Donkey, voiced by Eddie Murphy), Lord Farquaad has ominously reprised the cruel ghettoization of difference. Shrek scares the men away only to be disturbed by an influx of fairy-tale creatures who have been herded to the swamp (and told to stay there) by Lord Farquaad's men. The spectacle of the collection of fairy-tale creatures offers an alibied vision of disorganized polymorphousness and interspecies existence (always associated with animation), a comically uncanny appearance of childhood memories prefaced not uncoincidentally by the appearance of the Three Blind Mice, who, like Lord Farquaad, are anamorphized by means of huge cast shadows.

The disarray of the fairy-tale creatures and their insistent invasion of Shrek's personal space drives Shrek outside the swamp to seek their eviction. The only creature who knows where to go is Donkey, whose hip Sancho Panza accompanies the vaguely Quixote-like Shrek to Farquaad's Disneyesque theme park city. Forced into a tournament in which he and Donkey prevail, Shrek "wins" the right to rescue the Princess Fiona (voiced by Cameron Diaz), whom Lord Farquaad has chosen as his future bride, from her imprisonment in a dragon's keep. Shrek and Donkey rescue the Princess, during which time the dragon falls in love with Donkey, and the two comrades escort the Princess back to Lord Farquaad. Princess Fiona, however, is also secretly anamorphic and metamorphic. By day she is human; at night she morphs into an ogre. Shrek falls in love with the daytime version, but through a series of comic mistimings thinks she thinks he is repellent, so he turns her over to Lord Farquaad. Not wanting Lord Farquaad to see her after nightfall, the Princess insists on an immediate wedding. In the middle of the ceremony, however, the sun sets and Shrek, who has decided that he is in love with the Princess anyway, comes to retrieve her in a reprise of *The Graduate*. The rescue is enabled by Donkey's dragon girlfriend, who transports them to the castle, intervenes by eating Lord Farquaad, and watches as Princess Fiona transforms into an ogre.

The romance organizes the film's genders and species rather than the other way around. The film envisions the possibility of interspecies romance as it flirts with and ultimately rejects disorder in the realm of gender taxonomies, though it embraces mixed-species unions. Donkey and the dragon can be a couple as soon as Donkey realizes the dragon is a girl; Shrek falls in love with the Princess even when he thinks she is human. The film teeters between polymorphousness and taxonomy as it perpetually sorts among species, genders, and the stories from which the fairy-tale creatures emanate. The sorting process itself is modeled by the film's openly anamorphic and metamorphic moments as large shadows reduce to recognizable characters, as Fiona becomes an ogress, as a pumpkin is transformed into a carriage. These transformations span between literal anamorphosis, in which an out-of-proportion figure is lensed into proportion by a change in perspective, and metamorphosis, in which an object that seems to exist in one order (human, squash) instantly transforms into another (ogre, carriage). In *Shrek* these morphings often work in reverse, the monstrosity of the large shadow reducing to the monstrosity of the midget Farquaad, or the beauty of Fiona transforming to the ogre.

Shrek 2 (2004) further develops the role of the metamorphic, centering its plot around Shrek and Fiona's choice to become permanently ogre. In this sequel, Fiona's royal parents (voiced by Julie Andrews and John Cleese) invite Shrek and Fiona back to the kingdom of "Far Far Away" to celebrate their wedding. Her parents are surprised to see that the enchantment that had forced Fiona's circadian oscillation had resolved itself on the side of the ogre instead of the princess. Fiona's father, however, has some hidden dark deal with the Fairy Godmother (voiced by Jennifer Saunders), the practitioner who suggested Fiona's parents lock her in the tower in the first place. The Fairy Godmother's son, Prince Charming (voiced by Rupert Everett), was intended to rescue Fiona, but arrived long after Shrek had taken her away. The King and the Fairy Godmother plot to have Prince Charming re-rescue Fiona from ogre-dom. In the meantime, Shrek visits the Fairy Godmother's elaborate potion factory and takes a "Happily Ever After" Potion that turns him into a handsome prince and Donkey into a "valiant steed." Again, Shrek instead of Prince Charming rescues Fiona, and together they decide to return to the fun of being ogres.

In *Shrek 2* the metamorphic clearly becomes a process by which various taxonomies mingle. The King, whose pact with the Fairy Godmother is necessary to hide his metamorphic status as a frog, turns back into a frog at film's end, his wife commenting that he is a "better man" now than he has been for a long time. The ogre is a better man than the Prince, who cannot even be a "best man," and the agent of metamorphosis, the Fairy Godmother, is a commercialized, ambitious celebrity who uses her powers for her own gain. These characters' taxonomic statuses are inflected by their metamorphic capabilities, raising the question of exactly what their taxonomic affiliation really is. If one can turn into an ogre, then is one an ogre and a human by turns, or is one potentially both, or does one occupy some liminal ground in between? Is ogre an anamorphic version of human? These characters illustrate the ways no taxonomy is permanent, as well as the value of an interplay between the literal and the metaphorical, between status and value, appearance and essence as matters of temporality rather than depth and as those statuses inevitably layer onto and oscillate within single characters. Although *Shrek 2* never confuses taxonomic genders, the model of its species metamorphoses operates as a metaphor of a metamorphic gender regime insofar as it enables variety within a traditional quest/romance narrative structure.

That *Shrek*'s metamorphoses are often accomplished by means of a literal anamorphosis also enacts the relation between metamorphic and anamorphic regimes. A fairy-tale logic accounts for both *Shrek*'s range of taxonomies and their anamorphic revelations. The two regimes both appear as forms of morphing, working as decoys for each other, distracting as well from the film's eternal processes of sorting—human from fairy tale, royal from common, this princess from that. While the anamorphic is interpretive, insightful, and apparently revelatory, the metamorphic is temporal, organizing genders as complex, multiple, persisting regimes, statuses, and histories. The metamorphic is not merely a mode of transition nor the example that suggests the intrinsic multiplicity and instability of all genderings, but is a regime in which different gender possibilities are always equally immanent. The metamorphic, thus, is governed by the tension of becoming, by a present tense of perpetual instability understood in relation to a history of change—and in any cultural text, by the taxonomic exigencies of conventional narrative. The metamorphic means that we are never any single thing, but always both the potential of others and the history of many.

Anamorphosis brings the metamorphic into momentary focus as a gender regime on the way to becoming by making regimes intelligible one at a time and in relation to changing contexts, individual growth, and mechanisms of narrative revelation. As a visual trope and as a gender regime organized around the scopic and the analytic, anamorphosis involves the dual status of an image as both a distortion and a condensation, recognizable and collapsed, needing only the right set of perspectives to transform it from one image to another already imagined to abide inside. The way anamorphosis unfolds itself produces the illusion that some eminent form residing inside emerges through the realignment of perspective. The process of anamorphic morphing thus produces as a side effect an impression of depth rising to the surface, of inside coming out, of inscription becoming legible in the same way that the model of the flaccid tattooed penis described in Djuna Barnes's *Nightwood* can only be read as "Desdemona" when its subtending field is erect.[22] Many of the anamorphings in *Shrek* work to shrink rather than to enlarge, appearing to move in a direction opposite to the anamorphic expansion typical to cinemascope. We might also, however, understand them as diminishing both the status and stature of taxonomic binaries, reducing, for example, Farquaad's booming masculinity to an effect of special effects—his shadow, camera angle (often revealed as such), tricks of depth, and the ungainly disproportion between his huge head and tiny body anatomizing the faux finish elements of masculine masquerade, reducing it to a series of tricks. In this sense, all of the main characters of *Shrek* anatomize some masquerade, which is itself a mode of anamorphosis insofar as masquerade exists as an encodement in need of interpretation.

Renditions of metamorphosis often screen the process of change with spectacle. Whirling magic dust, spinning auroras, and distortions stand in and occlude, like cocoons, metamorphic processes themselves, rendering change through time instantaneous and magical. And, given the prominence of distortions in the Shrek films, metamorphoses often appear to arrive via anamorphoses. As a process masking a series of actions, metamorphosis is always reduced to the difference between its beginning and end, but the actions or processes of metamorphosis, which gloss over the mechanics of change, are themselves glossed over, masked by a magic represented magically. This masking attracts our attention to product—to the difference between the definitive forms of a character's beginning and end—as decoys distracting us from the un-located status and undefined middle-stage processes by which a subject appears to get from one regime to another. Perceived as transient and temporary, metamorphosis persists as an ontology we cannot see.

As a very slippery gender regime, metamorphosis appears, then, to provide a mode of transition between taxonomies, layering them atop one another, so that at any given time a being is neither one nor the other, but some liminal form. The function of transition, however, also works to distract us from metamorphosis's dynamic of amongness, of the coexistence of multiple shapes in which themselves represent multiple stages of development or times of existence. Changing form is less about category than about history. Metamorphosis appears to speed up history in relation to a sense of fated direction—the genetic program of the frog, or the mythical curse that governs Princess Fiona's form. As a gender regime, metamorphosis fronts a comingled temporality understood as ontological, enacting the possibility of no taxonomy and multiple coexisting genderings as an effect of a process of perpetual distraction through history.

In the most literal sense, we already understand gender as temporal in that we regard taxonomically gendered beings as different genders (always rendered as different "versions" of a gender) depending on what age they are. A girl, for example, is a different gender than a woman, and a woman different from an older woman. While taxonomic gender re-contains these differences with an oppositional binary, the differences function within the realm of kinship and desire as operative gender distinctions. What we might be able to enjoy with a woman or man we cannot enjoy with a boy or a girl. Developmental history accounts for the slow, almost imperceptible metamorphosis from one to the other of these stages or genders, but metamorphosis itself, as a temporal regime, is a matter of scale. Imperceptible when stretched through time, metamorphosis becomes visible and magical if time is sped up. The sequential habitation (for lack of a better word) of taxonomic genders is not really a sequence at all, but the historical layering of different taxonomies. No woman ever stops being a girl (or boy). In its sped-up version, metamorphosis both embodies and distracts us from the layered intergeneric regime that persists in relation to taxonomy.

Crossing Kind

In the extended *Shrek* narrative, heterosexuality secures kind, but the diegesis of the films consists of a large field of polymorphous diversity filtered through the fairy tale. Not only does this produce a very busy background full of mice, pigs, fairies, dwarves, bears, witches, gingerbread men, and fairy godmothers, but it also never relieves the possibility of immanent metamorphosis. Just as the films are dotted with anamorphic transformations, so metamorphoses proliferate. Pinocchio's nose grows, pumpkins turn into carriages, animals and baked goods talk, mirrors counsel, inanimate objects animate. In other words, in a world of fairy-tale creatures, the creatures reflect what technologies of representation are capable of representing and what we are already capable of imagining, not because DreamWorks pioneered the animated spoon, but because the crossing of kind and the mechanisms of metamorphosis already operated as comprehensible gender regimes.

Visual technologies such as cinematic animation enable the representation of such cross-kind entities as animated crockery, garrulous animals, prehensile hooves, literate pond scum, and willful natural phenomena. Crossing kind melds one identifiable order to another, making both visible at once while merging their capabilities. On the one hand this is a comic realization of the question of animation that Freud notes that Ernst Jentsch associated with the uncanny. The inanimate come alive. But crossing kind in this way also defers the uncertainty linked to the uncanny in favor of a decoy of personality expressed in the character of the animation—the literal style of movement—itself. Crossing kind becomes comic in the way that the inanimate and mechanical gain a quirky ontology.

The films' implied mode of address—that cartoons are for children—might also produce a version of the vantage regime linked to the angel, since the films position the audience in the vantage from which taxonomies can be envisaged as taxonomies. There are humans and fairy-tale creatures, animate beings and animated inanimate beings, metamorphic beings and anamorphic beings. However, the Shrek films' use of decoy, where one regime plays off and distracts from others, works against any more comprehensive vision of the commingling of taxonomies or regimes. The films thus simultaneously present the possibility of multiple coexisting gender regimes and normativize them via the romance narrative and decoying dynamics.

This domestication is a compensation linked to the systemic interrelation of gender regimes at a particular historical moment when the taxonomic itself has become openly unstable. The repetition of this domestication of metamorphosis responds to anxieties about a loss of kind, species, genre, taxonomy, and to the systemic revelation of taxonomy's paradox. Another way to understand this is that metamorphosis itself, though a gender regime of transition and change through time, is redeployed as a way to control change and secure taxonomy. The increasing prominence of the metamorphic in the Shrek films parallels a contemporaneous cultural fascination with personal metamorphoses, which work not as a way to expand multiplicity, but instead as a way to endorse normativity and essentially rid ourselves of the metamorphic altogether while seeming to endorse process as the route to personal fulfillment. *Shrek's* cartoonish metamorphoses are not so far away from makeover magic, but function more radically as possibility—as an opening up.

Postscript

Shrek Forever After, the last in the series, retroactively resignifies Shrek's polymorphous variety as a problem of temporality. Given the chance to relive one day in his life by a tricky Rumpelstiltskin, Shrek inadvertently trades away his entire life and must use the twenty-four hours to gain yet again "love's first kiss" with Fiona or cease to exist. This final *It's a Wonderful Life* retelling of the first film's romantic imperative suggests not only the desire to take advantage of the series' market popularity, but also some anxious sense that things are just too loose and need to be yet again secured to a very heteronormative story.

3 Temporality Still

We seem only to inch ahead, circling and re-circling, but still apparently tied to appearances discerned visually: metamorphosis, anamorphosis, taxonomizing. As gender regimes, these appearances front processes organized through different economies. The metamorphic is temporal. The anamorphic is a process of translation or digestion. The taxonomic is a perpetual sorting. The regimes appear to move one to another en route to some clarity, the taxonomic seeming to resolve the uncertainties posed by the other two. But another way of understanding their interrelation is that they coexist as inter-cooperative parts of a first-order system (a system that is open, a system that cannot see itself as a system). The regimes are inseparable even as their own processes and relations to one another might vary. The very difficulty in separating these regimes from one another—of discerning any sense of a clear, "pure" category (other than the illusions of the taxonomic)—is an attribute of their systemic relation, as each regime interacts with others and with environments altered by the constant shifting of regimes, signifiers, symbolic systems, imperatives, and narratives. For this reason, genderings' regimes appear in symptomatic but always transforming clumps that play out the relations among regimes. And all of this—regimes, clumps, processes—are perpetually reorganized by cultural narratives that produce, locate, contain, and deploy such systemic adjustments.

The first decade of the twenty-first century was preoccupied with the metamorphic under the narrative guise of the self-improving "makeover." This preoccupation suggests that makeovers represent some anxiety about taxonomy—about achieving clearly defined conventional categories as gender's taxonomic certainties continuously blur. Making over provides a narrative that organizes a useful multiplicity redistributed through narrative roles in the drama of the makeover itself, providing specific sites for regimes that become visible as such as a part of metamorphic processes. And makeovers also play on the notion that individuals are in charge of their own genderings, as makeovers enable the impression of one's taking control—except, of course, that no one tries to re-engender him- or herself as anything other than conventionally normative. If anything, makeovers represent the perpetuated rehearsal of something akin to a "normative performative" insofar as they make it seem as if sets of conventional acts result in the production of conventional genderings whose clarity we assume.

The Metamorphosis of Metamorphosis: Narrative Regimes

Reality television is one genre that exposes gender regimes organized around characters' narrative functions. Narrative deploys characters in roles of relative centrality; major characters take on roles of schematic primacy, while minor characters never quite get there. Major characters are "schematic" insofar as they appear to operate the scheme—they are the protagonists, winners, or, occasionally, primary villains. This schematic position constitutes a gender regime organized around narrative's transformative processes of intelligibility; central characters of uncertain fate find their way into clearly delineated roles in narratives of heterogeneous joinder and reproduction. These roles brand central characters with the necessary gender attributes of their respective heteronormative narrative functions. This conforming process appears to comply with taxonomic binary genders, but these genders might themselves be entangled with other regimes, as happens with heroic female protagonists, for example, or in gay love stories where the lovers are glossed as taxonomically binary through the opposition of superficial traits (one is brunette, the other blonde, for example). In a narrative gender regime, minor characters are "asymptotic" in that they never participate in the primary impetus toward joinder and resolution. These are the experts, helpers, and also-rans. These apparently derivative roles rebrand secondary characters as not quite taxonomically intelligible—as something else. This "something else," however, also reveals other operant gender regimes that may or may not be tied to the exigencies of heteronarrative resolution. It does not matter if these characters otherwise display normative social and/or taxonomic genders; by virtue of their roles they acquire the gloss of "not quite there."

Narrative is our very sense of what a story is as well as a way of reorganizing information into a paradigm through which knowledge and meaning appear to be produced. The basic pattern of narrative is our concept of sexual intercourse (and vice versa). Western narrative reiterates a dominant paradigm in which difference, defined oppositionally (male/female, black/white, pro/con, them/us, bad/good, active/passive, capital/labor), engages in conflict (foreplay), joins in battle (sex), and having come together, is victorious, or produces knowledge (discovery, insight), or gets married and has children, or dies (satisfaction). The paradigm produces the players as oppositional or "hetero" as a necessary condition for their figuratively coital battle and paradigmatic (re)production. In addition, these oppositions are organized according to a binary gendered paradigm in which the passive, ground, object is feminized and the active subject is masculinized.[1]

As the covert closing down of gender complexity, narrative dramatizes the relation between sexuality and gender as a matter of role. Organized as a binary structure, narrative is simultaneously a dynamic in which the imbalance of the beginning, figured as opposition, goes through a middling set of imbalances and mismatches (bad timing, misinformation, inappropriate pairings), aided often by a helper or sidekick who has no productive fate itself, to an end in balance and quiescent happiness. Narrative dynamics move from disturbance (understood as opposition) through a confused and chaotic middle to the balance and resolution of an end (or an end we recognize as an end because there is no unsettling opposition or residual chaos). This dynamic produces oppositional (and taxonomic gender) binaries as an effect of narrative itself. Narrative does not depend on gender binaries; it produces them. What happens, then, is that roles in narrative linked to specific functions are also linked to gender binaries because of their role in narrative, rather than the gendered taxonomy of the character. For example, the love story of two lesbians will schematically gender one of them as masculine, even if both are clearly feminine as in *Desert Hearts* or almost any couple in *The L Word*. The narrative of two cops who work together to solve crimes will schematically feminize one of the protagonists, usually the black one. Consider any of the Lethal Weapon films, any of the Die Hard films, *Training Day*, and *Swat*, to name just a few. Not only do these narratives require an oppositional difference in the first place (one lesbian is blonde, the other brunette, one cop is white, the other black), they schematically taxonomize the players according to their roles.[2] Evil enemies, though masculine, are always feminized, as happens with almost all the antagonists in James Bond films (see, for example, Ernst Stavro Blofeld), while evil females are masculinized (Rosa Klebb, for example, in *From Russia with Love*).

Aligned with narrative roles and structure, the schematic regime thus can play against the typical alignment of biology and social genderings (male with masculine, female with feminine) by reproducing binary genders as an effect of a character's narrative function. The feminine Ellen Ripley in the series of Alien films can be an action hero, for example. At the same time, the binary characteristics narratively associated with specific roles and functions (activity, goodness, agency) gloss those roles and functions with binary gender associations—active roles are masculine and passive roles are feminine. Schematic gender, thus, seems to reinforce normative gender binaries while sometimes producing a mismatch between the biological sex of a body and the gender associated with its function. For this reason, schematic gender is also ambivalent in that it enables a lack of alignment between nature and culture while providing a matrix of narrative sense within which it alibis and recuperates that misalignment.

The ambivalent operation of schematic gender hosts the other narrative gender regime—the asymptotic—defined by its differential relation to the schematic. The narrative function of the asymptotic is never quite to accede to the taxonomy of the major characters and functions around which narrative seems to be defined. The asymptotic regime characterizes secondary helper characters—

those who emerge at the beginning and in the middle of stories as purveyors of wisdom, information, and advice, and whose fate is to disappear before the end—to have no end, to not be bound in the paradigm's oppositional dynamics. Neither active nor passive, they persist in the middle in the site of confusion where the sorting organizations of taxonomy have not yet reasserted a distinct distribution of taxonomies and roles. They deviate often from traditional social assignments (e.g., they do not marry), and their narrative function is precisely to be both secondary and visionary. Although they most often manifest taxonomically binary sexes (they are clearly female or male), their functions and their secondary status in relation to primary actors makes it appear as if they are always only approaching some conformity to taxonomic gender binaries rather than embodying them—that is, they are not clearly or normatively masculine or feminine. This not-quite-there quality accounts not only for their asymptotic lack of participation in paradigms of joinder, but also often for their simultaneous situation in a regime of chimeric vantage that can envision the disposition of the narrative field itself. They narrate and warn; they see what the audience sees. These (usually) secondary characters often appear to be nonheterosexual; that is, something other than, for example, what the narrative's protagonist might demonstrate. Their nonheterosexuality, however, is an effect neither of actions nor of identity, but of an asymptotic relation to taxonomy itself (even if they mark themselves as literally homosexual). They are rendered as not quite as good nor as clear a taxonomic specimen as the protagonist, as second best, as approaching, but not quite there. The pleasure in this asymptotic regime is complex, combining as it does the chimeric vantage of a certain gender omniscience with the pleasures of rebelling against the constraints of normative convention.

Reality

Reality television makeovers expose the extent to which narrative processes organize and inflect gender regimes. As a persistent environment to both individual psychical sexuations and social negotiations of gender possibilities, narrative dynamics are part of the environmental material (signifiers, processes, feelings, etc.) that subjects interject, locating themselves in the positions narrative provides as part of any engendering. "Reality" makeovers anatomize the narrative environment of possible subject positionings in specific relation to a metamorphic gender regime, thus dramatizing a fantasy of conscious gender manipulation and correction.

The public rehearsal of reality television making over goes back to 1979, the moment when postwar housing began literally to fall apart and when *This Old House*, the PBS home-restoration program, first aired. Making over was never simply the humble process of rescuing, repairing, updating, and revivifying shabby structures or tasteless decors. It has always been at least ostensibly about a spectacularized metamorphosis from one status or condition to another, as the temporal ellipses intrinsic to television documentary focus the series on results. Although metamorphosis is the governing paradigm of the makeover and rapid change its magic, the lure of home improvement—and for that matter any other documentary of transformation, such as cooking shows, redecoration attempts, fashion shows, motorcycle- and car-building dramas, *The Joy of Painting*, and even close-ups of the mortuary—is the spectacle of work itself. The promise of metamorphosis is an alluring pretext for the pageant of how things go together, the spectacle of making, the predictability of structure, and the calming hypnosis of competence.[3]

But the makeover as the intrinsic material of "reality" television is more than this. In rehearsing the relation between part and whole, in partially anatomizing the mechanisms and processes that produce and maintain structure—the girders, frames, wiring, custom parts, mise en place, organized and generously equipped work spaces—the spectacle of work is ultimately about a continuous ritual reaffirmation of structure and category. Makeovers rediscover (and produce) a very familiar version of order located as the inevitable effect of virtuous process. The proliferation of these shows and their gradual slide into a second stage of the "reality" game gimmick (cf. NBC's *The Biggest Loser*) points to the way these shows, no matter what their instructional virtue, were finally all about a consumerized and normatively taxonomized subject. The shows not only endlessly reiterate the reassuring specter of the heteronarrative link between part and whole, work and product, investment and pay-off that shores up notions of structure, capitalism (or corporatism), and the patriarchal familial narrative, they also situate products as correlatives for their creators and owners, reflecting tastes, constituting a part of the de rigueur commodity identity thrust on the consuming public. By securing the connections between structure, process, product, and subjects, makeover shows appear to entangle viewers with the virtues and processes of work rather than with consumption itself, producing the illusion of identity premised on a fascination and alignment with creativity, skill, and process. The consumer, then, appears to assume a subject position in relation to the metamorphic, wielded by proficient shamans, enabled by corporate capitalism, and punctuated by flares of rejuvenated hope.

The morphing of the home and of the product (especially motor vehicles) was the commodity displacement of an impetus to morph the owner. In a massive fit of accessorizing, a first stage of reality makeovers reigned from the mid-1990s to the middle of the first decade of the twenty-first century. This first stage began the perpetual media reinforcement of a commoditized orthopedic shell that stands in as subjective identity, but which also produces a notion of the subject as a collection of consumption "habits" that locate each individual within a market grid of predilections, classes, and personality types. This subject, whose illusion of coherence is constituted by a commodity reciprocity, appears to splinter taxonomic binaries into a shower of possible categories—Deleuze and Guattari's "heteroclite"—while simultaneously reinforcing notions of the subject as hypertaxonomic, as a compendium of accrued categorical taxonomies. This commodity variety competes with and substitutes for the range of gender regimes that offer an infinite variety of genderings, substituting commodity for gender, and thus aligning gender taxonomies with sexual difference as a precondition for consumption.

The repeated drama of the first generation of cable "makeover" shows was a process by which normative consumer identities supplanted the agency of the subject, and in so doing slipped in taxonomic gender binaries as the condition of any metamorphosis, either as the substratum or the intended result. Most of this was displaced into the transformation of consumable objects such as homes, food, and vehicles. Some subjects, however, became the fodder for makeover and weight-loss shows whose trajectory was to transform these subjects overtly in Toula-like conversions from unattractive to normatively attractive—and coherently taxonomic. The result—the "reveal"—was the anticipated effect of the shows' concentrated labors, fulfilling and wondrous in itself. Not only was the fat girl slimmed and the house refurbished, the subject owners now happily matched their identities. All was, as far as the television audience could discern, brought together, the owners becoming more themselves than ever now that their houses, bodies, cars, dinners, and clothing styles matched their class, sex, age, and educational status. Subjectivity, consumer tastes, and identity were one and the same. The fantasy was one of subjective control and alignment, but this only occurred with a great deal of outside help. The corporeal subject became incorporated with the corporate with the help of hidden corporate weal.

The Subject of Identity

The concept of the subject represents a convenient fiction that aligns bodies (which are already fantasmatic) with consciousness. We imagine the subject to have desire and agency; we project onto it an assumption of separability constituted through historical narratives of development. The fiction of the subject manifests itself as both agency and identity, as the sense not only that one is who one is, but also that one knows who one is in culturally available categories. The apparent coalescence of subject and identity masks the perpetuated dynamic through which a subject continuously sorts, adjusts, responds, and re-narrates its negotiations among the range of available taxonomies, languages, histories, and rules (the symbolic), its delusion of conscious choice and agency, the field of available objects and images (the imaginary), its vulnerability to cuts, tears, and traumas (the real), and its unconscious and overdetermined selections, repetitions, and fears. As the symbolic, imaginary, and real, all knotted inextricably with one another, constantly change through time, the subject, moored in its self-production both to these orders and to the objects and drives through which it interprets difference and pleasure, changes as well.[4] The flexive relation between the subject's sense of speaking self and its unconscious, which it cannot know, is both the idiosyncratic product of its individual history and the introjection/projection of the symbolic/imaginary/real terms within which it lives. There is no central or core essence, but a process in constant change and adjustment, which, like a spinning spoked wheel, projects the illusion of presence and solidity. The subject finally is a fiction of a space or vortex, an ever-moving Red Queen from *Alice in Wonderland* keeping up with the moving background. At the same time, the subject is itself also a vortex, a complex interweaving of inside and outside (which are, of course, both neither) understood partially as a process of sorting or negation. The subject is imposed and taken up at the same moment, always out of time, any sense of "true inner self" coming from the illusion of subjective depth, clashes of temporality, and the delusions of choice produced by ever-shifting vectors of recognition.

In contrast to the subject, "identity" consists of those themes and objects selected in response to and as a part of the process of the subject's perpetual production, but delimited by the terms and objects available culturally. Although identity would seem to derive from a subject's identifications, the process is more complex than that, involving the basic processes of sexuation, a subject's own drives and objects, as well as complex narrative motivations for assuming certain positions and affiliations in relation to the terms available. Some of these terms, such as taxonomic gender or race, belong to and stand in for the binary structuration of language and legal systems and thus impress themselves as if inexorable, reproducing a sense of the obvious truth of their division. Others, such as ethnicity and class, which belong as well to symbolic schemes of division, may also define varying individual experience and history as subjects are located and locate themselves in particular symbolic and cultural locations. Yet other identity categories, such as tastes in music, clothing, and avocation, seem to represent idiosyncratic choices constituting identity and revealing the essence of the subject, but actually cohere to notions of age, class, region, genderings, and a wide range of subjective fantasies. These apparent choices are, as an effect of subjective process, already partially defined for the subject, as both fodder and product of its process. As an armoring fiction, "identity" is an orthopedic collation, a set of shifting totems referring elsewhere to some digestive dynamic, metamorphic in itself, interwound in Klein bottle fashion with the subject, speaking for and being spoken by it.

As simultaneously subjective definer and definition, identity seems to offer the solace of individuality while providing a mode of registration and delimitation. Identity makes the subject disappear in service of ideology, while at the same time appearing to endorse the individual's meaningful cultural position understood as a set of narratives (essentially stereotypes) and choices. Whether these narratives (of privilege, oppression, exception) apply is irrelevant insofar as taking on an "identity category" appears to harness individual differences in favor of the illusion of homogeneous categories. In offering a category and set of narratives to belong to, identity seems comforting, but it never quite fits anyone. It is a reassuring fiction whose advantage is that it actually enables a subject both to fit in and to be itself at the same time.

Identity is also orthopedic in the sense that it provides simultaneously the illusion of subjective coherence and a trompe l'oeil locus of displacement from which the fiction of the subject is projected and by which it is protected. What seems like an identity—a taste perceived as natural and essential—is already an effect of flexive subjective dynamics. Selected as a way to signal and protect, as a kind of offering to the gaze through whose vantage one sees oneself seeing oneself, these tastes project ourselves back to ourselves in a form that we like, one accepted by the flexive structure that produced the taste in the first place. When we gather these objects and themes, we end up with what appears to be a composite profile by which we are defined (see Facebook, for example), even though subjectively we always sense that like every other taxonomy, none of it quite fits. No matter how happily we enlist identity categories, such enlistments only defend against our essential alienation, the condition by which the subject never belongs.

Stage I: Schematic Stagings

Reality makeover shows, which prevailed from about 1979 to 2005, optimistically suggest that hard work is all that is necessary to make things "right"— that is, to make things fit into a vision of capitalist (and taxonomic) conformity. These shows deploy their characters simply as either the recipient central subject or the helper expert. Except in shows overtly focused on cosmetic body makeovers (*The Swan*, *Pimp My Ride*), these roles seem normative and equal in emphasis. In cosmetic makeovers, the helpers become more clearly helpers (i.e., not as primary as the objects of their ministrations), even though the helpers are the agents of change. As the makeover recipient becomes the central site of schematic narrative operation, the helpers become asymptotic, and their genderings, too, are a bit less taxonomically conforming, even if the characters are completely coherent within a taxonomic binary. The whole point of the cosmetic makeover is to take a sloppy subject verging on the incomprehensibly gendered and transform it into a clearly taxonomic "him" or "her" that the show then presents as if it were a rejuvenated and resplendent consumer item.

The second stage of reality makeovers, which became exhausted by the beginning of the second decade of the twenty-first century, features a redundant, predictable "contest" or "treatment" narrative as itself the means by which subjects might be rejuvenated. Top chefs, fashion designers, the overweight, aspiring fashion models, drug addicts, hoarders, restaurateurs, beauty parlor owners, bars and businesses, and law enforcement all participate in the same narrative trajectory that leads inexorably toward closure, rearranging its gender regimes along the way so that by the end all is conforming, commodified, and triumphant. The focus of all these reality shows is success; the model is corporate competition where all is fair, or salvation, where all is . . . fair. In relation to the lure of ultimate victory and big prize, each episode sorts virtue and vice, investment and sloth, worthiness and fatal error, agent and helper, indicating that winning the contest reflects real commodity value.

The first stage's repeated metamorphic merger of bodies with taxonomic binaries—of male with masculine and female with feminine—could occur only in an imaginary isolation somehow deemed intrinsic to the metamorphic process (a cocoon, for example), but actually necessary to the narrative of product that subtends and sustains the makeover as a positive experience. In this narrative, the noncompliant subject realizes his or her unhappiness, which is because the body just does not conform (e.g., the male is not masculine, biology clashes with the social); so, via application and selection, the lucky subject becomes the object of expert treatment. Helpers and shamans reshape the body, and the subject evokes the Rocky Balboa fable of fortitude and survival through the intermediate stages of pain, struggle, and working out. At the end, after having lost poundage and been refitted with hair, makeup, and clothing that contribute to the image of compliance, the subject is "revealed" to the "oooos and ahhhhs" of family, friends, and a television audience. A constant comparison between the pathetic before image (usually in sloppy, nondescript fitness garb) and the shining after image (in stylish clothing) comply as a magical Cinderella effect, but at the same time also presents the disappearance of the subject into a gender anonymity. All individuality gone, the remade subject looks more like everyone else than does everyone else. The triumph of the makeover is invisibility—and in the case of weight loss shows, "health."

At the same time, the isolation and fragmentation of the makeover body prevents any actual consciousness of the gender normativizing that is the goal of the process. While appearing to make visible the processes of transformation, makeovers become hard to see, occluded by the by-products of the process itself. The narrative shape of these shows makes its "payoff" the transformed subject's emergence in the ending "reveal," which defers any curiosity about mediate stages to the anticipated joy of the end. At the same time, there is ample testimony about hope, salvation, strength, and gratitude from huffing mid-morphees, as well as the spectacle of the priestly caste of morphers whose kind services are the salvation of order and the guarantors of happiness. Finally, of course, these makeover subjects are not really isolated at all, but the constant object of the camera view, never alone, revealing their most private moments.

The paradoxical message of the makeover is that gender normativity is difficult for anyone not naturally endowed. Masculinity and femininity require work: diet, workouts, makeup, clothing, attitude. Compliance with taxonomic binaries is anything but natural and anything but easy. There is never a question of subjects wanting to be made over into anything other than a strictly gender conforming being—no requests, for example, to be made into the perfect dyke, or a screaming queen, a motorcycle gang member, or even something like Don Knotts (best known for his portrayal of Barney Fife on *The Andy Griffith Show*). The work of metamorphosis, which occupies the bulk of these shows, is veiled, repetitive (the shows actually repeat sequences), and focused on the purveyors of change—the gay men, therapists, fitness instructors, fashion advisers, hairdressers, and makeup artists—who conduct the transformation, piece by piece. Not only does this clinicalize metamorphosis while pathologizing deviation from normative appearance, it also welds gender conformity to health and essence—and this is the real trick of the makeover. Instead of using these "repair" technologies to reflect, express, and reveal gender idiosyncrasy, the makeover shamans and the narrative of metamorphosis produce the illusion that the only problem that exists is that the normally gendered subject does not match his or her biological sex. There is no question at all about the status of gender itself, remarkable when some of the shamans themselves are openly gay.

Stage II: The Contest Treatment

In 2004 Bravo launched the first of several contest shows with *Project Runway*, a program in which aspiring young fashion designers compete in an elimination tournament for the opportunity to show a fashion line in New York's annual Bryant Park fashion extravaganza along with other valuable prizes. The year 2004 also saw the start of NBC's *The Biggest Loser*, a weight-loss contest show in which contestants compete to determine who can lose the most weight—sort of, as the necessities of game strategy made this show less about real industry and virtue and more about interpersonal rivalries, villains, and the kinds of selfishness lauded in corporate practices. Two years later, Bravo launched its *Top Chef* series, a show in which aspiring young chefs compete with one another in an elimination tournament for the title of "Top Chef." The Food Network launched its own contest series beginning in 2005 with *Food Network Challenge* and *The Next Food Network Star*, followed by *The Next Iron Chef* in 2007 and *Chopped* in 2009.

At the same time as this rise of the contest was the rise of the intervention, shows in which an expert comes on the scene to fix what is wrong with a restaurant, an addict, or a beauty parlor. The BBC launched *Ramsay's Kitchen Nightmares* in 2004, which was quickly picked up by Fox in the United States under the revised title *Kitchen Nightmares*. A&E Network commenced *Intervention* in 2005, which reiterated the narrative of addiction, intervention, and treatment for people afflicted by a range of harmful behaviors. In 2009, A&E launched *Hoarders*, a show which focused on the treatment of people afflicted with obsessive-compulsive hoarding behaviors. Bravo introduced its own intervention show with *Tabatha's Salon Takeover* in 2008, in which hairdresser Tabatha Coffey intervened in the substandard business practices of various beauty salons. The Food Network entered the scene with its own Ramsay copy, *Restaurant: Impossible* in 2011.

All of these "reality" genres, which focus on either a contest or treatment, represent the ascendancy of a narrative of talent and correction over the previous spectacles of makeover work. The contest narrative pretends, on the one hand, to be about fleshing out the most talented, while on the other hand it focuses on rewarding gamesmanship as somehow more valuable than mere talent. To win any of these shows, a contestant must be both talented and strategic—and willing to relinquish friendships, loyalties, and good ethics to do what it takes to win. The treatment narrative, rehearsed repeatedly in exactly the same form, establishes a subject's addiction to drugs, alcohol, or anorexia/bulimia, traces the potential etiology of the disease, musters the family in a group intervention in which they all confront the addict, where the addict then consents (or not) to treatment at a facility, and then the treatment either works or does not. The very end of the show informs the audience of the current status of the addict, providing a second closure to the first victory of getting the addict into treatment.

All of these shows trade the spectacles of work and process for the spectacle of interpersonal drama, which is even more rigidly orthopedic than the lure of work. Although the shows appear to focus on strategy and interpersonal dynamics, they persistently reorder types and kinds into their proper narrative functions—the schematically normative to their positions and the asymptotic to theirs. The normative gender and sexual orientation of contestants is no longer at issue, as the contest shows have especially made room for gay and lesbian contestants. In fact, *Project Runway* absolutely requires them, and given that in the early years of the show (before it moved to the Lifetime channel) it pandered to gay audiences, a number of its winners were overtly gay men. Other contest shows (e.g., *Top Chef* and *Chopped*) include both homosexual and hetero-sexual contestants, whose lives are inscribed as completely norma-tive in the small stories they must tell about why they are compet-ing and what a victory will mean to them, which usually includes some heteronormative paean to their nuclear family, children, or dead (or dying) parents. The contests are dominated by the repe-tition of these stories of normative motivation, as if somehow the contest of skill, which was once interesting, has given way to a series of pathetic motivational testimonials. Like the spectacle of work, these testimonials lure attention away from the other coextensive sorting processes, such as the way strategy trades for industry and talent—in fact, these stories tend to displace both the processes of industry and strategy as alibiing whatever is necessary to win. In this way, the schematic and asymptotic, the hetero and the homo, the taxonomically conformative and non-conformative are reor-ganized under the aegis of a dueling set of narratives, the familial as proper motivation for any victory or self-improvement (i.e., the heteronarrative itself), and gamesmanship as the sneaky, rewarded narrative of behaviors without ethics or value (capitalism). The for-mer narrative obscures the latter, which is, of course, the point. In treating all subjects as normative and rendering all of their narra-tives as familial, the story of gamesmanship sneakily trumps the story of industry. The effect of this is to render all equally within the constraints of a capitalist system openly dependent on families as reproductive units—no matter how comprised—while covertly valorizing and even justifying behaviors that win, without regard to any values whatsoever . . . except winning itself.

Storying Gender Regimes

As the second stage of reality television makeover persistently over- and/or doubly narrates every event, it continues to construct its contestants into the two narrative regimes of clearly schematic and asymptotic. Two quick examples of how this narrative gendering occurs in first- and second-stage reality shows demonstrate the relations between the schematic and the asymptotic gender regimes, as well as how shifting the emphases of narrative alters what might be schematized. In the first stage of makeover reality shows, *Queer Eye for the Straight Guy* clearly dramatizes the relation between the subject of normative metamorphoses and his helpers as a version of a typical heteronarrative, in which the protagonist is aided by some middling gay figure toward culminating success in romance. *Queer Eye for the Straight Guy*'s "Fab Five" occupy the role of shamans, the gender guides that conduct heteronormative protagonists through the liminal middling space-time of self-transformation. The process is clearly, almost cornily, a literal "hetero" narrative both in its shape and in the way it typically sets out heterosexual coupling as the goal of the makeover process, even if the makeover subject is already married. The show focuses on modes of metamorphosis—on redecoration, cosmetic improvement of appearance and grooming habits, tutoring in behaviors and consideration, and learning a "show" dish to prepare for one's girlfriend.

The project is to conform the nonconforming object of expert ministrations to a taxonomic masculinity so that he can couple more effectively than before, a project that makes quite apparent how sex, gender, narrative, and heteroideology work together. That the experts are openly—even hyperbolically—gay emphasizes the queerness of the middle as itself a fixed identity category in a narrative relation to the hetero. With no apparent love lives of their own in the show, the Fab Five flirt with their usually (thank goodness) non-homophobic subject man, serving as surrogates of almost every kind. The show ends with an extended ritualized reveal. First, we see the straight guy's house or apartment, room by room. Then, from their spiffy loft and with drinks in their hands, the Fab Five watch the new and improved straight guy on widescreen HDTV showering and shaving (using his new products), fixing his hair (zhuzhing), getting dressed, preparing the meal, lighting candles, and greeting his (usually) stunned paramour for a night of atypical romance in which the straight guy has become more than his typical doofus self.

The second-stage reality competition musters all protagonists, no matter how they are gendered or what their sexual preference, as figuratively heteronormative. Everyone—contestants, helpers, also-rans—becomes schematic (and sometimes those who begin as helpers end up as stars). *Iron Chef*'s Cat Cora, an openly lesbian celebrity chef, accedes to schematic femininity by the very fact of her tendency to win, especially in the stripped-down simplicity of the contest narrative. We like to think that her sexuality and participation in other gender regimes do not matter, but that is the way commodity culture currently re-contains threats by the erstwhile non-heteronormative. In *Project Runway*, another show likely to have a significant percentage of openly gay contestants, participant testimony, especially about family ("I'm doing this for my mother") resecures all non-heteronormative subjects within their own very conventional stories. This double narration makes it seem as if second-stage reality shows liberally feature all kinds of subjects, while they schematize them into normativity by means of their own saccharine narratives and increasingly prevalent product endorsements.

This narrative transposition of schematic and asymptotic gender regimes does not only happen in reality television. A quick example of the way narrative gender regimes can refigure the genderings of characters in a sitcom is the interplay among Charlie's (Charlie Sheen) inevitable hetero-trajectories in *Two and a Half Men*, the less successful attempts of his brother, Alan (Jon Cryer), and renditions of the maid, Berta (Conchata Ferrell). There is never any doubt about either Charlie's sexuality or his taxonomically binary masculinity. Although he gets himself into trouble repeatedly because of substance abuse, he never fails to get the girl (at least once). This contrasts with his brother Alan's iffy romantic success that comes, if at all, only after much soul-searching, anxiety, insecurity, and goofiness. Alan appears to be less normatively masculine than Charlie (even though there is nothing about his appearance that would signal anything other than normative masculinity). Alan evinces more a mix of gender regimes in his obsessive-compulsive behaviors, his lack of confidence, and his interest in interior decoration. His insecurities make Charlie look even more confident; Charlie's success makes Alan appear less manly, even though Alan is a father. The interplay between these two men is the interplay between a schematically gendered Charlie and the asymptotic Alan as the never quite. The jolly, buxom maid, Berta, is also asymptotic, offering wisecrack commentary, appearing as chimeric, and certainly not "traditionally" feminine, although she occasionally announces heterosexual desires.

Compensatory Obsessions

In all of this, genderings, which have been repeatedly layered, transformed, and repositioned, seem to lose all relevance. Cultural anxieties appear to shift from refinding normative taxonomic binaries, to enlisting a range of genderings in the service of family and corporate weal (which collapse into each other). But do not be fooled. Diverting attention from forced normality does not mean that such conformity is not still encouraged (or encouraged even more viciously as we begin to dress three-year-old girls as hookers). What this distraction and apparent acceptance means is that cultural narratives are deploying other tactics to contain that which seems to escape taxonomic binaries. This suggests an anxiety about category itself, reflected in the ways the reality contest narrative over-compensates. This tactic actually cannot lose. Either we simply muster everyone in the service of corporate participation, looking liberal, et cetera, or we distract attention from the ways in which gender norms are actually being enforced more viciously (eroding women's rights of reproductive choice, for example).

That reality shows from both stages are replayed daily, however, suggests that these genres are symptomatic of something else.

If we understand gender as a system of inter-influential, inter-constitutive, and co-productive regimes, then the obsessive repetition of the makeover and the contest suggests a process of compensation, a working harder in the site of heteronormativity to overcome some problem somewhere else. Makeovers, weight-loss regimens, and treatments overcompensate, which suggests that the heteronormative itself is insecure and must be constantly rese-cured. But what destabilizes the heteronormative, which is, given the work it obviously takes, already unstable?

We might look to other obvious contemporary sites of taxonomic overcompensation: right-wing politics, any mindless emphasis on the automatic virtues of the nuclear family, patriarchy, political agendas designed to enforce and reinforce the ideological advantages of marriage, and identity politics as the insistent taxonomizing and control of differences. One reason for these systematic overcompensations is that we are culturally anxious about the loss of category itself and the kind of structure it fronts and reproduces. This is one reason gay marriage, really a very minor matter and no change to structure at all, has been such a lightning rod. If we are afraid that categories of intelligibility are disappearing, our first line of defense is the symbolic site of heteronarrative itself—the joinder conclusion of taxonomic binary difference as the only means to a satisfying end. Gay marriage only *appears* to assault heteronarrative (though it actually reconfirms it), but this cultural heteronarrative is one already assaulted by larger systemic changes and shifts. The worry about gay marriage is itself only a symptom.

In a way, of course, structure has already given way to more systems ways of thinking in the larger sense of the term. Since systems and structure coexist, as in this gender scheme, are not they interdependent? And in this regard, is not my more "systems" approach to gender as regimes merely rescuing gender for system? Or was system always already there? If so, why be anxious? Systems thinking that emerges first in technology and science plays out a constant drama with structure and taxonomy. Systems make visible the multiplicities and complexities that structure obscures and/or re-contains. Systems, for example, splinter variations into separable phenomena rather than degrees of the same thing. Each variation in temperature requires a different degree of response and perhaps responses from different parts of a system. Structure understands genes, for example, as words that express, while system would understand genes as complex, interlocked, multi-stepped phenomena, where one gene works differently depending on its environment, position, age, and the chain of events within which it is provoked.

4 Social Algebras

It is a truth universally acknowledged, that a single man in possession of a good fortune must be in want of a wife.

—Jane Austen, *Pride and Prejudice*

Past Perfect

In retrospect, the turn of the twentieth century fixated not only on makeovers, but also on the apical figures—the ideal feminine, the ideal masculine—of a "social " gender regime which defined, in correlation with each other, the perfect type of each side of a taxonomic binary. Popular culture has long focused on such figures as the exemplary loci of instruction and desire. Celebrity culture has always produced iconic figures who, if they did not already, came to define the perfect "type" for the era even as these "types" obviously displayed different mixes of gender regimes. "Ideal" femininity, was exemplified by such icons as Marilyn Monroe and Joan Crawford—or Jackie Kennedy, Farrah Fawcett, Jennifer Aniston, or Kim Kardashian. The same variations occur among icons of perfect masculinity, whom we see less as examples of a gender ideal than as active agents whose masculinity is an attribute of their potency. But even these guys manifest different versions of the "perfect" masculine man. John Wayne differs from Sean Connery who differs from George Clooney, Denzel Washington, Benedict Cumberbatch, or Chris Hemsworth. If the first decade of the twenty-first century fixated on attempts to achieve taxonomic compliance by continuously trying to produce "ideal" or social versions of masculine and feminine, the last decades of the twentieth century meditated on what constituted those social ideals.

We can envision the site of the struggle for exemplary perfection, however, only retrospectively. At any contemporaneous moment, playing with gender taxonomies and especially hyperbolizing them (the drag of *Some Like It Hot*, Patsy Stone's feminine masquerade on *Absolutely Fabulous*) is generally a comic commentary on the impossibility of trying to comply with what appears to be a gender extreme. Or wait—the comic only emerges in relation to the feminine ideal. On the masculine side of social gender, clowns are exempla of failed masculinity: nerds, effeminate men, weaklings. Perfect masculinity is never funny.

In retrospect, endeavors at the social ideal also reveal something else: that the hyperbolized models of the feminine and the masculine are themselves perfect instances of femininity and masculinity and that females and males have a differential relation to the quadratic process fronted by the models themselves. This differential relation is itself the motor of a social regime whose quadratic organization both produces and accounts for some (but not all) gender asymmetries.

Two Fabulous

In an episode of *Absolutely Fabulous* (the over-the-top, tongue-in-cheek, girl-buddy sitcom written by Jennifer Saunders and originally aired on the BBC), the girls, Edina (Jennifer Saunders) and Patsy (Joanna Lumley), go to New York. On the Concorde, of course. Patsy is a hyperbolic version of the feminine—slender, blonde, leggy, and heavily made-up. On a New York street, two transvestites take her for another transvestite. The humor in that moment reflects the complex algebra of a social gender regime. The compulsion to reduce individuals to one of two positions in relation to the ideals that govern those positions is complicated in this scene by the canny perception that the ideal feminine is best exemplified by someone self-conscious of femininity as femininity, or as a kind of femininity squared, or better yet, a male. Acknowledging that femininity is always already multiplied by femininity, *Absolutely Fabulous* unrelentingly exposes all of the coefficients of '90s femininity, with too much money and time to spend on itself.

The revealing aspect of *Absolutely Fabulous* was its fan base, which, in my observation in American universities, was composed entirely of middle-class women and gay men. When I screened an episode of *Absolutely Fabulous* in a college classroom, for example, the female students would almost always think it hilarious and the male students (with few exceptions) would not understand it at all. This division in reception was not simply because the show focuses almost entirely on its female regulars—Edina, Patsy, Edina's daughter Saffie, Edina's secretary Bubble, and Edina's mother—though this would seem to support a theory of reception based on simple same-sex identifications. The show exposes the quadratic dynamics of femininity itself, something those who are located in relation to the feminine know and those located in relation to the masculine know only as an imperative (and therefore never really a joke): that femininity itself is a joke insofar as it is by definition hyperbolic, doubled, extreme, and never possible. For those on the side of the feminine, making fun of this feminine dilemma by multiplying it again is hilarious. For those on the side of the masculine, those multiplications are annoying noise to be displaced onto women as character flaws.

The Strange Platonism of Modern Life

The regime of social gender is the familiar version of conventional, normative "gender" that is the subject of sociology, women's studies, popular cultural renditions of subjective positioning, psychology, religion, and even science. In the United States, it is imagined to be the apt signifier of biological sex, even though we already know that such an alignment rarely occurs (hence the need for the taxonomic). The social regime is the observable manifestation of the inequities, inclinations, compensations, and other adjustments of a social process as it perpetually negotiates multiple, conflicting interests and ideologies displaced onto the individual as a register of self-expression. As the apparently social embellishment of the taxonomic's imaginary biological substrate, social gender is only the delusion of an elaboration, like the relation of gender-specific clothes to a sexed body. That this social regime appears to be merely the accessory of a greater subjective truth—its sign and expression—is the reductive effect of social gender's algebra. In this algebra, social gender appears to be resolving toward the definitive and quiescent nature of a more "scientific" taxonomic imagined to be real instead of ideal, possible and material instead of contingent, unreachable, and abstract. Social gender's paradoxical and reductive dynamics, thus, have a gravity that compels the reduction of all terms to an equation in an attempt to capture the fluid complexities of such trite concepts as "gender role," "sex role stereotype," "gender appropriate," and "gender bias."

Myths of subjective positioning in Western culture, but also in many non-Western cultures, are embroideries of this gender algebra as a compulsion toward a reduction (or solution) within a set. This compulsion persists as a social operation, a pressure toward resolution and intelligibility that seems to emanate from all points—from cultural institutions, individual "essence," and individual will as well as from the choices available to medical, juridical, and lately Transportation Security Administration discourses. This compulsion squeezes subjects toward one of the two possible ideals that constitute the set, not as a matter of locating subjects in a taxonomic binary, but as a matter of proper signification. Social gender myths, which circulate as the ordinary, street-level, pink/blue, endlessly reiterate, reinforce, and revise the imperatives of a set of binary ideals. These gender myths are the parole of social gender, the teaming possibilities expressing either masculinity or femininity from culture to culture through time. These myths exist in relation to the langue of gender ideals—the patterns, roles, and paradigms that reach toward two glowing exemplary models that correlate fantasmatically with a binary sexual taxonomy. These social models are platonic insofar as they situate themselves as apparently archetypal, permanent, ideal, and unrealizable, and insofar as they hover as the imaginary paradigms into which we reduce all characterological phenomena. Of course, the actual content of these ideals is contingent and historical instead of permanent and universal, but located as ideals, they emanate an aura of essential truth that solicits compliance in a dynamic of familial imperative and social obligation. That multiple cultural discourses—religion, the state, science, art, literature, film, advertising, and clothing—treat these ideals as the truths from which society (and even life) itself springs obscures the ways society produces the ideals in the first place as the imaginary correlative of male/female taxonomies, as the content defining structures such as the family that, produced by culture, seem to preexist and exceed it.

That these imaginary archetypes occupy the idealistic regime of social gender creates a paradox. On the one hand, these ideals offer a model of perfection toward which beings aspire or toward which the socius pushes and manipulates its subjects, whether they aspire or not. On the other hand, by definition, these ideals are unattainable; no one can reach them. So if imaginary ideals govern the possibilities of subjectivity, subjects are put in the position of never really being able to be what they are compelled to be. This means that from the start, a gender regime organized around the ideals driving social compulsion shares in an asymptotic dynamic, never achieving its aspiration, never solving the equation of the relations between feminine and masculine ideals—especially insofar as the relations between the two are thought to be intrinsically incommensurate: "men are from Mars, women are from Venus." But unlike an asymptotic regime in which gender itself appears as a reaching rather than a being there, social gender is the perpetual delusion of realizing its own terms as it vainly reaches for them; it is the definitive mirage of a solution and balancing that cannot be achieved.

As a compulsive regime operating in the stretch between ideals and individual manifestations of imaginary archetypes, social gender's dynamic is characterized by paradox itself, by a bidirectional and contradictory impetus, moving two ways at once, and never really getting anywhere. One direction is reduction, a consolidation into intelligibility and compliance with impossible ideals. The other direction is augmentation, an understanding of the process of engenderment as a series of additions, of literally appending things to bodies as a means of compliance with idealization. Understood as forms of "expression"—as an outer manifestation of an inner subjective truth—this appending process takes the form of clothing styles, accessories, makeup, the development of the physique, and, most recently, its literalization in plastic surgery procedures such as breast, gluteal, calf, and pectoral augmentations. The entire process of compulsion is like focusing a lens, both lengthening and shortening to get a sharp view that is always already distorted by the possibilities inherent to the lens itself.

The paradoxical two-way process of social gender compels toward reduction in a fashion that is quadratic—it solves for two different axes—in the essential interrelation between the ideals of femininity and masculinity on an x-axis, which represents femininity on the "minus" or "not all" side and masculinity on the positive or "all" side. The parabolic relation between success and failure is represented on the y-axis. These are not envaluations, though of course culturally they are, but rather are positions in Lacan's scheme of sexuation insofar as they reflect, too literally, the operation of beliefs in the possibility of all/not all that Lacan aligns with genders but not sexes.

This quadratic equation is less an analogy of gender complementarity than a direct expression of the complex and contradictory logics at work in the busy system of the social regime. This quadratic relation is one of algebra's most rudimentary operations: "A set together with a pair of binary operations defined on the set [feminine, masculine]. Usually, the set and the operations include an identity element, and the operations are commutative or associative."[1] The set—humanity—is defined by a pair of binary operations (masculinity, femininity [in our culture already conveniently labeled XX and XY to comply with a genetic imaginary]), which include a gendered "identity element" and whose operations are "commutative or associative." "Commutative" means that elements of the set are moved to one side or the other; they are turned from one thing into the other. "Associative" means that elements close to one side or the other are attached thereto. Quadratic equations, various ways to complete the square (to search for the perfect proportion), always have two unknowns, x and y, whose solutions must be mapped in relation to one another on an x-pole and a y-pole. The result is a proportion or a conic section: a circle, an ellipse, or a parabola. The circle and ellipse seem complete, while the parabola is an arc that produces either asymptosis or a falling away.

Within the social regime, three different relations represent three different, but coexisting and superimposed, sets of relations

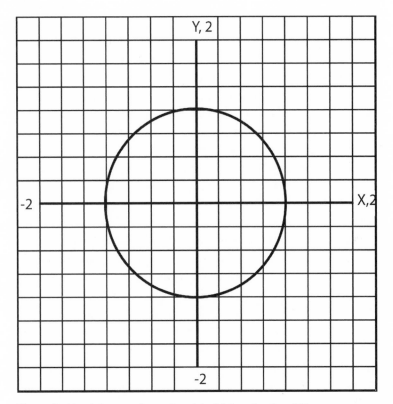

Figure 2. Absolute complementary ideal ($x^2 + y^2 + 1 = 10$).

between x and y, where x and y represent "perfect" femininity and masculinity. The first and simplest equation is the realm of the absolute ideal where the poles x and y transverse each other. In the ideal in which x and y are seen as equal coproducers (that is, on the same side of the equation), their relation produces a section of a circle— the yin/yang of total binary complementarity—using the equation $x^2 + y^2 + 1 = 10$. The circle's expression of symmetry results from the addition of the squares of both terms, plus 1, the signifier of wholeness.

We might understand squaring (y^2, x^2) as something like the masculine masculine, which takes the imaginary form of masculinity expressed in and through a male body, or the feminine feminine, which would seem to layer feminine signifiers on a female body.

Such squaring also refers to the ways social gender regimes themselves are the doublings produced by paradox (moving in opposite directions at the same time) and/or the illusion of accruals or layerings (gender coefficients such as clothing, accessories, mannerisms, body styles—exemplified in the figure of a muscled man riding a horse and smoking a cigar) by which the effects of social gender are produced and manifested. The squaring reflects an idealized and complementary relation of coordinated equality, offered as ideal in dualistic or Manichean understandings of phenomena and resulting, perhaps no so coincidentally, in a figure that grounds a yin/yang. This equation of complete complementarity exists in tension with the gender asymmetries that govern most gender regimes as well as processes of subjective sexuation. This complementarity is the myth that grounds the idea that genders complete one another.

But, also and at the same time, as happens in relation to this unreachable set of ideals, the two terms are not coequal producers, but exist in a relation of equivocation in which one side (x^2) is defined in relation to the other (y), and is therefore parasitic and always reaching toward that other. This produces a second equation, which results in a parabola where each term, x and y, exists at a point relative to the other in a trajectory that inclines toward and leans away from their balance.

The asymmetry of this second equation represents the dynamic in which the poles, x and y, represent the two conflicting movements that constitute the social regime as such: either aspiring to but never reaching the ideal (on the y-axis), or falling away from the ideal. The y-pole represents the platonic ideal of two specific complementary genders, masculine and feminine, conjoined perfectly at the parabola's apex. The x-pole represents the movement toward or away from that ideal as the condition of the possibility of either femininity or masculinity. In this equation, the x-side is also multiplied by a coefficient and augmented by a value. But why make this so complicated? Because social gender is a complex, flexive system of perpetual adjustments and relations arranged around and constituting multiple conflicting paradigms. It is not that there are genders and they negotiate these contradictions; the contradictions and the complex interrelations constitute the regime of social gender itself.

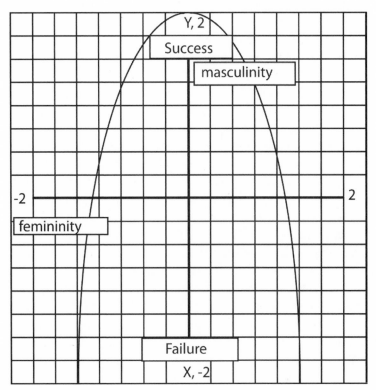

Figure 3. Asymmetry ($y = x^2 + x + n$).

The terms by which femininity squared plus augmentation equals masculinity symbolizes Lacan's characterization of the feminine as the position that believes there is "not all." The feminine side exists in an asymptotic relation to the y-axis of "success," or the achievement of any perfectly feminine state. By itself, the feminine side needs help; in the social regime, femininity is that which seems doubled—that is, self-conscious and bearing the marks of its labor—and must be squared, added to a coefficient, and augmented by a value. This final value is very much like Lacan's notion of the "petit object a," the temporary and transient object that seems to fulfill desire. This can be an actual object such as a purse, or fetish objects such as lingerie or shoes, or signifiers of any of the multiple registers or modes that inflect or incline genders in certain directions—toward, for example, a race, class, ethnicity, age, sexual style, religion, and other cues by which we mark or deduce subjective situation. In their most ossified form, these filtering modes and accessories constitute an identity politics that graph positionalities across a range of class or wealth privilege (understood itself as quadratic). In their more flexible use, these modes mix and mingle and appear, at least, to reflect the eccentricities of the subject who wields them, constituting (or at least appearing to signal) the identifications imagined to produce a "gender identity."

This second equation maps the essential asymmetries that persist between the social gender ideals of femininity and masculinity as an effect of their interdependency in the play of difference itself, where the notion of difference is premised on the presence somewhere of an imaginary phallic signifier. Femininity squared, multiplied by the "petit object a," and augmented by yet another value pairs finally with ideal masculinity as the intrinsic character of social gender. Femininity must look as if it is the result of effort, even if that result is looking effortless. The work of masculinity becomes increasingly visible only as it begins to fail because the masculine, mythically, begins at the apex. Increasing supplementation (money, muscles, facial hair, etc.) functions to prevent falling away rather than enabling a getting there. Hence facial hair, buff bodies, and guns, though clearly compensatory, are not intrinsic elements of masculinity, but are, rather, signs of a propping up, of a need to re-signify that the something that is always missing is not missing.

This third version of the equation also results in a parabola, with its apex located just right of the y-pole on the masculine side. Femininity, located on the "upward" side of the parabola, always reaches toward but never achieves the apex, while masculinity, at the top and on the downward slope, is at the parabolic apex and can only fall away. When the three equations are combined, the result is social gender as a paradox that manifests itself as oscillating between the ideal completeness of the circle and the asymmetry of superimposed parabolas, a relation in which itself would be expressed as a parabola. Social gender simultaneously inclines toward and falls away from its ideals, like a bell curve or what we understand to be the law of averages, or Stephen Jay Gould's "full house."[2] The so-

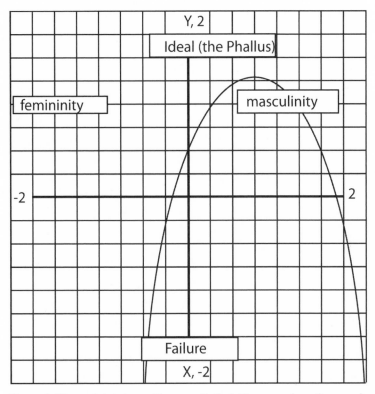

Figure 4. The social regime with masculinity falling away ($y = x^2 + x + n$).

cial is simultaneously symmetrical and asymmetrical, its dynamic paradoxical and self-contradictory in a process of constant reduction predefined by specific fields of possibility that nonetheless can never be realized. It is an ideal with no content and no possibility of achievement that dominates the imaginary and that morphs and changes through histories and cultures as an urge toward the impossible reduction of its contradictory dynamics. We can change the values for x and y and still have the same relative dynamics.

As the dynamics of social gender coexist and pull against one another, social gender seems both obvious and enigmatic at the same time. The complexity of these dynamics also suggests why there is an urge toward an idealizing reduction as a way to avoid the complexities of the regime's self-contradictory dynamic. But the equations do not tell the whole story of this complex dynamic, in part because the superficial styles that constitute the accessories of social gender shift through time. To understand how those forms work as equations of movement rather than as static representations, one would need to understand these geometries as fluid. The regime of social gender is indeed a mechanics of fluids, not existing, as Luce Irigaray suggests, only on the side of the feminine, but as the dynamic of the entire regime.[3] The equations for hydraulics are far more complex than the relatively simple and potentially obfuscatory quadratic equations listed here, but consider such concepts of fluid movement as turbulence, splash, and viscosity as describing the interrelation among ideal, myth, the compulsion toward reduction, the impossibility of compliance, and the omnipresence of gender-signifying accessories.

As a dynamic of correlated attitudes in relation to a single parabolic arc, social versions of femininity and masculinity are not complementary positions, nor are they binary. They are legible as multiple versions articulated in and through complex webs of signifiers that locate individuals on a parabola produced by the interrelations of two terms on an imaginary grid. Their relative locations on the parabolic slopes of the equation reflect the way the two categories of social gender relate to each other—kinetic and static, failing and achieved, striving and precarious, success in perpetual failure and insecure in perilous success. This maps an interdependent relational economy that describes the dynamics of social femininity and masculinity as vectors of reduction, but it also describes the intrinsic asymmetries observed by Irigaray and others: where masculinity is singular, delusively believing there can be an "all" and femininity never quite there and not believing there is a "there" at which to be.

Quadratics through History

How else to understand the persistent coexistence of contradictory models—the yin/yang of perfect complementarity and the obvious asymmetries of sex/gender? Only if we understand these two sides as inter-constitutional does the coexistence of these models make much sense. In line with Lacan's reinterpretation of the relative cultural envaluation of feminine and masculine as sexuations defined along multiple axes, a social gender regime constantly processes these multiple axes in relation to one another. The equations are relatively static; only the signifiers of the codes shift through time. So we can easily understand Marilyn Monroe's version of ideal femininity, even though today someone who displayed her style literally would be a travesty. At the same time, at any moment there are cues that would signify ideal femininity and that would define that position in different social contexts.

These "ideals" coexist and constantly change, not only as the effects of commodity fashion but also as the complex production of the all the elements by which gender is produced at any given time and place. So in a 1960s culture in which elegance was defined by a certain fashion sense, and femininity reached toward Bambi-dom, and physical beauty was defined by full-figured-ness, Marilyn Monroe would be perfect and Jane Russell not Bambi enough. Arguably, at the current moment, perfect femininity requires the addition of a baby bump (the "+" supplements, e.g., Kate Middleton, Kim Kardashian) that aligns perfect feminine beauty with an increasingly insistent heteroreproductive narrative.

$$y = x^2 + x(a) + a$$

Although femininity and masculinity belong equally to this paradoxical set of dynamics and processes, they do not participate in equal ways. The symmetry of the complementary binary is an idealization whose unreachability is cast onto the side of the feminine as the place of failure. That is why femininity operates on the side of the coefficient, visibly squared even though, of course, we understand that masculinity has its own squarings and coefficients. Catching up and ever failing is the definition of femininity: greater work for greater failure, all on the x-pole, so the y-pole can stand up straight and tall. This relates to a Lacanian notion of the relation between the Phallus and gender: that the two genders have a differential relation to the Phallus as a signifier. The Phallus is the signifier that alibis asymmetrical displacements, and symbolically grounds the social regime's economy by always providing the first coefficient that disrupts the idealized circle and turns it into a parabola. All asymptotic movement is displaced into the feminine as the site of lack, the function through which the delusion of masculine stability is produced. For this reason, the Phallus must be located on the side of the feminine as that which multiplies and lenses her, but which the feminine cannot even have the delusion of wielding. The feminine, thus, is wielded, modified, multiplied by the phallic signifier.

Although masculinity, too, participates in and is produced through the paradoxical two-way movement between ideal and failure, we imagine its economy as singular and envision its augmentation as supplementing instead of completing. This perception exists even as the evident overcompensations of masculinity make us fully aware that no penis is large enough, no man manly enough. The asymmetrical relation between femininity and masculinity plays out on the feminine side as femininity's problem, in part because, as Irigaray points out, both masculinity and femininity, when simply reversed, are really terms of the same $(x = y)$, and because social genders each have their own "internal" logics and dynamics that perpetually work together in a complex fashion to produce and balance this "same."[4]

If we understand the social regime as simultaneously moving toward (x) and falling away (y) from ideals, this dynamic appears on the side of the feminine as work. Work is an intrinsic effect (and also ostensible cause) of femininity's constant failure. The work of femininity is poised as the energy (understood as significations) necessary to reduce disorganization toward one term of an ideal gender binary. Western forms of femininity, almost regardless of race, class, or age, rove between processes of reduction and augmentation, losing weight and wearing earrings, shaving body hair and having breast implants. These bodily operations are less about the final perfect reduction of the being to the ideal of femininity than they are about the production of the feminine subject as always undergoing the processes of becoming more feminine. The feminine subject is not the product of work, but the effect of working. The more perpetual these bodily adjustments, the more intrinsically feminine they are and the more ideally feminine the subject who engages daily in applying makeup, coiffing, depilating, dieting, dressing stylishly, wearing jewelry, doing or having nails done, donning perfume, restricting movement, and tottering on high heels.

Sexing and the Single Girl; or, Always a Bridesmaid . . .

In the past two decades, the status of femininity as work has most recently become self-consciously visible in a series of comic texts focused on single women. Although the styles may change, the process has remained surprisingly constant. Such mainstream entertainments as *Sex and the City*, *Absolutely Fabulous*, and most recently *Bridesmaids* make openly apparent the intrinsic kineticism of femininity. In all of these popular cultural texts, the female subject is confronted with a series of disjunctions: between her body and cultural expectations about the proper feminine form, between her desires and "proper" desires, between her joy in singletude and the devaluation of single women, between what she thinks she is and what prescriptions about femininity suggest she should be, between self-comfort and cultural urges toward self-improvement. A lot of apparatus rushes to the fissures produced by these contradictions in all of these texts. All evoke self-help, dieting, and pop psychology as potential and often-sought mediators and patches. Self-analysis and self-critique become preoccupying modes of existence and the substance of many conversations and interchanges. The gangling apparatus produces unrest, a kineticism that comes to stand as femininity itself, as the impossibility of the ideal perpetuates a more or less roving desire that slides from men to food, to proper body image to comfort, and yet can never be comfortable with any of these.

In a final tautological turn, femininity's kineticism, then, accounts for the singleness, for the girl who can never settle down, a restlessness that loops the single girl back into the hunt, since it is "a truth universally acknowledged," et cetera. This kineticism also prevents the female subject from ever actually being a subject if we understand the subject as a sort of fixed, defined entity. The feminine subject is overtly the subject in process, taken as unfinished. Unfinished because she is feminine or because she is single. Single because she is insufficiently feminine. Unfinished femininity becomes self-conscious, and conscious of itself as a production, as not all, conscious of itself as a commodity, as a point and condition of exchange.

Although its self-conscious processes all seem aimed at achieving some kind of feminine ideal, they actually constitute a lifestyle in themselves, founded on a never-ending labor with the mirage of a specific goal, and hence a secure and satisfying process. But they also suggest a subject with a kind of capitalistic urge to invest in the production of femininity itself in hopes of a return in the form of romance, the dividend of heterosexuality (whether straight or gay). On the one hand, the feminine subject desires to comply with cultural ideals of femininity that would presumably make her an object of exchange. On the other, she is a desiring subject who wants a quick exchange—instant gratification in the form of things beyond the pleasures of mating: food, booze, cigarettes, sleep, comfort, and the company of women. Even heterosexual marriage is a supplement for social femininity, providing an augmentation that enhances at least presumptions about the subject wife's femininity.

The struggle to achieve femininity (which itself reveals the complicity of self-help and capitalism) becomes the essence of femininity—a femininity that can never be itself, but is instead a kind of circling indirection always veering toward femininity as the essence of femininity. Femininity is a cottage industry, a self-production that always fails, or rather always succeeds in its failure, if the essence of femininity *is* its inevitable failure. Women who are too perfect—who succeed at feminizing themselves—are no longer feminine, but masqueraders, hiding that hard-core Rivièresque masculinity, being mistaken, as Patsy was, for transvestites.[5] The most perfect femininity—a femininity poised as complete—is the terrain of male drag queens whose transformative labors lead them to an end fulfilling in itself. Femininity is a kind of indirection, pointing always toward an ideal, while all the time consisting of the process itself.

Although it is easy to point to such iconic examples of the perfectly feminine (such as Marilyn Monroe or Beyoncé), the position of such an ideal has itself become doubled, self-conscious, self-multiplied to the point where any representation of the "perfect" feminine is always a self-conscious production of its ultimate impossibility. While *Ab Fab*'s Edina, Patsy, and even Saffie comically labor around the ideal of femininity as manifested through the gluttonies of commodity culture, their most recent "coda" episodes (2012) dramatize the ultimate exhaustion of this commodified version as itself a travesty of the ideal that got away. More recent texts that focus on contrasting versions of femininity, such as *Bridesmaids* (2011), offer a range of versions of femininity in which the one deemed most "ideal" is also the character most reviled. *Bridesmaids* offers a spectrum of femininities as the ground for its comic play on the "also-rans"—the bridesmaids at friend Lillian's (Maya Rudolph) wedding. The bridesmaids, including Annie (Kristen Wiig), Helen (Rose Byrne), Rita (Wendi McLendon-Covey), and Megan (Melissa McCarthy) among others, are not the failed alternatives to Lillian's romantic success. Instead, they figure, together with Lillian, femininities understood precisely as degrees of economic and social success, competence, and masculinization. The most successful, wealthy, and classically "feminine" of them all, Helen, is the most reviled by the film's protagonist, Annie, who envies her perfection. Lillian is a practical, unpretentious, down-to-earth character whose ability to see people for who they are locates her in a slightly chimeric position. Rita is a married, faded beauty whose previous feminine perfection has already disappeared in favor of maternal cynicism. Megan is a rough-and-ready, tough, "masculine" female whose inappropriate heartiness, lack of boundaries, and manly carriage locate her as the sexual "top" to the air marshal Jon's (Ben Falcone) bottom. Annie, whose point of view the film represents, is a failed baker, full of quirks and self-destructive tendencies, and who most frequently and visibly engages in the visible work of femininity.

Like *Ab Fab*, *Bridesmaids* anatomizes femininity, but more overtly as a range in relation to the masculine against which the film compares this femininity. Just as femininity is glossed by wealth, race, girth, and behavior, so the film's males are arrayed in relation to a kind of masculine perfection best embodied by Officer Nathan Rhodes (Chris O'Dowd), whose immigrant Irish patience accompanies his gentle wooing of Annie. Like the film's variety of feminine exempla, the film's males display varying degrees of masculine poise, defined primarily through their relative imperturbability. Even the bizarre Gil (Matt Lucas), Annie's roommate, firmly holds the line when it comes to Annie's behavior, kicking her out of the apartment. The film imagines masculinity as that which holds its own in relation to the women who constantly buffet it with insecurities, whims, and idiotic complications. It is probably no coincidence that two men who end up coupled with the bridesmaids are in law enforcement. And like the women, the men are glossed with details of ethnic and physical difference, from Rhodes's Irish accent to Jon's small stature. In all of this variety, *Bridesmaids* presents a recent view of a continued feminine struggle where no ideal is ideal in contrast to a masculinity that, accessorized with guns, is still unassailed, even if it consents to being the bottom.

Where Did Marilyn Go?

Marilyn Monroe has become a toddler. In recent years, the process of perpetual feminizing work appears in the overdocumented protocols of child beauty pageants. The reality show *Toddlers and Tiaras* repeatedly rehearses the hard work necessary to transform little girls into stylish, feminine minxes, highlighting especially the artificiality of this femininity. In this context, the feminizing that might seem to be an automatic travesty given the age of the contestants is surprisingly serious—the displacement of maternal wishes for that which has either passed them by or which they have no possibility of ever achieving. The program is almost entirely about the beautification process, highlighting the augmentative tricks necessary to make little girls competitive in beauty pageants that reward outdated ideals of female beauty while approaching the hyperbole of the drag queen. Masquerading as Marilyn or Madonna, or any one of a number of recognizable past paragons of the feminine, these little girls show this social femininity up as a masquerade, even as they demonstrate the lingering hold of previous feminine incarnations. The toddlers' pageant regalia are curiously anachronistic, effecting something like "southern belle" meets Zsa Zsa Gabor, all displaced onto prepubescent bodies rife for pedophiliac delectation.

The Array

When I asked my Facebook friends what they thought might be a current version of ideal femininity, the answers ranged from Tina

Fey to Lena Dunham, from Beyoncé to Meryl Streep or Rachel Ray. But there were also questions about the meaning of my query. Whereas in the 1960s the question of the ideal woman would have made sense, it may no longer—and not just for academics. This does not mean that the quadratic relation between the ideals of femininity and masculinity no longer operates, but that shifts in media and the commodified stratification of generational audiences elevates age as a central variable. Adding age to the equation produces multiple possibilities that locate both femininity and masculinity according to a range of trends. The "trending" version consists of a collection of types, all of which manifest some aspect of femininity or masculinity, but in which there is only one vaguely ideal example. These collections envision themselves as social gender as well as envision the collection of itself as an ideal. Alibiing this multiplicity with a market logic that suggests that there might be multiple ideals for multiple audiences, even these ranges betray the basic dynamic by which social femininity and masculinity interact: femininity is still work and masculinity is still all about the threat of falling away.

This sense of multiple ideals plays out in popular cultural texts that begin late in the first decade of the twenty-first century. Both mainstream cinema and television sitcoms begin focusing on these collections of types, almost de rigueur. Genders now come in groups. There are few vehicles aimed at young adult audiences that do not include clumps of varied examples of masculinity and femininity. But the dynamics by which social femininity and masculinity contrast are more starkly visible in texts from the first decade of the twenty-first century that play out anxieties about categories, differences, and ideals themselves as the first generation of young adults emerges from a culture that has tried to protect them from feeling bad about themselves.

Delusive Dressing Down

The labor of femininity, something always seen as a means to end, constitutes social femininity. The feminine woman, who in never really being feminine is always feminine, seeks advice from material offering instruction about how to be feminine from self-help books and maybe talk shows (with their makeovers). This provides the illusion of some control for the wannabe femininity candidate, giving her an ersatz sense of empowerment and independence that verges on feminism. Feminism (even though using that term is really unfeminine and even taboo) becomes the source of strength and resolution needed to surmount the tribulations of an ever-failing femininity in a world that demands indirection from its females. Feminism contributes to an illusion of agency, while the process of feminizing purifies feminism by redirecting it toward the preparation of the bride. That may also be how feminism ceases to be a social movement with political aims for a group and instead becomes an individual philosophy focusing on self-improvement and assertiveness in the arena of the self or in the slightly enlarged theater of diplomatic heterosexual relations. Finally, by wedding the process of the subject to the fervor of doctrine—to agency as perpetual engendering—femininity's insincerity gains the stamp of sincerity.

Turn-of-the-twenty-first-century texts about single, always feminine women—*Bridget Jones's Diary, Sex and the City, Absolutely Fabulous*—strip away the pretended pretext of femininity ostensibly to denude the process of its manufacture as an operation of agency, the same agency that makes the woman a writer or a public relations agent. Stripping away the obviously superficial and insincere vestiges of femininity—makeup, high heels—produces the illusion that what one sees is the "real," that is, an authentic woman in the process of her feminization. But like femininity itself, the striptease or denudement *is* the woman. The agenic power made visible by an appeal to self-oriented feminism turns out to be what drives the social regime's illusion engine, producing a perpetual motion machine dedicated to the stalled repetitions of the spinster's holding pattern. The feminine subject comes into being as an effect of this striptease, existing in deixis—the "not all" in reference to the "all"—enacted in the various frames by which she is presented, or presents herself. Femininity is aware of itself as always striving, commodified by accessories. The algebraic ax squared, ax^2.

Social femininity's perpetual process of becoming feminine suggests why female protagonists in turn-of-the-twenty-first-century texts are often writers who write about the process of being a single female. The presence of the diary apparatus in *Bridget Jones's Diary* and *Bridget Jones: The Edge of Reason* or the insights of Carrie Bradshaw (Sarah Jessica Parker) in *Sex and the City* enacts social femininity as a process aware of itself as a process. Bridget Jones (Renée Zellweger) writes a diary about her failures and her weight; Carrie Bradshaw's newspaper column is an insider's view of the single-girl experience in the murky maelstrom of the metropolitan dating scene. The films' rendition of the writing process with its voice-over narrative—both *Bridget Jones* and *Sex and the City* frame diegetic narrative with voice-over readings of writing in process—serves as a distracting presentation of the female voice. The voice is a guarantee of the personal, simulating a denuding revelation of the "real" female whose feminizing processes the writing documents. This produces a perpetual cycle of feminizing as the character in the process of perpetual feminization reveals herself to be in the process of perpetual feminization, et cetera.

Framed by scrivening female characters, both the two Bridget Jones films and *Sex and the City* present the spectacle of the feminine subject in process as a phenomenon about which there is a retrospective consciousness of the feminine subject always in process. Not only does the characters' writing reflect the framing intimacy of personal observation on culture, it also produces the illusion of the feminine subject as the object of its own scrutiny, producing another version of self-multiplication or squaring (x^2). Oscillating between the agenic frame of authorial consciousness and the self-conscious processes of constant striving, the social feminine subject circulates through the parabolas of a regime that finally always hovers in the tension between partial and complete and appears to move in a single direction from the former to the latter. This movement is legible, coherent, and compliant with the directionality of all narratives of production—and narrative itself. But this sense of left-to-right process coexists with the dynamic of its undoing, produced in the relation among the frames of self-conscious self-production. Because social femininity is intrinsically a working toward, the writing woman is already the essence of femininity insofar as the writing is both part of the work processes of feminizing and testimony to striving. Bridget Jones's diary writing is always the confession of her failure to accede to the feminine ideal. In writing her failure, Bridget also succeeds in incarnating femininity as that which must strive and never get there.

There is, however, a difference between Bridget Jones's comic struggles as a feminine subject in process and the slick, apparently finished femininity of *Sex and the City*'s four minxes, which recalls in its unfortunately too-sincere version, the excesses of the *Ab Fab* ladies. If *Bridget Jones's Diary* is about the production of femininity as always failing, then *Sex and the City* is less about femininity than it is about the production of feminine sexuality (hence the title). *Sex and the City*'s heroines rarely worry about their appearance, style, or attractiveness except in relation to age. Their insecurities tend to be about behavior rather than appearance. With seemingly and para-doxically "complete" feminine subjects, the revelation of the minuet of sexuality, illustrated by *Sex and the City* as the process of mating in all of its variations, displaces social gender's pressures to achieve an ideal with oscillating and unsure desires.

Sex and the City's illusion of finished femininity commodifies femininity as agency, and its feminizing is almost always a de-feminizing. The ensembled and coiffed single girl comes apart: she drops her purse, gets splashed (as Carrie does in the title sequence), or the various plotlines of her daily existence unravel. In this nar-rative, undoings become punishments for hubris, for a kind of fem-inine overreaching. The ladies live, thus, in a dynamic of constant compulsion and retribution. One can achieve something close to a perfect femininity, but one must work to maintain it or it will come apart. In fact, being an agenic subject makes a girl's femininity come apart unless it is increasingly trussed up. This is perhaps one reason why feminine subjects who wield agency are often represented in leather, tight skirts, or skin-tight pants, and why the image of the décolletage represents an uncontrollable femininity so well. The cleavage is not only the alluring effect of the seam or gap, as Roland Barthes extols in *The Pleasure of the Text*, it is also the visual counter-part of femininity's unfinished quality, its inability to control what it seems to be controlling, the uneasy relation between agency and process, between potential and kinetic energy.[6]

Because femininity is never there (except in those rare "ideal"

cases) processes of feminizing spin by-products in the form of perversities—of desires, appearances, and positions that deviate from
the parabola. These by-products are perverse not only because they
veer from the track toward the ideal, but also because they exist on
the way to and from the idealized conditions of heterosexuality. Although we can easily understand that these sites of partial accession
and completion exist—and we permit them to exist because we understand them to be merely passing and temporary—what do they
look like? Is the not-quite-ideally feminine really the status of someone like Toula in *My Big Fat Greek Wedding* before her makeover, or
the snorting irreverence of Agent Gracie Hart (Sandra Bullock) in
Miss Congeniality, which is much akin to Melissa McCarthy's version of femininity in *Bridesmaids*? What other gender regimes do
these share in? What registers of desire? Is femininity in the making
simply a process toward an ideal, or do these manifestations represent genderings that belong to multiple regimes?

In *Sex and the City* the relations among women like Carrie,
Samantha, and Miranda gain a vaguely lesbian cast, while their relations with men threaten to veer into a brand of homosex buddy-
dom. This careening is safely controlled in *Sex and the City* through
the convention of the girl-to-girl meal, which allows some diegetic
airing of feelings and the surrogate of eating as the end of desire, the
presence of a distracting token gay male (already present in both *Sex
and the City* and *Bridget Jones*) who embodies a more perfect feminine
sensibility, and story lines of experimentation (mostly Samantha's
role), which contain all variety of "perversity" (everything from sex
for sex's sake to lesbian sex to three-ways with gay male couples or
other women). Samantha's experimentation is more titillating than
threatening precisely because she is also the closest of all to a social
feminine ideal.

In relation to the sexual and sartorial perversities produced as a
by-product of process, the aspiring dynamic of ideal femininity is
also necessary to sustain a fiction of heterosexuality. This heterosexuality represents the merger of complementary opposites that
retrospectively achieves an ideal version of the social feminine
from a femininity that has, up to that point, merely tried hard. But
if we imagine that this ideal femininity produced as an effect of

heterosexual success is located at the apex of the parabola, such ideal social femininity exists at the same locus as ideal social masculinity. This means that if we take heterosexuality to mean the merger of ideal femininity and masculinity (at least in a kind of doll-like Ken and Barbie vision of such), then heterosexuality is actually the merger of two versions of the same. And insofar as ideal femininity is often best performed by male drag queens, heterosexuality may actually represent a merger of masculine with masculine—in other words the recombination of apical singular categories (social masculinity, male), which are always one (and in relation to what Irigaray formulates as "not one").[7]

But who says heterosexuality is the merger of social ideals? Are not most heterosexual unions the merger of the less than ideal? This quotidian heterosexuality shadows the "perfect" version not only insofar as the partners are always reminded of their distance from the ideal social gender apex, but also insofar as the dynamics of joinder envision these incomplete beings as completing each other. Heterosexuality works because when the partners are not perfect, the feminine side props up the masculine side. This is the function of social gender.

From the side of the feminine, the fantasy of perfect heterosexual union occupies the site of ultimate fulfillment. But because femininity is the state of never quite being feminine, heterosexuality is the state of never quite being fulfilled. This means that femininity as exemplified by Bridget Jones and our *Sex and the City* NYC girls is a state of constant desire and striving mitigated by the co-presence of feminine signifiers as distractions from the fact that the feminine subject is never where she seems to be. The overt framings of the narratives reiterate the ways the coefficients of femininity are themselves framings, a deixis pointing to the authenticity of the feminine subject while distracting from any actual objective vision. The ploy of distraction is an intrinsic part of the tricks of indirection that govern these anatomies of the feminine subject. Distraction, the art of making someone pay attention to something that is not really the point so that those things that are the point can be produced, is part of the indirection enacted in *Sex and the City, Absolutely Fabulous*, and *Bridget Jones's Diary*. Femininity, always in process, is also always in the process of distracting the consumer away from its feminizing by means of its performance of the feminizing process as itself a physical spectacle. Thus clothing, primping, and makeup are distractions from the subject while, at the same time, they constitute the feminine aspect of the regime of social gender. This is not because these distractions produce the surface appearance of femininity; it is because the very means by which they distract attention away from the feminine subject in process mimics the processes from which they distract. They distract us from the distraction that constitutes the production of a femininity always in process. Like the diary genre when aimed toward a reader other than self, femininity is a process that deflects itself as a way of constituting itself.

This is more than simple narcissism (the unfortunate conclusion a mirror analogy may create) or the vertiginous effects of a self-conscious awareness of being looked at looking at oneself being seen, though these regimes also participate. This complex distraction is the essence of the squaring operation of social gender's compulsion toward reduction. Femininity as always striving and failing—as incomplete—manifests itself as the distraction of an uncompletable production. Even though fashion models and media figures would appear to present completed and perfect versions of the feminine ideal, such perfection constitutes their role in the equation. They present the ideal that can never be reached as reachable by someone. They approach the paradox of the "masculine" "one who has it all," establishing the illusion that there is a feminine that has it all, a formation that turns femininity into masculinity.

Girls Will Be . . . ; or, The New Ideal

There is always Heidi Klum, the always already put together, even in supposedly casual shots captured by opportunistic paparazzi. Perhaps she teeters at the top of the parabola. Looking back to the turn-of-the-century narratives that try to process the processing of the impossible feminine, it is easy to see these figures as striving. Recall that the first ten years of the twenty-first century is also the decade of the makeover, which makes self-improving work a major theme. But what happens to the ideal feminine as the goal of the makeover—and the ideal feminine as that which consists in work—when we pass the makeover stage, as arguably we have?

It is currently the era of the "girl." There are a plethora of recent "girl" television shows, ranging from the sitcoms *New Girl* with Zooey Deschanel, to the HBO series *Girls* with Lena Dunham, to 2 *Broke Girls*, *Gossip Girl*, *Gilmore Girls*, the film *Mean Girls*, to *The Girl with the Dragon Tattoo*. The "girl" is an age-defined process, again the one who must strive to achieve femininity *as itself* the femininity it strives for. Age is the new work, and yet the girl who is not yet there is already there by virtue of her process of not yet getting there. Even *Gilmore Girls'* clever mother, Lorelei (Lauren Graham), is still imaged as a girl—single, disputing with parents, living like a teen. The emergence of the "girl" does not put ideas of "ideal" femininity on hold; instead, the girl redefines the process of this ideal as an impossible maturity that substitutes for the laborious cosmetic processes of the previous versions. The girl is, impossibly, approaching the "all."

Coefficiency

What could an "all" of femininity possibly be? If the feminine is the posture that does not believe that anyone has it all, then the feminine that has it all should spectacularly not have it all. The all that "perfect" femininity might entail, then, would be to incarnate the Phallus itself as a form of all (insofar as the Phallus itself stands for a signifier that pretends to stand for the signifier of some sort of completion somewhere even though no one ever gets there). Ideal femininity becomes the Phallus instead of becoming masculine, and in so doing also becomes an appurtenance of masculinity. The pageantry of fashion shows, or more massively, the series of red carpet awards shows, is the yearly parade of the social feminine ideal in relation to which all strivings and failures have meaning. Squaring such feminine ideals is like a male driving a Corvette or being Trumpishly wealthy. If in the 1970s feminists complained that events such as the "Miss America" pageant perpetuated an impossible and oppressive femininity, that was, of course, exactly the point insofar as ideal femininity's impossibility, taken literally, is oppressive.

Even the lyrics of the "Miss America" anthem pronounce her "our ideal." The dynamic that characterizes the regime of social gender exists in everyone's inability to embody that ideal for more than a few minutes—if that. That is, unless you are six years old, a drag queen, or most recently a "hot" girl (who is only hot because she is always imaged in the context of a range of other girls in relation to whom she is the hottest).

The paradox of this process is quite clear: identity expressed through taste and understood as individual is anything but unique. Instead, it constitutes itself through sets of commodity signifiers that crassly impart class, race, ethnicity, age, education, and other attributes and positions in a standardized vocabulary. Although these signifiers can be deployed creatively—the sure sign of anxious individuality is the inept mixture of signifiers that makes a "comment," such as Lady Gaga wearing a meat dress—they carry with them the ambivalent taint of market signification. That is, no commodity accessory (and all accessories are that) can ever leave its signification of commodity behind, nor its original sets of identitarian associations. Femininity in process is always an appendage of this commodity signification, especially as it tries to escape it.

The net signification of this accessorizing tends to be misunderstood as this fiction we call "identity," the appearance of which is produced through the layerings of a commodity vocabulary. In this way, what we take as social femininity is always already situated as an effect of taste, which we imagine is an effect of identity position, expressed through choices that we pretend are free. The layering of motives urges the acknowledgment that femininity itself has multiple versions, coproduced by other discrete identitarian categories such as race, class, ethnicity, age, ability, sexual preference, et cetera. Insofar as gender is systemic, it obviously shapes itself and is shaped by a range of cultural signifiers. But understanding, for example, black femininity differently than white femininity (apart from the impossibility of either as an inclusive or defining category in itself) is partly an effect of the range of commodity signifiers different social groups deem appropriate and possible for their constituents. These signifiers such as hairstyle, for example, are situated at the conjunction of biology (hair type), class (what amenities one can afford), and, more broadly, cultural perceptions about social gender ideals that are themselves inflected by complex, often self-contradictory and inter-constituting understandings of racial or class possibility. At the same time, such figures as Beyoncé, Halle Berry, and Lucy Liu can operate as embodiments of ideal femininity more broadly.

Situated, thus, as the myth of individual choice expressing, finally, the illusion of individual interiority tantamount to identity, these commodity coefficients are preselected as possibilities, defined by the actions of the socius, marketed to certain groups as identity signifiers, and displaced into the potentials of differentiated bodies as their specific mode of reaching for an impossible ideal. The more difficult, costly, and painful an attribute, the more highly we value it. Hence, any hairstyle that forces the painful and unnatural disposition of hair will constitute a valued coefficient for any individual who has hair that does not easily comply, but means nothing for individuals whose hair accommodates those dispositions easily. Black women may have difficulty with ultra-smooth straight hair, but for many white women such hair is the easiest (if never convenient) possibility. Or declaring that women should have dark skin forces the use of dangerous procedures for skin darkening difficult for very fair women (and hence overvalued), but meaningless for women who are naturally dark (but whose coefficient may discern among skin tones).

That femininity's coefficients are often commodity signifiers connoting (if they do not openly denote) race, class, ethnicity, age, religion, et cetera, makes it appear as if femininity itself is constituted by these other categories, while at the same time producing the impression that these commodity signifiers merely frame an authentic feminine hidden within. Although individual subjects are indeed inflected and formed by the various environments within which they exist, femininity as a social regime is expressed in its ever-failing process in terms of these coefficient signifiers and their relation to the particular bodies they both produce and frame. Class, where the investments of commodity culture are greatest, may well be the most evident coefficient of all of the commodity possibilities. We gauge class through the extent to which feminine subjects exhibitionistically participate in the fashion system, which means, of course, that with class, feminine exhibitionism is a display performed as if unself-conscious, as if the lady were born wearing the designer fashions about which she is careless and presumably unself-conscious. The increasing numbers of consumers who purchase simulations of style in the studied marketings of Old Navy, or other wannabes who still carelessly disport the striving middle-class icons of designers, nonetheless mark their class as striving. The adjective "cheap," deployed in relation to a gender coefficient, applies only to femininity insofar as feminine striving is defined in terms of the commodity value of its accessories. "Cheapness" persists as the mark of failed striving. The cheap, in other words, is that which aspires to class but does not make it because its striving is visible. Cheap *is* femininity.

The New Girls

The past ten years has hosted a shift in the striving dynamics of both makeovers and the possibility of any singular embodiment of a feminine "ideal." Reflecting and enacting the range of positions available on the upward curve of the social gender parabola, the more recent focus on "girl" groups positions feminine striving as both an effect of immaturity and as realized by the collaging effect of multiple feminine versions in a group. This group strategy, a feature of films and television shows aimed at twentysomethings, features group members helping one another overcome the weaknesses of each individual, all the while also accepting such weaknesses as mere idiosyncrasies. The group both heals itself and enacts an "I'm OK, you're OK" kind of politic that appears to dispose of any notion of ideal as old-fashioned. Paradoxically, of course, all of the members of the group are well aware of the ideal toward which they strive; their failures to get there are what group comfort is all about. The tactic of grouping female character types simultaneously acknowledges an ideal, assuages all failures by suggesting the ideal is impossible, and then, by combining its versions, presents the ideal as a utopian community. Or the series of "mean girls" films presents the characters who embody the social ideal of femininity as, well, mean. In the earliest of these, *Heathers* (1988), social feminine perfection is simply cruel, while in the later *Mean Girls* (2004), such ideals are dubbed "The Plastics," suggesting a defensive shift from the displacement of cruelty onto the ideal as a source of suffering to regarding those who seem to comply with a social feminine ideal as fake.

The group phenomenon thus offers both achievement and am- bivalence about achievement, the resident pressures of a hovering ideal and its dismissal, but still, in all of this group dynamic, social femininity remains a striving. This is the case in any of the plethora of girl-group television shows that have emerged since the advent of *Absolutely Fabulous*: consider the television series *Ally McBeal*, *Gilmore Girls*, *Sex and the City*, and *Girls*, and the film *Bridesmaids*.

$y = 1$

In relation to social femininity's constitutive kineticism, social masculinity, as the other side or slope of the equation, begins at the apex of the parabola and threatens to slide down. Masculinity, whether threatened by cultural norms or not, begins with the ideal threatened only by the perpetually potential risk of loss, castration, imagined in the social regime as a falling away from the masculine ideal itself. Where femininity is unrelentingly striving, ambitious, and ever failing, masculinity is conservative and wary because any move it might make could force it from the top, render it less than singular, and set it sliding down the struggling slope, the obverse mirror of femininity's laborious asymptosis. Men are always already masculine whether they are or not, and it is up to them to lose it.

The social version of heterosexuality thus exists at the paradoxi- cal point at the top of the parabola where the feminine ideal and the unmarred masculine coincide. As the quadratics of the dynamic suggest, sometimes this joinder may take the form of a drag queen, produce a heterosexuality more like an imaginary yin/yang, or even offer the specter of an Aristophanean doubled being.[8] Because of the kinetic dynamic of femininity, however, the appearance of static bal- ance at the ideal top of the parabola accrues to the side of the mas- culine. As singular and achieved, masculinity deploys the upward slope—the feminine—as its propping, magnifying, aggrandizing appurtenance. The prop of ideal masculinity is ideal femininity. The closer to the ideal his feminine consort (ax^2) is, the more masculine the male is. Paradoxically (again), this produces phenomena such as Playboy Bunnies, fashion models, and expensive escorts—that is, the "ideal" feminine as already a masculine magnifier. It also produces an overt equation between the ideal feminine and the Phallus, as the girl operates in the same propping way as does a Ferrari. The Phallus—this portable signifier—haunts and informs what might constitute appropriate masculine compensations—tools, guns, cars, motorcycles, muscles, cigars, or sports equipment.

What we understand to be masculine fashions and accessories do not function as coefficients as they do on the side of the feminine. While femininity is over-accessorized, masculinity is always already overcompensated since any prop redoubles a masculinity already imagined to be there. These props, like fetishes, work two ways: they reflect, repeat, and signal agency while also marking slippage. The man who needs a cigar is both the man whose cigar reflects an ever-present masculinity and the man who needs a compensatory signifier because he is beginning to slide away from the apex. In this ambivalent logic, the most masculine subject is the subject who needs no props. But what possible vestige of subject is that? Even denuded masculine subjects are already accessorized if only with the penis/phallus itself or with hypertrophic musculatures, which reflect the same ambivalent reflection/compensation economy as the cigar—or for that matter the truck, the motorcycle, the pinkie ring, the gun, the mustache, the boots, the tie, the tattoo, et cetera. Feminine accessories are coefficients that signify striving; masculine accessories are props that signify an ambivalent relation to the static. The masculine both is and is not where it is.

Social masculinity's props provide an imaginary traction that resists the always-imminent skip down the parabolic slope. While social femininity strives and works, social masculinity repeats and resists. If femininity can never get there, masculinity can never stay there. Women are punished for not being sufficiently feminine; men are occasionally rewarded for having slipped, their fall from ideal masculinity revealing a more gentle and "human" side. But men are also taunted for having slipped down the slope, their slide a reminder of masculinity's inevitable failure. The more threatened social masculinity might be as a cultural certainty, the more props are necessary to secure its position at the top. This may be one explanation for the current craze for guns and the zealous defense of their procurement and ownership. Masculinity is always slipping.

The constitutive ambivalence of social masculinity reflects the contradictory coexistence of the two differently defined parabolic equations, the one reflecting the reduction toward masculinity as singular and as the term through which femininity is defined (i.e., the idealized top of the parabola), and the other the paradox of the ideal itself, which can never be reached. On the top of a downward slope, the dynamics of the masculine social equation work out to ambivalence, to being two places at once, both ideal and sliding away, unitary and repeated by same. In popular culture, social masculinity splits itself into the two forms of this ambivalence instead of combining and playing out the ambivalence of the possibilities within single figures. This splitting produces vignettes of social masculine stability in contrast to social femininity's constant failures.

Like social femininity, social masculinity has ideals that change with the race, ethnic origin, age, and social position of individuals, though class is a major patch of masculine ice. Each version of social masculinity is equally ideal, from the athlete to the businessman, from the well-appointed laborer to the playboy. Masculinity exists as something like the band Village People, with varieties associated with various racial, cultural, age, and class positionings. Although these varieties are not equally valued and strive against one another, they are all ideally masculine. The point is that all of these versions represent some manifestation of a masculine ideal, while femininity, though it has variations, tends to cling to one impossible wealthy, thin, young ideal.

One form masculinity takes is the ideal of the unitary, masterful, always already masculine man whose props signal a full, long, and complete masculine subject. This appears in such figures as various James Bonds (perhaps the most long-lived and quintessential), or either the Frank Sinatra or George Clooney versions of Danny Ocean of the *Ocean's Eleven, Twelve*, or *Thirteen* films, both of whom wield mastery through style and cleverness. Earlier embodiments of this full sophisticated masculinity are Cary Grant, Rock Hudson, and James Garner. Contemporary versions of well-rounded and fully fitted masculinity are Daniel Craig, George Clooney, Denzel Washington, and Brad Pitt. Another version is various muscular heroes, including professional athletes and action protagonists such as Bruce Willis in the Die Hard films, or Keanu Reeves in The Matrix series, or even Arnold Schwarzenegger in *True Lies* or *Eraser*, or Jackie Chan, who provides a special case of ethnic adjustment. Earlier versions of a manly hero are John Wayne, Gary Cooper, Steve McQueen, and Clint Eastwood. Schwarzenegger, who has recently ambivalently slid up and down the slope (up because he has shown what a real stud he is, down because his peccadilloes reveal his distance from any ideal), tends to be a travesty of this masculinity, as does the early muscular Sylvester Stallone. The muscular, masculine hero wields mastery through the body itself as a self-contained, disciplined machine, evinced through the protagonist's mastery over other men and machines.

The cultural vestige of the "sliding" side of social masculinity's ambivalence manifests itself in sitcom versions of comic marriage and paternity in the pervasive figure of the henpecked husband, ranging from *All in the Family* to *Modern Family* and everything in between. Comic husbands always have strong wives. The domesticated male is delusively bound into the complementary yin/yang dynamic of the imaginary circle (see Figure 1) instead of the asymmetrical dynamic of the two other social gender parabolas (Figures 2 and 3). If singleness produces less successful femininity for the female, marriage provokes a slide away from the singular ideal for the male, but a slide that accomplishes various adjustments. Masculinity itself takes on a comic form, which works in various ways to reestablish the originary masculine ideal. The tussle between wife and husband becomes a battle between the feminine's attempts to ascend and the masculine's attempts to conserve, masculinity defined by the various ploys by which the husbands attempt to escape wifely vigilance and control. This last tendency would seem to make masculinity a function of femininity or even the effect of a relation (which it is anyway), but it also locates masculinity as both culpable and OK as it is.

Bromance

Less lensed by the makeover, contemporary social masculinity has nonetheless been remade in the varietal spectrum exemplified by girl groups. Along with holdover figures of singular masculinity that range from the suave to the muscular to the slacker (i.e., Jeff Lebowski of *The Big Lebowski*), guy group sitcoms and films display a similar constitutive variety as girl groups. Such sitcoms as *How I Met Your Mother* and *The Big Bang Theory*, and films such as the entire Ocean's series, *Knocked Up*, *The Hangover*, and *I Love You, Man* present masculinity as a matter of contrasting individual versions. Most of these versions lack something, marked by some obvious idiosyncrasy—the *Ocean's Eleven* group comprises a cockney accent (Don Cheadle), sweaty palms (Eddie Jemison), perpetual snacking (Brad Pitt), sibling rivalry (Scott Caan and Casey Affleck), hesitation (Matt Damon), and love (George Clooney). This group is pitted against the perfectly powerful masculine man, Andy Garcia, who has both casinos and Clooney's girl (Julia Roberts) and whose only weakness—greed—is also his strength. Through three different films, the composite group fights the Man and finally wins.

More recent guy group films aimed at young adults repeat this composite tactic, offering as protagonist not the most securely and evidently masculine (and also perennially single) of the groups (in both *Knocked Up* and *I Love You, Man* played by Jason Segel), but the more vulnerable, but perhaps less stoically masculine sidekick-type character, Seth Rogen in *Knocked Up* and Paul Rudd in *I Love You, Man*. The films' supporting groups of characters, each member characterized by some evident tic or physical flaw, provide both a variety of versions and contrast to the protagonist, who finally emerges as having always been, at least potentially, perfectly masculine. *The Big Bang Theory* varies this formula by pitting a group of nerds whose masculinities again represent a variety of travesties of stereotypical masculine traits—the control freak, the tastelessly sexist, the shy and inarticulate, and the sadly-interested-in-fashion guy who cannot talk to women—against the "ideal" femininity of their waitress neighbor, Penny. In representing different versions of masculinity, this group of misfits actually produces both a critique of American masculinity and its own revised version of an ideal. The sitcom is largely ambivalent about most of its topics: masculinity, intelligence, femininity, sex. But all of these texts, as in the girl group texts, define social gender as a matter of a multiple group expression where together the players may produce a composite vision of what social gender means, how it functions, and what it looks like. Any man is only as masculine as the sum of his posse.

Bond. James Bond.

But to return to the singular example of non-lapsarian social masculinity, the top of the parabola is personified by the figure of James Bond in his various cinematic vestiges. Occupying a site of imaginary masculine competence for more than fifty years, the filmic Bond exemplifies ideal masculinity where all appurtenances are tools to be wielded and where the male evinces power through a full and complete ideal masculinity. Because this masculine ideal needs no coefficient, style is a signifier of an intrinsic mastery, doubling what we already know is there. Bond's style also signifies mastery—the imaginary "all"—reflected by the masculinity it appears to produce. As an extension of his being, Bond's style is the correctly innate, thoroughly appropriate vestige of the social masculine ideal welded to masculine prerogative, exercised as masculinity itself. Style reflects Bond's authority, which then authorizes his style in a self-cycling logic where what is reflected by style produces the sense of "all"-ness the style reflects.

A semiology of Bond's haberdashery reveals nattiness, propriety, versatility, careless wealth, and in the case of the Sean Connery Bond an acre of leg proudly displayed. See, for example, Bond padding through Goldfinger's Miami hotel in *Goldfinger* in his very brief beach holiday outfit. Carelessness is the key tone—not a carelessness akin to sloppiness, but carelessness in the not having to think at all about impeccability. This carelessness translates to a naturalness or innate capacity for self-presentation, which itself bespeaks confidence, security, and mastery, not as attributes gained through hard labor or study, but as intrinsic to Bond as ideally and securely masculine. Bond does not have to worry about what to wear, or even apparently, about what to pack. Rather, he always has the proper clothing for any occasion, clothing sometimes mysteriously supplied, and always cared for. When Bond returns from the casino or removes the jumpsuit from atop his tuxedo, he always scrupulously hangs his jacket, tosses it folded properly on his bed, and adjusts his bow tie. Bond has two modes of dress: formal and coordinated casual, the latter less evident as his adventures seem always to require at least a sports jacket and tie.

But consider the meaning of this sartorial propriety. The Bond figure accomplishes the most challenging tasks while dressed up. This is not simply about some historical formality of dress we have recently abandoned. Even in the 1960s when the Connery Bond was fashion-plating his way across the Alps, the golf course, or the high-rise Vegas penthouse (to which he mountaineers in a tux), other manly heroes (e.g., Steve McQueen, Clint Eastwood) accomplish their tasks in a more leisure-suited, work-clothed, off-the-rack style. Only the Rat Pack is as natty as Bond, but not nearly as classy. The tendency toward the informal only increases toward the end of the twentieth century, so that lately the be-tuxed Daniel Craig incarnation of Bond is even more unusual, the ubiquitous evening clothes operating as an even more pointed reference to ideal masculinity as an operation of class, suavity, and savoir faire. The ideally masculine can be dressed up without losing his masculinity. The man makes the clothes; the clothes do not make the man.

But even for Bond, the clothes are not the only thing that makes the man ideally masculine. Add his sartorial security to a semiosis of carriage—Bond never hesitates, looks as if he feels out of place, or seems not to know what to do socially—synecdochized by the way Bond deploys his eyes and shoulders (the Connery Bond and perhaps the Pierce Brosnan Bond, but only sporadically the Roger Moore Bond, whose overplay of the cynical occasionally registers as a kind of simpering insecurity), and the effect is efficacious presence. Bond is the man who is most in place where he is out of place, the man whose style says he belongs, the man who belongs by virtue of not belonging—by virtue of his not even having to master the rudiments by which mastery itself is signaled. Bond's physical style—

his clothing and body language—signify mastery as never having been an issue. It was always already there.

Bond's efficacious style is the means of his success at both the gambling tables and the bedroom—two sites not as unrelated as they might seem. Bond approaches gambling—or undertakes its challenge—without even flinching, just as he undertakes the bedroom duties thrust on him as a British secret agent. Gambling is a figure of the same natural mastery as Bond's haberdashery as well as a figure of Bond's relation to male adversaries. With the stakes on the table, Bond dominates effortlessly precisely because he never flinches. For Bond, gambling is not a gamble, but an extension of the natural ideality of masculinity. In the battle of the lowering horns, Bond never even bows his head. For Bond, women are tools wielded by a master whose masculine irresistibility always undermines his less masculine opposition. And so, too, are his carefully orchestrated, multifunctional accessories—the lighters, watches, pens, cuff links, briefcases, shoes, and cigarette cases—which quite literally get him out of any tricky situation as a most literal operation of style.

Even the various Bonds' ideal masculinity is poised ambivalently as it occupies two contradictory positions at the same time: it is singular and perfect just as it struggles not to fail. Masculinity's ambivalence reflects, as its Oedipal underpinnings might suggest, an element of bidirectional temporality missing from the side of the feminine, which can only go forward. One way to resolve social masculinity's ambivalence is through chronology—through the dramas of Oedipus and the challenges of Nemi.[9] In the Oedipal myth, there is a before and an after in relation to which the ambivalent positions (ideal, sliding away) of the masculine line-up. Ideal masculinity exists as the before, as pre-lapsarian, pre-castration, and Mosaic. Masculinity sliding away exists as the after, the post-knowledge, post-castration site of memory and lesson. For this reason, versions of ideal masculinity are often represented as anachronistic, as harking back to a purer, less castrated before. Bond's style, for example, is retro in the sense that even the most recent, 2012 Bond film, *Skyfall*, hints at the clean-lined casual formality of classic 1960s suavity. This style is not coincidentally also associated with Frank Sinatra and the Rat Pack, and with romanticized renditions of American mobsters, from *The Godfather*, which itself refers to an earlier, post-WWII, pre-RICO (and pre-leisure suit) mode of dress, completely ensembled if not formal, jaunty in a sportster fashion, to *The Sopranos*.

Enter then George Clooney in his reprise of Sinatra's role in the much-altered remake of *Ocean's Eleven*. Less state-identified than Bond, Clooney takes over the incarnation of masculine ideality as increasingly internalized. With Clooney in the role of Danny Ocean, the ideal masculine becomes a matter of soft-spoken control tinged with humor and ineffable good looks. Like the Connery Bond, Clooney's masculinity is mainly a matter of carriage and the performance of control, but Clooney performs this as a matter of contained and constricted movement—by the tilt of his head and the understatement of his voice. Inclined slightly, Clooney's head deflects direct attention, making him impenetrable and unreachable. When he looks directly at either a character or the camera, the effect is a startling relief in the performance of an upright frankness that dispels the occasional sense of guilt or shame Clooney's brooding masculinity might seem to hide. His humor, like Connery's, is always the performance of mastery in relation to other men. Clooney, however, never acts alone in the Ocean's series. The posse of the less-than-ideally masculine sidekicks already allies him to the variety of versions.

Musclemen and Husbandry

Which brings us to the curious paradox of the muscular hero whose crass version of masculinity is the always already overcompensated. Teetering between ideality and lack, muscular heroes would seem to incarnate a social masculine ideal expressed through the body itself as a signifier of masculinity insofar as masculinity equates with physical power. While Bond's and Clooney's perfect masculinity is internal and revealed only by understatement, the masculinity of muscular heroes is visible as the body itself. Unless muscular heroes also perform versions of an inherent masculine mastery, their muscularity becomes a signifier of lack and compensation.[10] For most sports heroes whose realm of ideality exists primarily in the demonstration of skills, muscularity functions as an extension of the mastery of skills that enables a player to triumph over other men.

For film protagonists whose effectiveness seems to rely almost entirely on muscularity—figures such as Arnold Schwarzenegger, Vin Diesel, and Sylvester Stallone—muscularity does not guarantee masculine ideality, but rather the struggle to avoid slippage. This struggle takes the form of the perpetual physical battle against muscular and/or well-financed adversaries, a battle whose seriatim form presents masculinity as the Nemic tussle with a string of challengers. The terms of the battle pronounce an ultimate failure, the eventual defeat of the champion; and so this muscular narrative always prefigures its own demise, its own position on the decline, if not now, then in the future. In contrast to the version of ideal social masculinity (James Bond, Danny Ocean) that appears to be anachronistic, masculinity on the decline always looks forward to its defeat and fends off that defeat through muscularity itself.

Muscularity, then, is itself an ambivalent signifier, exhibiting a spectacularized male body that both does and does not stand for idealized masculinity. The muscularity itself is too overt, too compensatory, too prop-like. In their muscular redoubling of the male body, muscles also signal that perhaps this version of masculinity is not innate, but compensates for something missing, some slippage covered over by muscles put on and worn like feminine fashion. As props instead of signifiers of something within, muscles have fetishistic qualities. They stand in as the something there in place of the nothing there we fear. Muscles are mechanisms of disavowal. An economy of muscular display belongs to the regime of the vertiginous—to the regime of a self-conscious seeing oneself being seen as a gender. It also inclines to the side of the feminine insofar as the body becomes a phallus in a process of visible striving, which is curiously and paradoxically feminine.

The obverse of this muscularity is the figure of the suburban husband, whose popular figurations range from the suave incarnations of Cary Grant, James Garner, and Rock Hudson to the deliberately doofus-y comic personae of Tim Allen, Ray Romano, Kevin James, Ty Burrell, and other sitcom husbands. These figures represent masculinity as a paradox; henpecked, it slips away; in slipping away, its generosity resecures it. This masculinity is produced by its relations with the feminine as a mechanism by which masculinity is challenged, disrupted, shown as lacking, and solidified. In fact, one definition of comedy may well be this process of masculine salvation on the slippery slope.

Bros and Nerds

Like the girl group version of contemporary social femininity, social masculinity is also now a group affair. Groups include multiple masculine types: geeks, the nonaggressive, the slobs, the immature, the cool. Guys in groups play tricks on one another, showing one another up as vulnerable. These tricks are also ways that the more securely masculine continue to secure their masculinity—by displacing their own fears onto weaker friends. So the *New Girl*'s three male roommates constantly undermine one another. Ben's housemates in *Knocked Up* bet one another that Martin (Martin Starr) cannot not cut his beard and hair. The guys in groups in *I Love You, Man* are constantly competing with one another. These all depict masculinity as a competition to be won by two possibilities: (1) There is the guy who is able to ignore all the other guys and do his own thing. This guy is usually generous and understanding to his male friends but ends up single. He is usually the friend of the protagonist—Brad Pitt in *Ocean's Eleven* or Jason Segel in almost any movie he is in. (2) Then there is guy who finds a way to achieve a good relationship with the woman he loves. This guy displays an unthreatened masculinity able to work with femininity—George Clooney in *Ocean's Eleven*, Seth Rogen in *Knocked Up*, and Paul Rudd in *I Love You, Man*. In the group economy, these two versions are ultimately interdependent. This is a compromise formation that permits the singular self-sufficient and complete male to engage with the feminine without harm.

The most complex version of group recuperation of a social masculine ideal is that presented by *The Big Bang Theory*. Four self-defined geeks in a social group that might be conceived of as the realm of the "already slipped" rescue one another from this slippage by rescuing one another from slippage. The central figure, Leonard (Johnny Galecki), seems most securely masculine, undermined only by his short stature, interest in science, and various ailments (asthma, lactose intolerance, tendency toward injury). His roommate, Sheldon Cooper (Jim Parsons), is the least securely masculine (and most potentially gay) as he affects an asexuality allied with an unrelenting ego combined with a version of obsessive-compulsive disorder. The girl is there for his having, but he strives (like a girl) to win the Nobel Prize as he spends his time being picky, germ-phobic, and completely narcissistic (a trait also associated with femininity). Leonard and Sheldon's two friends, Howard Wolowitz (Simon Helberg) and Raj Koothrappali (Kunal Nayyar), represent other versions of less than ideal social masculinity. Howard is a tiny man who began the series as a shameless sexist predator (with little success), but who continues on later in the series as a married astronaut. Raj defines himself as a "metrosexual" with a familiarity with fashion, potpourris, and cuisine, who repeatedly declaims his heterosexuality, but who has difficulty finding someone who will date him.

Taken singly, each character seems not to embody any version of ideal social masculinity, but as the characters interact (most often in the two couples defined by their living arrangements), they make up for one another's flaws and inabilities. Leonard helps an unwilling Sheldon date Amy (Mayim Bialik) and tone down his OCD. Sheldon pushes Leonard toward more academic success even as he despairs of Leonard's relationship with neighbor Penny (Kaley Cuoco-Sweeting)—a despair that makes Leonard's success with the ultrahot Penny seem all the more valiant. Howard helps Raj; Raj supports Howard even as he seems not to support him by falling in love with Howard's wife, Bernadette (Melissa Rauch). The combination of envy, support, critique, and friendship combine to make the group a study in social masculinity since 2007. Even though no individual ever seems to accede to Bond status, together their relationships illustrate both versions of social masculinity and the ways such masculinity can be recuperated from a notion that slippage unmans them. *Big Bang*'s group of guys eventually operates this system of exemplification and recuperation in relation to a group of females, whose own self-presentations, like most recent girl groups, enact the varieties that gather around the ideal.

5 Scopic Folding, Layered Economies

Gender regimes have a scopic dimension insofar as genders are modes of both unconscious and conscious display. This scopic dimension, however, multiplies, layering hologrammatically in such a way as to produce a series of illusions that present two or more sides at once.[1] Not only does this layering invite processes of decoding and translation, it also links the scopic to dynamics organized around different economies, objects, and processes—attitudes. Anamorphosis, for example, requires a figuratively digestive dynamic insofar as others "take in" and decode its distortions. We apprehend the metamorphic visually, but its dynamic relies on duration. The taxonomic is a perpetual sorting that digs at a truth imagined to undergird appearances, but which arrives at some conformative coherence with a binary imaginary.

The other side of looking is being seen. Here the gaze, as the sense of being seen, operates as a part of the desire that underwrites the dynamic of seeing oneself see oneself and seeing oneself see oneself being seen. On the one hand this vertiginous spiral links to a desire to be the desire of the other, and on the other to a mise en abime that distracts from the taxonomical incoherence at the core of all subjects. While appearing to point to the essence of a subject, gender regimes always point away, distracting with ideal images. In this sense gender regimes are all stains—the something to see in the place of nothing to see, offered to those who look in place of the subject who is somewhere else.

The Gender of Fluids

In "The Mechanics of Fluids" Luce Irigaray asks, "And so far as the organism is concerned, what happens if the mirror provides nothing to see?"[2] Or too much? Both instances are the same. The spectacle of sexual difference is nothing to see or something to see. Or is it? What if it is something and something more, one and too many? Nothing is the scenario imagined for the girl when the phallus is thought to be what she is looking for, or in the alternative, too many—the drama never imagined except as Medusan, except as a twirl of writing snakes winking back. Irigaray's comment initiates the conclusion in "The Mechanics of Fluids," in which she asserts the symbolic (and also not so) repression of the figure of the sexualized woman as a condition of theorizing subjectivity. Arguments such as Irigaray's object to and simultaneously reproduce the asymmetrical logic of binaries. The persistence of the one is at the expense of the other. Solids rule, an inclination producing and produced by our ignorance of fluids. Binary structures cannot help themselves—they are inevitably unitary. The mirage of two is the solid perception of one, whose singularity is perpetuated by the simultaneous repression and evocation of the other.

But as always, the two of sexual difference is also always three. So, if we can only perceive two from the vantage of some third place, then how can two only be one? For Irigaray, two as one is an effect of language and symbolization. The economy of the binary is singular in that what might be understood as the other is merely a necessary attribute of the one. We know white is white because it is not black; black is necessary to certify white's whiteness. The other is a complement, a site of displacement where the shadowy and fantasmatic "not all" and "not I" lurk their looks back. The envious regard of this other onto whom the subtending ejecta of the one have been lavished replays a master/slave dialectic, a power differential hallucinated as the product of difference itself.

Appealing to the fluid is a strategy by which one stone is killed by two or more birds. The figure of fluidity does not, however, serve as a gender regime, but instead as a way of contemplating one's relation to regimes. Characterizing as untheorized and unsymbolizable that which is simultaneously repressed and pressed into the service of the one—using, in other words, liquid as the figuration of neglect and structural impossibility—theories rescuing the "other" as not one try simultaneously to show up and evade the complementary logic of difference and structure. The "two is one" paradox of structure (such as deployed in broad cultural readings of genders as complementary) requires such metaphorical solutions as fluidity to oppose the logic of one with a figurative economy of many without necessarily reconsidering the (structural) logic by which this is so. Popular feminist strategies for rescuing, balancing, or revising the apparent hegemony of the one—making women visible, extolling an essentialist version of female virtues—end up buying into the binary again. So have the ever-burgeoning inclusivities of the "queer," the "other," to the normative. Recuperating or asserting the equivalence of the other by speaking as a woman or a queer, for example, spectacularly reinforces the binary logic by which the woman or queer cannot speak in the first place. It might seem that so speaking would shake up the system, would perform some uncanny and destabilizing reminder. "I am woman/queer, hear me roar." The problem is that asserting the presence and existence of that other also reaffirms the functions of otherness. The more woman speaks as woman or queer as queer, the more binary logic is stabilized, no matter what she or those queer others might say.

We imagine that the figure of the fluid, then, may oppose the solidity of binary structure with the trickle of a different economy. Woman is not the "other"; women are others to this "other." The error is, of course, that no woman is ever a "woman" to begin with. Thinking in terms of a stolidly binary gender system or conflating the gender system with sexual difference are parts of the impetus of the taxonomic regime—of sorting and compacting variety into binary, hierarchical classifications. If we understand the difference between feminine and masculine in terms of a logic of sexuation, the "feminine" beloved is the one who knows there is no one who is all. The "masculine" lover believes that somewhere someone is all. Belief in the one (or not) is ultimately an unconscious positioning in relation to the intersection of knowing and being—an epistemology. The fluid assaults the crystalline character of this epistemology by suggesting not only that knowing is not everything, but that everything knows, but not everything. Not only is there no one who has all, there is no one who knows all, and there is no all to have or know. Evoking the uncapturable, the fluid, supple, unlocatable, and changeable as an economy that evades the crystalline, bifurcating apertures of structure, Irigaray's metaphor hints at something else and supplies a framing other to the other, which, of course, if we are not careful, might ironically reproduce the stubbornly duplicitous economy of structure all over again. Now there are solids and fluids. Now there is binary gender and something that is not binary gender. It is all still one and the same, unless we see fluidity as a way of thinking—perhaps as a complex, recursive system (and even that threatens to collapse back to a systems/structure dichotomy). Regimes collapse into categories like ice cream flavors.

In itself, the figure of the fluid still seems liberatory, melting the arrogant and icy pinnacle of a singularity always defined as phallic. But the Phallus is also curiously portable, the accessory whose secret is that it, too, is not one, but infinitely proliferated, a sham, the signifier signifying that there is no signified. We know this because even at that prime moment of subjectivity, figured as an Oedipal moment of castration anxiety, the one realization made by the regrettably always-masculine subject is that the Phallus is evasive. It can be removed. It can show up on someone's nose. You can have more than one. It can change size. Girls can have it, and they can have more than one.

The singularity of a binary economy may well be designed to repress not the "other" of woman, but the possibility of proliferations and instabilities sometimes figured as or dislocated into woman as other, but constituting a generalized, slippery, non-oppositional polymorphous non-other "other" shared by female subjects as well. If somewhere there is someone who has it all—God, the president, the CEO of Goldman Sachs—then the rest of us are not all. The effect, as Irigaray and others point out, is an internalized self-hatred displaced onto the feminine as the representative not all, not because she really is not all (because no one is all), but because the insight of the feminine is that there is no all to be. The other effect of believing one has it all is a continued cleaving to the binary economy by which those who believe that one can have all accept the fantasy of oneness.

Pointing toward a polymorphousness, the figure of the fluid occupies an eccentric position in relation to the insistent taxonomies of binary gender systems. On the one hand it would seem to represent a completely alternative economy. On another hand it already frames the binary as its other. On a third hand (perhaps hands, too, proliferate), it depends on binary categories for its sense—even paradoxically—in order to exceed, outstrip, reform, reorganize, resituate, redeploy, redefine, or reinvent them. The fluid is curiously a "re-": redemptive perhaps, but also a reiteration, a reflection, and a repetition.

Revisiting the House of Mirrors

This "re-" character refracts a self-consciousness about gender expressed variously as rebellion and hope, but not veering far from gender in its binary taxonomical guise. This gender self-consciousness, whose intellectual project has been spurred and proliferated partly as an effect of interpretations of Judith Butler's *Gender Trouble: Feminism and the Subversion of Identity*,[3] constitutes a gender regime whose dynamic is bound up in reflection—a looking at oneself looking at oneself being looked at in an apparent performance of gender fluidity. This fluidity involves the conscious performance (or actually wielding) of taxonomic gender signifiers (conventional binary gender attributes) that themselves perform two contradictory functions. As the stuff of mimesis, these signifiers signify the lack of essential connection between bodies and genders. But, as repeated in the paratextual discourses of these performances, such signifiers are understood to refer in both direct and circuitous ways to some subjective essence, some self-defining set of characteristics of personal identity. The discursive evocation of any gender regime as "fluid" refers not to the kind of alternative economy suggested by Irigaray, but to some practice of fantasmatic subjective mobility. Subjects' gender transits are accomplished by imitation—by a putting on—an imitation that endorses the conscious will and triumphant agency of a subject whose deployment of gender signifiers represents some (though hardly direct or unmediated) truth about the wielders' relation to difference—that they are indifferent and over-deferential. They may consciously claim to have the advantage of Tiresian (and angelic) vantage, but their vista is the stock range of gender roles operated like an elegant puppet show that slides into self-revelation. What these practices may reveal, however, is the subject's fantasies of genderings in relation to a perceived desire of the other.

Fluidity, then, does not characterize any species of gender regime organized around the figure of polymorphous flow, but, rather, it fixes flow as directional, moving from subjective truth (which is the fantasy that the subject wields gender signifiers at will rather than those signifiers tying to unconscious drives and desires as well as to the effects of subjective sexuation) to practices of representation and mimesis, to the evocation of the other as witnessing audience that finally dramatizes the subject's repetitive fixation on its own echoing moments of gender signification. The looking that organizes the positional regime of vantage is turned back on itself.

Recall that the term "performance" itself is ambiguous (but not fluid), meaning both an act of conscious imitation, enactment, and artistry—a deliberate exhibition—and also a functioning or execution (as in the performance of an engine). The voluntary and conscious aspects of performance become entangled with the enactive possibilities of the linguistic performative as defined by J. L. Austin, producing a gender scenario in which it seems as if one can, by virtue of performing, wield gender, become through repetition what one performs, and at the same time rediscover the inessential and constructed nature of gender roles as they are socially constituted.[4] However, in this account of gender as a performative, gender refers to the lack of correlation between bodies and genders and its evocation is post-subjective. The allegory of performance assumes an already-formed (and gendered) subject—one already sexuated as lover or beloved. Displaced from the unconscious to consciousness, this fantasy of control underwrites a vertiginous gender regime that redoubles the epistemological stakes of narrative regimes and elicits the gaze as guarantor. This gaze, however, is not the unlocated sense of being seen, but it is the subject's persistent interpellation of audiences to the performance.

Vertiginous "performative" gender is, thus, the appearance of a secondary set of identity/identifications with only the illusion of consciousness and will exercised within an unquestioned pool of binary gender choices. Although many drag king performers, for example, believe themselves to be gender mobile, others see their performance as a form of self-expressive artistry, signaling some real identity, or both simultaneously. Display and witnesses are necessary to certify the subject's gender mobility. Both ends of this spectrum need an audience, a watching other whose regard guarantees the efficacy of performance as the imitation of a gender as well as its parodic commentary. As a gender regime, this complex layering of the seeing of oneself with the "to be seen" emerges from and produces a vertiginous dynamic of reflection, repetition, and the decoying sleight of hand that defers knowing whether one has it all or knows one cannot have it. It feigns a deferral of sexuation itself while displaying its sexuation.

Because the engenderment of subjects is far more complex, unconscious, and involuntary than either a "performative" or melancholic process (the introjection of loss—the loss of all, for example), this scenario of willed and wielded gender provides a fantasy of agency within what seem to be the restrictive limitations of social and taxonomic gender regimes. Focusing on genders' inessential characters, such performative fancies rarely question the pool of signifiers from which they might draw, sticking to familiar, caricatured, binary, taxonomic categories. In so doing, they produce a regime that asymptotically endeavors to perform a corrective scenario understood as *in se* resistant and radical. Wielding gender signifiers—facial hair, clothing, body language, makeup, and strategic paddings—produces the illusion that gender is superficial, malleable, and playful. It should, therefore, not be determinative, restrictive, or essentialized. And so, the gender outlaw demonstrates that gender is not natural but does not interrogate what genders are available, assuming and acting in relation to the binaries of the taxonomic (male/female) and the social (masculine/feminine)—unless, like Kate Bornstein or MilDRED (more on the latter below), they see themselves as gender fluid, itself a position that persists within the dynamic of seeing oneself being seen being gender fluid.

This gender fluidity curiously becomes situated, again through performance, as essence and personal identity. When this happens, performance is no longer performance in the first meaning, but it is instead a very sincere version of performance in the second. It turns into something like our strange contemporary notion that art is merely an extension or authentic expression of the author's persona. These performances are finally reaffirmations of a self (yes, a real, essential, maybe fluid, maybe Tiresian self) made in relation to that self, but needing an audience (an other) to witness and reflect back the self seeing the self perform the self. Our fascination with various versions of this performing—drag, transgender, and transsexuality (when evoked as performance)—is itself a symptom of a fascination with a far more subtle interplay of regimes as has become more visible and apparent. Transsexuality, offered as a fairly clumsy spectacle of metamorphosis in medical documentaries, actually follows behind our imaginary of gender mobility, which is multiply inflected rather than binary. *Venus Boyz* (2002), a documentary film made primarily about drag kings, slides inexorably from a celebration of transgender into a meditation on versions of transsexuality as a mode of surgically realizing the gender fluidity of the performer. This surgical sincerity, which results in an intriguing range of body permutations (breasts and penis, no breasts and no penis, no breasts and enlarged clitoris, etc.), fixes the body to a gender identity even as that gender may no longer be taxonomically coherent. Although individuals understand their genders as fluid and other to the other, there is still an impetus to make bodies reflect coherent genders and vice versa. Why should drag as a performance slide into transgender or transsexuality? What is it about the vertiginous that demands an ultimate sincerity, or at least the idea that the body expresses an inner truth?

Bringing to the stage an already complexly ambivalent scenario, the regime of self-conscious gender performance involves the multiplication of the sites of regard in relation to one another as the delusive effect of subjective agency in the throes of self-expression. Performing genders is not the intrinsic mode of subjective engenderment or an indication that gender is not essential, but it is instead ultimately a mode of self-regard in the act of self-conscious gender performance. Performing genders requires two looks: self-regard as an intrinsic part of the pleasure of performing, and the gaze (the sense one is being looked at) as that which certifies one's own self-regard. There are at least two implications to this multiplied self-consciousness. First, the dynamic of this gender regime is a vertiginous dynamic of reverberation as self looking at self being seen looking at self. Mirror image mirrors mirror image. Second, the genders performed belong to the taxonomic and the social; that is, vertiginous gender performance works only with the binary taxonomic regimes already available, even if this regime is synecdochized by movable gender signifiers. Its logic is always about the simultaneous authenticity/inauthenticity of the other.

This means that the dynamic of a vertiginous gender regime is an effect of layered iteration, of repeating in various forms signifiers that are already there. In addition to iteration, this vertiginous regime also requires reiteration since its use of gender as a citation is ambivalently poised between iteration's recontextualization and something that is exactly as it has been. The voguing of the 1980s was mesmerizing in the exactitude of its capture of frozen slides of cultural types defined as much by class, occupation, and sexual type as by gender—the businessman, the college student, the beauty queen.[5] In contrast, drag kings perform simultaneously a version of parodical mobility, the conscious performance of gender mobility as a fact in itself (mobility and a consciousness of mobility), and gender sincerity. The vertiginous regime's evocation of an *ab original* authenticity (a subject who in fact does have a gender) is itself ambivalent, halfhearted, and glancing, appealing to thoroughly contextualized and ephemeral gender signifiers as if they persist in the sacred in- and out-of-time hangar of permanent gender effects. Thus, in its endless reverberations, a vertiginous gender regime works like a series of quoted quotes in which each iteration is different in that its repetition is contextually relocated in relation to previous iterations, but in which each is also a nod to an exact replication at once both timeless and historical.

All of these iterations reflect gender performance back to the performer whose gender regime is produced precisely as an effect of watching oneself being seen seeing oneself in relation to one or another binary gender signifier. This dynamic represents the exponential multiplication of the regime of vantage while at the same time situating itself in a structural paradox. Vertiginous gender yawns toward the return of taxonomies to the subject as if from outside, operating as the displaced effect of the perception of being seen, of catching oneself in the act of seeing oneself being seen operating gender as the vortex from which gender emerges even as gender is understood simultaneously as both the object of will and subjective essence.

Obviously the redundant elegance of the vertiginous is also very messy, its hall-of-mirrors dynamic seeming to go in opposing directions and to emanate from contradictory conceptions of gender all at the same time. It is both an agenic operation and the mise en abime of a delusive subjective essence. It divorces gender from the body but weds it to subjective truth. The former subtends acts of performing, the latter marks the performance as sincere—and essentially no longer a performance at all. What we might understand as gender itself in all of this is that gender signifiers function as a mode of regulation and organization, harnessing the energies that fan isomerically from the various vectors of consciousness. A vertiginous gender regime, however, not only reiterates gender signifiers, it also makes visible what binary taxonomic regimes do. The contingent and ambivalent status of this vertiginous regime constitutes its tensions while its fascinations with itself seduce the regard of others. The vertiginous deploys exhibitionism as an inherent part of its dynamic—it is a show-off begging to be seen—but the eyes most crucial to its theater are its own.

Ab-Staining

Seeing itself being seen, enfolding itself finally within the seductive aura of narcissism, vertiginous gender occupies small, contained dimensions wrapped in on themselves. Vertiginous gender is a regime that collapses inward, containing itself in its own self-reflective architecture. It thus finally takes on the appearance of the stain, the "something to be looked at" that impersonates "the place of being looked at."[6] With its dynamic of infinite self-regard presented as soliciting the look of others, this vertiginous regime appears to offer itself to the gaze, to the sense of being seen. The sense of being looked at takes the outward-directed imperative of narcissism (look at me looking at myself) and turns it into an inward-directed consciousness of narcissism's demand (I see myself ordering you to look at me looking at myself). In the regime of the vertiginous, this inversion is multiplied. Offering a performance of taxonomic signifiers as well as codes from the social regime, feminine masqueraders, drag performers, transvestites, transsexuals, androgynes, goth teens, and gender rebels of various sorts deploy such signifiers to various ends. These performances often also include hyperbolic displays of social femininity or masculinity, and acknowledge, elicit, and even require the look of another gender "performance" as a evidence of agenic will, of the subject's ultimate power over taxonomy. Performing taxonomies so as to be seen as agenic works only if one sees oneself as being seen as agenic—only where one's agency is reaffirmed by the nod of the other.

But the other's nod never comes because there is no outside to the performance. Instead, the gaze solicited is a self-regard understood as self-consciousness that solicits self-regard, ad infinitum. This folding-in glistens and provokes, but its performance disappears into the staining insight of subjective vulnerability. Through this house of self-regarding mirrors, vertiginous gender reveals its constituting dynamic as the continuous performance of subjective desire in the throes of reaching for what it can never be. This has nothing to do with wishing to be or knowing oneself to be genders not in accord with biology—it has nothing to do with formulations such as "female masculinity," for example. Rather, it has everything to do with trying to fool taxonomy via a performance of agency so iterated that such frustrated agency can finally be felt as real—not as a real gender, but as real agency. If performing signifies agency and choice; and if that performing is observed, accepted, and even applauded (or booed) by others; and if the performing subject sees itself being seen as agenic, and sees itself seeing itself being seen as agenic, then through the series of repeated and receding gazing self-regards, that subject might grasp the untraceability of its agenic failures as a successful illusion of success. This inwinding process has the same effects even if the performance is ironic.

Doing Gender

In *GenderQueer*, gender activist Riki Wilchins makes clear the self-conscious etiology of vertiginous gender. "According to theorist Judith Butler," Wilchins says, "gender refers not to something we *are*, but to something we *do*, which, through extended repetition and because of the vigorous suppression of all exceptions, achieves the appearance of a sort of coherent psychic substance."[7] Glossing thus engenderment, Wilchins goes on to explain what the gender is that is "done": "Gender is a system of meanings and symbols—and the rules, privileges, and punishments pertaining to their use—for power and sexuality: masculinity and femininity, strength and vulnerability, action and passivity, dominance and weakness. To gender something simply means investing it with one of two meanings."[8]

For Wilchins, as for other gender activists, one "does" gender; that is, one operates the system of "meanings and symbols." But of course, it is not as simple as that, for gender "doing" must be transgressive to be seen, and being seen as doing gender is necessary, not to any sense of psychic coherence but to reverberate an assurance of agency to the doer. To be fair, though a prolific commentator and spokesperson, Wilchins does not claim to be a scholar, and her interpretation of Butler's work moves the entire process even more definitively into the realm of subjective consciousness (without, of course, accounting for how subjects can ever be subjects without gender). Wilchins's rendition of Butler is, however, typical of popular misreadings and appropriations of *Gender Trouble* through which Butler's work loses its subtleties. Vertiginous gender activism has a way of referring ultimately to some psychic truth of the performer, even if that psychic truth is the will to agency. Vertiginous gender has a will to workshop; it must constantly solicit the gaze. Vertiginous gender, then, thrives in a system in which the commodity image exceeds its value, in which the commodity becomes the signifier of itself.

For our delectation, then, vertiginous gender must put itself on the market as a commodity to be consumed as a way of ensuring that it can see itself being seen—can see itself essentially as a product. As Dennis Allen has observed, "Exchange value has migrated and now resides in people, each of whom becomes both his or her own producer/subject and an object of consumption for someone else."[9] The exchange value of the gender performer is determined by the extent to which the performer can simultaneously perform gender agency (the ability to wield and merge gender signifiers) and gender illusion (the appearance of taxonomic gender at odds with biological sex), whose artful re-presentation also indicates gender agency. What is ultimately being exchanged, however, is an economy of consciousness understood through the vector of sight, but oscillating endlessly between the performers' evocation of a consciousness of self-consciousness and the audience's self-consciousness of a consciousness of self-consciousness.

This oscillating economy sparkles between objectification and desire, but most importantly this commodity exchange, as Allen observes, "no longer substitutes for social relations," as Marx would have it.[10] "Instead," Allen continues, "it *becomes* the very principle of social relations, which are transformed into an endless circulation of shifting positionalities of product and consumer," in this instance between the performer and the audience, where the performer is already its own audience.[11] As a condition of gender performance, the performer encapsulates the subject/object and exchange relations of commodity culture as a self-enclosed dynamic from which the performance derives its significance, but which in order to signify agency must be endlessly reiterated through a series of reinforcing frames. In this way, the dynamics of commodity perpetuate the dynamic of seeing oneself being seen seeing oneself, repeating infinitely outward the vertiginous dynamic that also simultaneously iterates toward an inward vanishing point.

At the same moment in the first decade of the twenty-first century that makeovers filled the reality television menu, gender performers were an educational hot commodity. For example, drag king MilDRED ("MilDRED Love Experience & Trade; and D.R.E.D. Productions and P.I.M.P. Productions Daring Reality Every Day"), offered DRED's services to "speak, perform, heal and workshop at your school, group, school, organization [*sic*]."[12] MilDRED's website was headed by the epigram, "When one allows one's truth to shine . . ." (quoting herself). MilDRED offers such shows as "MilDRED! The GoD/Dess in Me—Scary Beautiful and Drunk on Self-Love © 2004." The description of the show offers liberation and insight: "The soul begins to experience an enlightenment once they embrace their feminine, masculine and total energies." MilDRED charges $4,000 for these performances, and they are attractive to and consumed by GLBT student groups.

Why GLBT groups would have found themselves the supposedly avid consumers of this version of gender enlightenment points toward how this vertiginous regime has functioned as the interpretive example of a perpetual misunderstanding of more intellectual arguments about gender and subjectivity within a larger cultural matrix focused partially on metamorphosis. The vertiginous is the logical end point of the makeover's appeal to agency. Exceeding the modest ambitions of taxonomic compliance, gender performers demonstrate how all subjects can simply wield gender signifiers to become whatever they want—and along the way show up the accessory character of gender signifiers themselves. Gender performers seem to provide a tangible, entertaining, resistant, in-your-face example of what all of that '90s theory is saying. Except, of course, in going one step too far to literalize it all, they miss the point, but also show how any theory of engenderment as performative only accounts for one gender regime—the vertiginous—among many. Gender performances depend greatly on a whirling iteration of consciousness, and it becomes clear our daily relation to gender lacks such vertiginous energy. We are typically more or less gendered within multiple gender regimes without even knowing it. And if gender is chatoyant, multiple, and inter-inflective instead of simply binary, we are all transgender and the concept loses any liberatory or agenic traction.

In the first decade of the twenty-first century, the vertiginous functioned as the response to the metamorphic makeover. The vertiginous connection between gender activisms of various kinds and nonheterosexual sexualities enabled a displacement of sexuality and desire into gender, where gender was the oppressed truth of a self who wishes to be desired. The sense was that it was important for sexual minorities to witness and absorb any sense of agency and challenge where agency was located as objective—as the attribute of the desired object. Happily participating in the economy of the vertiginous, GLBT spectators read agency not only in the performance, but also as an effect of having booked it in the first place. The problem with all of this is not only the way vertiginous gender is a decoy, providing a riveting dynamic that situates agency as the delusive but unattainable end of self-conscious gender performance, but also in the ways such performance distracts from the possibility of thinking beyond its own self-cycling model.

We See Boys Being Boys Being Boys . . .

Drag kings and drag queens, though they share in the economy of the vertiginous, act in and through this regime differently, mostly because of the asymmetries inherent to the binary taxonomies they have taken on. The cultural asymmetricality of masculinity and femininity renders drag king practices more radical and transgressive than the performances of drag queens, whose revelation that femininity is a masculine affair seems merely to reiterate a long-known truth. Drag queens belong to gay male community conventions. Their claims to agency short-circuit at the point where subjective essence emerges if we understand that femininity was always a version of masculinity. Masculinity, however, was never a version of femininity and so drag kings offer a challenging look back, the sense of the greater torqueing of taxonomies.

Because the vertiginous regime must be seen wielding gender and because live performances are not always possible, the photograph becomes a primary register of drag king performances. Photos of drag kings often actively solicit the look by looking back, by signifying in the look at the camera the subjects' consciousness of being seen—and being seen as wielding gender signifiers. There is never a question of real trompe l'oeil—that we really mistake these posed photos as, say, biological men or even as necessarily masculine. That is beside the point. The point is to admire the virtuosity with which the gender signifiers are performed, which means that the illusion can and should not be total. At the same time, because vertiginous gender is about seeing oneself being seen doing rather than being, the photos mark an instance of the intersection of being seen and seeing oneself being seen. They are the metonymic document by which their performing—and the dynamic of seeing themselves being seen—is perpetually recertified. Thus the photograph is the primary synecdoche of the drag king whose domain is less visual than the object of sight.

In drag king group photos, participants perform drag-kingness by deploying the eyes and the hands—and almost all of these group portraits deploy the same semiotics. A group portrait of the San Diego Drag Kings Club in 2006, for example, shows a collection of drag kings all affecting a James Dean "what of it" pose.[13] All look directly into the camera, and not one of them smiles (not smiling means looking tough, which means looking masculine). The photo enacts the spiraling framing of the vertiginous. The center figure of the photograph, a tattooed, kneeling, goateed, arm-banded chap, provides the two-fingered "rock on" gesture, with both hands held chest high. His four fingers point inward toward his face in a centering triangle in whose graphic middle is what looks like a horn necklace signifying phallicism. The other figures deploy their hands to gesture toward their crotches, and the figure on the far right has his hands in his pockets (and is the only one to do so). Separate figures framing a center, the portrait spirals from a center of phallic performance outward toward the inwardly disappearing pocketed hands, which in this case are buried in a pair of bib overalls with the bib, too, hanging down to veil the crotch, the real disappearing framing vortex of the image.

While group photographs do image portable gender signifiers—belt buckles, facial hair, clothing, arm bands, tattoos, hats, sunglasses, jewelry—these signifiers are less important than the way the portraits image the guys' interactions, not as males, but as kings that point to their gender performance itself as performance. "Look at us standing around like guys," the portraits exclaim, and pretty queer guys at that. The vertiginous regime has a both/and ambivalence—it has the phallus, and it knows it is a joke. The duplicity of the look is all about inveigling the look back, not as a casual glance, but as a double take, which begins the series of framings by which vertiginous gender is produced.

The portraits' posing and signifiers produce the image of soliciting self-contemplation. Lookers look, and inevitably they look at the image of drag kings looking at themselves being looked at, instantly completing the cycle and certifying not the masculinity of the king but the inward/outward vertiginous spiral of the regime itself. The question is not "Are these guys?" but rather, "How do these female people produce the illusion of masculinity?" This leads, if the looker looks again, to a reading of signifiers and the unconscious tracing of the portrait's spiral, which is ultimately not about making the looker conscious of his or her own gender assumptions or an admiration of the kings' ballsy transgressiveness, but instead is about cementing, via this spiraling enframing, the relation between outer and inner, between display and pose. In the mere act of looking, the looker completes the commodity dynamic by which subjects become desired objects seeing themselves being seen seeing themselves who model the scopic regime of their drives. Although the drive is linked to subjects' feelings of lover or beloved and the ways they deploy signifiers to signal that position, the vertiginous regime is less about transgender than it is about gender as a dynamic by which desire and display enwrap in the scopic field as subjects to the gaze. The inner "essence" is expressed in and through that dynamic that ends up encompassed by the act of looking, which produces the portrait's subjects at least as momentary objects of scrutiny and consumption.

Drag Drag (Drag²)

There is, of course, a very long history of drag whose practices range from sincere attempts to pass as another sex, to uncanny imitations or embodiments, to popular cultural examples of figures whose clumsy comic drag—or drag of drag—actually emphasizes what appears to be the essential (usually) masculinity of the operator. In contrast with a twenty-first-century interest in gender bending or even with longer gay cultural traditions of various drag forms, these popular cultural figures have ulterior motives for their drag. This version of drag does not belong to the regime of the vertiginous;

these figures are not seeing themselves being seen being a gender, but rather want not to be seen as the reassuring stable underlying gender they are or they feign insanity as itself the obvious conclusion to be made if there is some gender problem. These instances of drag[2] work to certify not the gendering of the appearance, but the unquestioned underlying gender of the wielder.

Tony Curtis's "Josephine" and Jack Lemmon's "Geraldine" in *Some Like It Hot* (1959), for example, are musicians who masquerade as women to hide from the mob. While Josephine rapidly sheds her drag persona (to undertake other, more masculine, upper-class gender performances), Geraldine clings to his drag, allowing the continued attentions of suitor, Osgood Fielding (Joe E. Brown). Geraldine performs a curious half-drag. He is quite capable of feigning feminine mannerisms (although they are clumsy enough for everyone to know they are feigned) and occasionally even slide into a pastiche of sincere feminine behavior and positioning, but he is unable to walk in high heels or rid himself of the continued assertion of masculine body moves. Geraldine is, thus, more an example of a gender layering, where one taxonomic gender is clearly layered onto something else, the authenticity of which becomes an unquestioned male ground. Even the two men's willingness to undertake the masquerade bespeaks a certain confidence in an underlying masculine truth, one that becomes perhaps less certain as Geraldine begins to like being a girl.

The two musicians also contrast with what might be deemed the epitome of femininity in the figure of Marilyn Monroe, as her gendering operates both taxonomically and socially to provide a model of perfect femininity. In contrast to Monroe's "Sugar," Josephine and Geraldine figure other gender regimes from the vertiginous consciousness of their undertaking to the metamorphic, or in-process character of their impersonations, to the asymptosis of their legibility as female (or male). Their drag is a comforting drag, repeatedly securing an underlying masculinity as that which cannot quite operate femininity.

A similar drag[2] phenomenon appears in the character of Maxwell Q. Klinger in the long-running sitcom *M*A*S*H* (1972–83). With a comically hyperbolically masculine body—hairy and big-nosed—Klinger's drag is a ruse to get a Section 8 discharge. But, like Jack Lemmon's Geraldine, Klinger becomes interested in fashion and feminine style, expertly operating his wardrobe more as an end in itself, the contrast between body and clothes ever insistently guaranteeing his underlying masculinity. This drag^2 is reassuring—gender taxonomies can stay in place even when threatened. Femininity is something the masculine can wield without threat either to the masculine operator or to taxonomic clarity. This drag^2 phenomenon persists for decades as a placeholder for any challenge to binary taxonomy or for the free operation of gender regimes outside of the taxonomic. While signaling some anxiety, drag^2 quells the anxiety it signals. At the same time, significantly, there is no resonant female-to-masculine version of this, which suggests again the asymmetries of binary taxonomies. Drag drag's male to feminine is comic and unthreatening; it is a lessening of prestige and power. In this context, we can only take female to masculine as a serious threat; there is no comic version.[14]

Queen for a Day

Because the taxonomic and social gender regimes—the realms of masculinity and femininity and their groups of associated culturally resonant signifiers—is asymmetrical, and because vertiginous gender plays on the arbitrary associations between taxonomy and social gender, being a drag king is never as "authentic" and unmarked as being a drag queen. Since femininity is always already masculinity, no one operates femininity better than men do. Drag queen, too, is a part of the regime of vertiginous gender, but its spiraling trade of self-conscious address works slightly differently, provoking not so much the eye as the ear. Drag queens usually produce a more total visual illusion of social gender than do drag kings, and they represent a larger spectrum of performance economies. There are beer-bellied guys in the burlesque comic review who don only enough hints of femininity to make their buddies laugh (drag drag); transvestites who cross-dress for libidinal reasons; female impersonators with illusionist panache who revivify iconic female performers such as Barbra Streisand, Judy Garland, and Marilyn Monroe (who themselves evoke a similar, but differently constructed, vertiginous dynamic of the feminine in contemplation of itself as the feminine); and transvestite sex workers whose vertiginity enables an elaborate lure, decoy, and disavowal economy that is ultimately a commodity. This range is partly enabled by the conventional and campy function of the drag queen in gay male culture, which means that the vertiginous spiral of regard, though still a necessary component of being the object of desire, is less about inner truth and more about the agenic command of a masculine subjectivity itself, which defines and openly dares to undertake the feminine.

As a sociocultural phenomenon, the drag queen preexists the recent two decades' more conscious impersonations spurred by agenic wishes' ideas of gender as performance promise. Cross-dressing itself has a long history in which its relative functions in the gender system change. In the late twentieth and early twenty-first centuries, drag functions as a necessary vortex within gay male community, offering the site of feminine operation as the texture that both appropriates and deflects femininity from the homosocial and male homosexual scene. Its performance is more about control than agency, about keeping the feminine at bay through the illusion of its strategic deployment as a communal ritual and, for some, as a regime of gender itself, understood as the position of the camp object of desire (which is a cover for wanting to be the real object of desire of [gay] men, a desiring economy that plays precisely through gender regimes as a mode of direct indirection). By assuming the dynamic site of the one who watches herself being watched watching herself as feminine, the drag queen perpetually defers the known phallic secret that secures the performance as such, while the performance produces the illusion of the truth of the secret (pssst—the phallus is there). This is essentially a dynamic of gentle disavowal, which is itself conscious rather than repressed. The "I know but all the same" of disavowal operates in the regime of vertiginous drag queens as "I know I know you know, but all the same."[15] This doubling self-consciousness has the effect of perpetually displacing the phallus as a mode of guarantee. Unlike the drag king, who produces the illusion of phallic ownership (of *having*) premised on phallic signification and deferral of disavowal, the drag queen produces the illusion of phallic *being* premised on the perpetual deferment of the phallus that we know we know is there somewhere.

The Phallus is a synecdoche that organizes the imaginary of the social and taxonomic signifiers deployed in the vertiginous regime. One has the object of desire or is that object, whatever that object is. And whatever that object is, the subject can never grasp it, which is why vertiginous gender regimes trick gendering into producing an illusion of the object's presence in what is ultimately an economy of desire that turns on itself. The vertiginous poses itself to be seen in specific relation to the postures of having or being. Vertiginous dynamics of self-conscious framing, misdirection, and perpetual delay play around the imaginary figure of a phallus somewhere. Drag queens render this delay in a performance of femininity that simultaneously obscures and points toward its own hidden object, making the terms of deferment and delay fairly literal. Because the drag version of perfect femininity *is* the Phallus, a drag queen both is the Phallus and has the phallus (insofar as anyone can)—a phallus that can be heard, though it cannot be seen. Drag only works if we know it is drag; an audience must have the signifiers of a phallus somewhere in the dress. In this sense the commodity status of the drag queen works in exactly the opposite direction of the drag king. The drag queen already has some imaginary vestige of the object of desire she must hide in order to take its place, whereas the drag king must produce a paradigm of self-conscious self-regard as a way to become the bearer of the phallus and the object of desire.

Many drag queens produce a fairly thorough illusion of parabolically perfect social femininity, though the performance itself is always marked as one through some hyperbolic or campy doubling of effect (too much makeup, a feather boa) so that drag queens' performance of femininity is the performance of femininity's status as already performance. Mainstreamed drag queens such as Dame Edna Everage perform what is arguably not femininity, but a version of the drag queen that makes an obvious link between drag performance and campy personality. The drag queen's vertiginous unraveling exists at the point where the drag queen speaks, or often does not—lip-synching instead or merely becoming someone else. These two manifestations—lip-synching and obvious impersonation—are actually the same phenomenon insofar as they produce the illusion of the perpetual displacement of signifiers, which, as with drag kings, disappears into a vortex of self-conscious inter-referentiality through which the vertiginous economy never emerges from itself. So the Judy Garland impersonator perpetuates the shifting significations of Judy Garland-ness by lip-synching to her songs. Drag queens such as Harvey Fierstein, who break this illusion and thereby toss the vortex into a different whirl of self-consciousness, do so by speaking.

The voice then, no matter how modulated, will always refer to the terms by which the vertiginous dynamic works, producing the illusion of a hidden subject whose wielding of femininity is a self-directed wielding of gender signifiers disappearing into the phallus; or, in the case of the drag king, often exposing its lie. Making obvious the circulating inter-referential modes of gender, the emergence of the drag queen's voice secures the mastery of the object of desire by seeming to break the illusion by which the subject becomes the object. In this way, the vertiginous regime of the drag queen becomes a regime organized by sound in addition to its self-conscious self-regard and phallic geographies.

The category of the drag queen is itself so multiple that the phenomenon—if it can even be considered a single phenomenon—itself shows the interlacing of multiple gender regimes. The differences between drag queens who perform in camp club settings, the more studied performances of impersonators, and libidinally invested transvestites demonstrate the ways gender regimes necessarily interweave and inter-constitute one another. Campy drag queens do not endeavor to produce anything like a total illusion of femininity. Their performance is a performance of personality and of camp itself as an indication of agency. The campy drag queen leans toward a chimeric "vantage" regime, as that constitutes the perspective from which gender signifiers can be seen to be performed. These "homely" drag queens (homely because they are canny and familiar, because the effect of their layerings is often infelicitous) literally drag the entire realm of the sociocultural with them as the focus of commentary, accomplished through vantage and the illusion that they occupy the outer edges of their vertiginity, emerging from or just beginning the whirl of self-regard.

In addition, we also understand campy queens as a particular mode of gay male positioning, veering toward the feminine in aspiration and inclination, but completely within a homosexual rather than a transsexual economy. Harvey Fierstein and Nathan Lane both perform this version, and it is the one most represented in mainstream popular culture, mostly because it situates its self-consciousness of being seen as a self-consciousness of the practice itself as a social rather than personal commentary—even as we might also understand that positioning as a revelation of some vortex of self. In this context, drag becomes a mode of empowerment, a style of social commentary, of occupying the Tiresian site of vantage instead of the hot, humpy compliant status of conforming masculinity.

In contrast to the campy drag queen, female impersonators are performers who aspire to a totality of illusion with varying ambition and degrees of success. Character performers—those who impersonate historical figures—tend to rely on signifiers associated with that person both to produce the illusion and to deflect attention from the places where it fails. These impersonators are anaclitic, linking onto the perpetuated persona of a specific version of femininity—that of Barbra Streisand or Judy Garland or Carol Channing—both performing it and providing a canny reading of the gender regimes that constitute that persona. While being a campy drag queen refers to individual gender regimes (primarily the vertiginous, but also chimeric vantage, social, and even anamorphic and metamorphic regimes), female impersonation ranges from being the agenic operation of the vertiginous to being a performance with reference only to a performer's talent. It may or may not have any connection to the performer's link to a male homosexual economy, but it does render a self-conscious commentary on femininity as well as on agency—not necessarily as the agency of the subject wielding gender as an expression of subjective truth, but as the agency of one who can wield gender as an effect of a capability or talent.

In contrast to this, transvestism in the register of the fetish displays a libidinal quality linked to the signifiers of social and taxonomic gender regimes. It is less about agency than about desire, and its economy of desire is less the desire to be the object of the desire of others than the desire to be the object of one's own desire.

Transforming oneself into the impression of the "other" taxonomic gender is the self-production of self as other in a heterosexual economy. The direction of this address is toward the self, but in a short-circuiting rather than vertiginous manner. The transvestic version of the vertiginous can stop at its own self-regard (especially when transvestism is practiced in private), which is sufficient to produce a desiring dynamic. That it may offer itself to the gaze merges it with a more extended vertiginousness.

Other, equally unspectacularized transvestic practices do not participate in a vertiginous regime at all, or only barely, as their object is to pass unseen as a gender. This transvestism is about social gender and operates a dynamic of paradigmatic compliance understood as fitting—fitting into the clothing, finding clothing that "fits" temperament and personality, using dress as a way of "fitting" into one clear category or another. This transvestism is about "being taken for" rather than "being seen as," and as such is both metamorphic and anamorphic, embodying change through time and producing a corrected view. Oft-cited examples of this version of transvestism come from the histories of women who successfully cross-dressed and served in the army or married women and lived as men.

Female impersonators and transvestites who operate in venues other than in private or on the stage often participate in a more elaborate decoying economy organized around being a commodity that enacts a complex phallic hide-and-seek for the benefit of sexual partners. Perpetually deferring and hiding the phallus in order to be the Phallus becomes a practice of offering this fetishistic illusion to sexual partners who are aroused by this complex politic of disavowal. These are men who must deny homosexuality and phallic inclination through their complex negotiation of desire in and through the vertiginous. They can believe that their partner is a woman even while they know she is not and thereby avoid the fears, phobias, and evaporation of desire that may come from an encounter with phallic absence. The interplay in David Hwang's stage drama *M. Butterfly*[16] is a good example of this phenomenon, as are the transvestite sex workers who have famously ensnared Hollywood celebrities with a marked homophobic penchant.[17]

The entire vertiginous dynamic, however, with the exception of the campy drag queen whose masculinity, more the goal of performance, is produced as an underlying illusion, depends on never hearing the voice. Aurality (or the essential lack of it) plays out their being heard while not speaking. The voice, like the phallus, is perpetually hidden, though unlike the illusive Phallus, it threatens a far too immediate short circuit of the whole vertiginous affair. For this reason, the voice, too, must constantly be deferred in favor of another gender signifier—a recording, for example, or gestures. As long as we do not hear female impersonators and transvestites speak, the economy of their seeing themselves being seen being a gender can persist as both agenic performance and gender mastery. The voice, cracking, wavering, missing its registers, emerges as a signifier of the out-of-control, the unrepressible, which both certifies the presence of the deferred phallus (or at least testosterone) that perpetuates the vertiginous, but also, and at the same time, stops the circulation of self-conscious regard. The visual economy of seeing oneself being seen seeing oneself operating gender never matches an aural economy. Sight and sound thus clash in a perpetual mismatch, a catachresis that produces the aural as the perpetual absence on which it depends. What this means is that the aural must operate as the auxiliary of the vertiginous, but it must operate as an absence that, like the phallus, is present only by virtue of never being heard. The vertiginous is thus an inverted synesthesia. What cannot be is the sound of the phallus as support for the perpetual circulation of an economy of commodified self-reflection.

6 The Fixer

Taxonomy is the impetus by which we always try to re-sort genders' multiples back into two coherent categories aligned with sexual difference as the condition of genders' comprehension within the multiple cultural structures that seem both to produce and to rely on complementarity and distinct categorization. With their two boxes (and now occasionally three), questionnaires require that we all sort ourselves. The cultural imperative for this taxonomic reduction is a symbolic order (patriarchy, capitalism, reproduction) as that which persistently and desperately tries to produce, coerce, and hold onto an alignment among bodies, genders, and sexual functions by which it thinks (and we think) it operates. If in fact the Symbolic did operate as a stable, unperturbed, and unperturbable aegis, it would not be so worried about disciplining its varieties into cadres. Taxonomy is the work we do to deny chaotic variety in favor of a fantasy of order.

But while individuals are required to sort themselves officially, everyone sorts others as a condition of desire itself. Is this person the type that allies with my fantasy? How do I know?

Class Parts

The flowers' leaves . . . serve as bridal beds which the Creator has so gloriously arranged, adorned with such noble bed curtains, and perfumed with so many soft scents that the bridegroom with his bride there celebrate their nuptials with so much the greater solemnity.[1]

In an enlightening age of burgeoning collection, Swedish physician and botanist Carl Linnaeus devised a taxonomy of all living things that he believed revealed "the Divine Order of God's Creation" through nature. Beginning with plants, Linnaeus produced what he called "an artificial classification" that grouped plants according to the configurations of their reproductive organs. Using a binomial naming system, Linnaeus drew a plant's first name or "genus" from its male organs and its second name or "order" from its female organs. Based on an accepted myth of sexual reproduction that always already sorts beings into binary, complementary, yet asymmetrical kinds, Linnaeus's *Systema Naturae* (1735)[2] fixes nature in a marital scenario that derives from the biblical Genesis but extends through an elaborate hierarchical system of ever broader similarity.

Linnaeus's system points not toward the truth of plants or the biosphere generally, but rather toward the binary hierarchical imperatives of what is imagined to be human sexual difference imposed on the world as the rationale for the taxonomic processes that merely rebound to the truth of the patriarchal myth by which they are sorted. Taxonomy reflects and proves the ideology that founds it. With a Linnaean taxonomy, the biosphere reconfirms the shaky foundations of a heterosexual patriarchy that only unsteadily manages to privilege the male over the female, the donor over the gestator. As long as the biosphere can reconfirm a clearly irrational human social order, not only do all the myths of culture seem to reflect some divine inspiration, but that social order is also preserved from any challenge on the basis of logic, science, fairness, good sense, et cetera. To produce this self-affirming tautology, the ostensibly "objective" protocols of sorting and naming are modes of dividing and assigning based on "observed" morphologies that ignore the bias of the selection criteria themselves. Why sexual organs and not modes of digestion or breathing? Why interpret sexual organs as "male" and "female" according to the human species? What about organisms that can deploy alternative modes of reproduction or nourishment simultaneously, such as paramecia or Venus flytraps? The binarism of the founding paradigm—this and not that—produces a system of artificial clarity and absolutism that renders sexual organs and reproduction central, visible, and important, while other possibilities such as olfactory capabilities or circulation become minor and invisible. Organizing these groups into hierarchical taxa produces an imaginary kinship and line of derivation that will later serve Darwin's ideas of evolution. Taxonomic classification fronts an entire narrative of species' history, development, value, and relation founded on an imaginary of bi-sexed reproduction as the key commonality of all living things.

Modes of taxonomic classification, however, are always paradoxical. On the one hand, they represent the essence of living things and their relations to one another as derived from ostensibly "detached" observation. Classifications order a worldview they take as already orderly, reinforced by a system of nomenclature that works in the same way as patriarchal naming systems: male first, female second, showing relation and imaginary evolutionary lineage through a family tree structure. Poised as empirical and objective, taxonomy is the product of a scientific practice that incorporates the assumptions and interests of patriarchal kinship systems and capitalist social orderings as already present and immanent in the order of things, shoring up and stabilizing these systems as always already natural and "nature" as the already orderly.

On the other hand, nothing really fits its classification. What appear to be categories derived from the observation of nature are inflected from the start with a particular value system that depends on the division of entities into a complementary, reproductive dichotomy. The binary character of taxonomy, while reflecting and subtending patriarchy and capitalism, actually derives from a particular universalized narrative of reproduction understood as the complementary contribution of two interlocking entities, with one—the male—superseding and utilizing the other—the female. The generalization of this simplistic, heterosexual, patriarchal reproductive model as the basis for all categorization predicts from the start a plethora of ill-fitted sortings. Linnaeus, for example, had to devise a class for plants that lacked obvious sexual organs, which he dubbed "Class Cryptogamia" or "plants with a hidden marriage."[3] Even the apparently sexless were subject to the reproductive regime. But why use reproduction as the basis for taxonomy in the first place?

In 1749 the Count de Buffon, another noted biologist, defined species as "a group of organisms capable of breeding and producing fertile offspring."[4] If two entities of presumably different species reproduce fertile offspring, they retroactively (and tautologically) constitute the same species. No species can really be known for certain ahead of time. The narrative of reproduction with its defining imprimatur also grounds a series of misapprehensions. As Simone de Beauvoir argues in *The Second Sex*, taxonomically binary sexes are hardly even "natural" in the entire context of the biosphere, which is characterized by a range of reproductive mechanisms and sexual capabilities. "Males and females," she says, "are two types of individuals which are differentiated within a species for the function of reproduction; they can be defined only correlatively. But first it must be noted that even the *division* of a species into two sexes is not always clear-cut."[5] Pointing out the myriad forms of naturally occurring reproduction—cell multiplication, fission, blastogenesis, parthenogenesis—de Beauvoir concludes that "biology certainly demonstrates the existence of sexual differentiation, but from the point of view of any end to be attained the science could not infer such differentiation from the structure of the cell nor from the laws of cellular multiplication, nor from any basic phenomenon."[6] Even the production of two kinds of gametes (sperm and eggs), she continues, "does not necessarily imply the existence of two distinct sexes," since both can be produced by the same individual.[7] Pointing out that asexual and sexual reproductive modes coexist, de Beauvoir comments on the bias that privileges sexual over asexual modes of reproduction, which constructs a narrative of the evolutionary superiority of the sexual and thus sees the asexual and hermaphroditic as primitive and "degenerate."[8] "All we can say for sure," she continues, "is that these two modes of reproduction coexist in nature, that they both succeed in accomplishing the survival of the species concerned, and that the differentiation of the gametes, like that of the organisms producing them, appears to be accidental."[9]

The ideological character of sex and species classifications that derive from a model of heterosexual reproduction is evident if we try to think about such processes the other way around, starting with species already divided into two definitive types. Thinking of reproduction as emerging from a preexisting division of all species into two clearly defined sexes does not make sense without narrative providing a reason for the complementarity of parts and hence their classifying protocols. All taxonomic binaries spring from an underlying narrative of heterosexual reproduction as it authorizes complementary divisions based on the imagined parsing of a preexisting whole, a whole then reassembled as an effect of reproduction. This tautology, the whole underwriting complementary halves necessary to the whole, produces a particular understanding of what might constitute a binary as already complementary and interlocking. Instead of reflecting some observed truth about the natural incidence of binary categories, taxonomies systematically impose the same narrative and the same binaries on all organic phenomena.

Taxonomy's job as a gender regime is to sort and secure its binary aegis even at the level of the idiosyncratic and the individual. Taxonomy defines difference as variations of one of two categories, and so enables other binary logics such as kinship, capitalism, politics, and various philosophical systems to function as if they already reflected a natural truth. Taxonomy's dynamic is aggressive as it assimilates variety into a rigid scheme of sameness; it is digestive insofar as it perpetually processes variety into culturally usable bits.

Taxonomy Is Destiny

Like any other gender regime, taxonomy is both a dynamic and an effect. We tend to see sex (as opposed to gender) as natural (as opposed to cultural), immutable (as opposed to changing through time), standard, and normal because we see it as both cause and effect of a biological reproductive process, which we situate, at least by some accounts, as the default definition of life (that which can reproduce itself). We perceive variations in biological sex as abnormal, but as still sortable "mistakes" of nature. These are only "mistakes," however, if we think that sexual binaries are the only normalcy possible. Sex "mistakes" can be resolved back to the binaries, but the lack of reproductive possibility that often accompanies biological variations sidelines these versions as evolutionary castoffs, as non-participants in the long pageant of "man," and, thus, partially justifies conforming treatments. Because individuals with apparently compliant sexual morphology might also lack reproductive possibility, we fix them as well, encouraging the industries of reproductive technology whose effects help otherwise sterile mothers "feel" like "real women." The medical establishment has long participated in enforcing (and forcing) sexual taxonomies, especially as they relate to reproduction, and not because of any population scarcity. Although we understand reproduction as an "instinct" and a basic human right, to what extent does a reproductive model (rather than instinct) participate in a retroactive sexing? To what extent is "instinct" an alibi of taxonomy?

The confusion between the "scientific" sortings of taxonomy and the compulsive reductions of the social regime emerges clearly in the contingent area where nature is unabashedly natural—where naturally occurring, nonbinary intersexual forms appear. To call this "natural" is not to locate intersexual beings as somehow in a privileged relation to nature, but to suggest the ways the "objective" protocols of taxonomies are most obviously anything but a science based on "nature." For a long period of time in the post–World War II era, since sophisticated surgeries have been available, children born with various genital "anomalies" were (and still often are) deemed "abnormal" and in need of surgical interventions to produce a morphological conformity to a binary typology within a fairly narrow taxonomic version of sex, imagined as linking taxonomic and social gender. The idea, most publicly bruited by John Money, was that any confusion about gender that would undoubtedly emanate from atypical genitalia would be psychically and socially damaging, so early surgical intervention was necessary to eliminate any possible gender confusion.[10] Biology had to conform to social dictates in a medical discourse that assumed gender emanates from sex. Thus, males with insufficiently developed penises would be castrated and raised as girls. Girls with enlarged clitorises would also be castrated and raised as girls, all in the belief that being genitally different would be a social and emotional trauma no child could bear. Although some of these anomalies are potentially harmful, surgeries were often suggested for cosmetic reasons.

The gender privileged by Money over even the possibility of individual sexual satisfaction is clearly a part of the social gender regime, where the body itself functions as an accessory and/or prop to an imaginary sexual difference. But this is in the face of the fact that the body's "sex" has never had to match assigned social gender. The underlying rationale for this sex/gender conformity is an effect of merging the sex of a body to social gender in a fairly simplistic, literal way. The imperative to sexual conformity outweighs nature and supersedes individual rights to sexual pleasure and to living in the non-life-threatening forms in which they were born. Do not, in other words, correct a conformist culture; correct instead those who seem to deviate. Make sure that sex and gender provide a unified, legible continuum from body to identity, even though they obviously do not and never have. It is not the child we worry about; rather, it is the culture itself that is at stake.

Intersexuality, like Cryptogamia, is a naturally occurring phenomenon, just as is the incidence of infertility among otherwise genitally and genetically conforming beings. Not all intersexed beings are infertile, nor are all "normal" beings fertile, so reproduction becomes so much more an evident alibi instead of a principle. The fact intersexual beings exist in statistically significant numbers (more, say, than one per one thousand births) suggests that taxonomies relying on binary gender produce the binary rather than reflect any naturally occurring state of affairs.[11] If at one point genitalia were determinative of sex, when genitalia proved misleading—when more sophisticated knowledge meant that the body could no longer be depended on to reveal sexual essence, as in the case of certain forms of hermaphroditism and intersexuality—genotypes became the determining factor. But, in fact, genotypes are never themselves direct indicators of sex and certainly not of clear-cut, binary sexual divisions. Humans are born with a variety of "sexual" genotypes, from XYY males to XXY females. The interactions of hormones with developing fetuses also produce a variety of sex/genital manifestations in which genital morphology does not match any genotype. This variety, however, is reduced to a particular kind of cause/effect narrative of bad timing and copying mistakes.

The intersex movement has presented a highly effective public education program raising awareness about the kinds of damage surgical interventions produce. Genotypic essence gives way to social regimes that deploy the appearance of external genitalia as indicators of essence. As a generation of feminist commentators has made clear, not even the body is devoid of cultural readings, and what stands for "nature" and "science" are always heavily inflected, if not themselves produced by ideologies and cultural myths. The treatment of intersexuals demonstrates the extent to which taxonomies based on physiology are never scientific but are, as Donna Haraway, Anne Fausto-Sterling, and Simone de Beauvoir have all pointed out in different ways, highly social.[12] The example of the intersexual also demonstrates the extent to which even sex determinations based on physiology change through time. What seems adequate to an infant (though still an unthinkable mayhem) develops and may emerge as something else during and after puberty. Intersexuals who have been "conformed" may well cease to conform as they grow up, wishing to become their original sex despite the surgical elimination of genitalia and/or hormone therapies. Or hidden forms of hermaphroditism may emerge, as in Jeffrey Eugenides's novel *Middlesex*,[13] in which the protagonist, raised as a female, realizes that he/she is a hermaphrodite.

Taxonomy tethers any free play of category under a mantle of science and within the realm of an over-normativized "nature" whose "mistakes," though "natural," are to be corrected by advances of technology. Why can't intersexuals just be intersexuals? What is it about taxonomies that makes them so rigidly binary in the face of a rather wide scathe of inconsistencies and clear evidence that natural forms are not binary at all? This is the purpose of the taxonomizing in the first place—to produce, as if "natural," an orderly "nature" that subtends cultural ideologies. But no one is typical, depending, of course, on the scale of one's examinations. "Nature" is full of "mistakes." Not only is the "natural" confounded with the "functional" insofar as functionality itself is defined within the hetero-reproductive narratives of kinship and capitalism, subjects must be clearly sexed/gendered to function within these binary systems—even if the subjects are sterile and even if they could be quite happy without conforming at all.

The reproductive narrative that organizes sexual divisions (and founds them) is thus less "natural" than the effect of a way of thinking that depends upon and reproduces binaries, and which in turn defines these binaries as simultaneously complementary and asymmetrical in value and function. The narratives deployed to describe the relative functions of the gametes are micro-narrative fables of gender ideology featuring a big bumbling, passive egg matrix and an adventurous, hardy, conquering sperm. This, of course, elides the immense number of sperm it takes to do the job and the millions that must perish in the task whose model of "male" expendability has been selectively ignored—as has the fact that mothers pass more genetic material to offspring than fathers do.[14] The point is, however, that gamete fables merely reiterate cultural ideologies of gender rather than the other way around, something that makes sense when we think of what we are asking gametes to do. We do not base other ideologies on cellular function, for example, and if we did, we might have a world dominated by socialism (where capitalism is best exemplified by cancer).

Taxonomy Always Has a Remainder

Sexual reproduction is *one* narrative of reproduction, not *the* narrative. Why, then, is the complementary hierarchical binary narrative so persistent? One possible answer is that our version of hetero-narrative reproduction fronts a paradigm of production as the joining of binarized differences. De Beauvoir comments that in Hegel's idea, "for the uniting processes to be accomplished, there must first be sexual differentiation, . . . one feels in it all too distinctly the predetermination to find in every operation the three terms of the syllogism."[15] If, as de Beauvoir argues, "nature" follows the exigencies of philosophy, what does this philosophy itself front? Does Hegel take his notion of synthesis from "rational" process, or is it an apt description of the exigencies of emergent capitalism? Does Hegel's idea, summarized by de Beauvoir, that sexuality is a mode of belonging to a "genre," represent a sophisticated psychological observation or an ideological constraint?[16] "The sense of kind," he says, "is produced in the subject as an effect which offsets this disproportionate sense of his individual reality, as a desire to find the sense of himself in another individual of his species through union with this other, to complete himself and thus to incorporate the kind (*genre*) within his own nature and bring it into existence. This is copulation."[17]

Hegel's explanation provides some insight into what is at stake in the heteronarrative: the colonization of otherness as a mode of self-definition and completion. This is not because individuals actually know themselves better in some sort of structural contrast to something different, but reflects instead the idea that certain individuals benefit from taking over others and deploying what is projected as the other's difference as a way of erasing their own uncertainty. This "othering" systematically described in the twentieth century in critiques of colonialism, racism, and sexism inevitably locates the "other" as something to be used for self-completion and negating comparison. The subject benefiting from this "othering" is almost always understood to be a white, Western male whose subjective status as primary and dominant is augmented by his use of the other to fill not only his bed, but also his congregations and his coffers. Naturalizing, thus, the exploitation of differently classed workers, women, and non-white or non-European, colonial subjects, the idea of the "naturalness" of genus and joinder with "other" is a convenient alibi for the acts by which a dominant category benefits (an "other" through which the dominant category has become dominant in the first place). And in all of that, this othering subject probably does not know himself better at all; he has just collected about him all that he "knows" he is not. But, indeed, they are "others" he can exploit to his benefit.

The drive to taxonomy, then, is defined by cultural paradigms of othering and exploitation. Taxonomy is overdetermined as a mode of oppositional differentiation that reduces variation to binaries that are also asymmetrical. This asymmetricality is an effect and perhaps the goal of taxonomizing, rebounding from the othering that produces binary divisions in the first place. Is taxonomizing itself a product of a process of projection onto an other used to secure self-definition? Is taxonomy co-opted by intersubjective colonizations? Or does the furious drive to appropriate the other actually produce taxonomy as the empirical process that meets its needs while screening the largely subjective benefits of the project? Certainly, the emergence of forms of taxonomizing began with the Greeks, such as Aristotle's use of the category of the "genus," which predates later European colonizing zeitgeists. The taxonomic project of Linnaeus, however, in line with burgeoning Enlightenment science, is both driven by and cooperates with the height of European colonizing activity in combination with the growth of industry and capital.

The power differential outlined by Hegel is certainly crucial to the colonizing for which taxonomy is finally used. Not only would eighteenth-century museum collections, which sprang up to accommodate the global loot of the empire, benefit from a system of categorization, they also put such detritus in its place—as curiosities, evidence of a lack of civilization, and testimony to the adventurous bravery of the empire's emissaries. Othering on display as science and natural history objectifies and essentially digests cultural differences as the objects of empirical scrutiny. The cannibalizing effects of taxonomy put the artifacts of anything "other" to the nourishing use of Western institutions whose subsequent rendering of otherness takes on the asymmetrical binary structure by which otherness is disarmed and demoted.

According to Hegel, the other is "an object which is itself such a subject."[18] The individual who feels a lack is inadequate "in its single actuality." This lack produces, according to Hegel, "drives to have its self-feeling only in the other of its genus, and to integrate itself through union with the other. Through this mediation the concrete generality joins together with itself and yields individual reality."[19] Although it is unclear whether this "other of its genus" is produced by the drive to self-feeling or preexists such drive, the dynamic Hegel describes is oddly similar to one Sigmund Freud offers in *Beyond the Pleasure Principle* as a way to account for his notion of "eros," a force similar to Hegel's "drive." Using Plato's retelling of Aristophanes's story in the *Symposium* of the originary state of beings as doubled,[20] Freud situates reproduction as a drive to rejoin what had been, at some prehistoric era, another "half," defining the origin of sexuality as "*a need to restore an earlier state of things*."[21] Aristophanes's story maps a primeval situation in which all beings were doubled, each man and woman having two attached bodies, and one being composed of man and woman attached. A threatened Zeus decided to render these doubled beings asunder, which resulted in the constant desire for reunification.

Freud follows the ramifications of this story to the conclusion that the sexual instinct might be a remnant of the breaking apart of life into fragments, represented in its "most highly concentrated form" in the "germ cells."[22] Sexual difference, thus, becomes the fragmentation of an *ab original* wholeness, which does not in itself carry any notion of asymmetricality. Notions of completeness are always already doubled, which means that individuals are not halves, but two single parts of a doubled whole, two-third's of which are composed, according to Aristophanes's story, of same-sex doubles. Freud, however, backs off from this explanation without ever rejecting it: "It may be asked whether and how far I am myself convinced of the truth of the hypotheses that have been set out in these pages. My answer would be that I am not convinced myself and that I do not seek to persuade other people to believe in them. Or, more precisely, that I do not know how far I believe in them."[23]

Both Hegel and Freud attempt to account for sexual reproduction as an innate drive that somehow requires an objectified other. This drive is always about a single subject and its struggles toward self-realization. It is never about the necessarily subjected other. Although Freud's use of Aristophanes's story would figure the other as somehow mutually engaged in the process, both Freud and Hegel finally envision the sexual drive as narcissistically invested—that is, as part of a libidinal force toward self-actualization and preservation. For Hegel, sexual difference defines genus, while for Freud in *Beyond the Pleasure Principle*, the other provides a rejuvenating difference that defers the death instinct, preserving life in the face of a desire for quiescence.[24]

In both cases, the necessity for an other produces a taxonomic urgency, a need to separate beings into self and other, where the self is always and definitively the site of power. Although both accounts gesture toward a vague mutuality, the centering of the subject in itself produces an asymmetry, predicated on the singularity of point of view. Power becomes the fictional attribute of the one who sees the other. Sight becomes the slim origin of objectifying othering. What both Hegel and Freud cast as accounts of a basic reproductive instinct are really assertions of a scopophilic model that itself screens and alibis another paradigm: that of cannibalizing and digesting the other within a capitalist industrial model. The "other" has a use value and gets used up.

As a cover story for assimilation, scopophilia is a way of distancing subjects from objects, a way of distracting from the processes of ingestion and digestion at the heart of taxonomy. Although taxonomy itself appears as a binary sorting based on a visual, preexistent sexual difference, the entire taxonomic process is also a way of spitting things back out as other as an effect of their digestion and assimilation. The other of this process—the disempowered, objectified part of the asymmetrical binary—becomes abject and uncanny as well as the site of disorganizations and threatening polymorphousness barely constrained by repeated taxonomizing and coatings of ideology. The other, then, is the turd of taxonomy, whose holographic status changes from excremental to reproductive. The turd is the baby, digestion is reproduction, and the model of ingestion and assimilation is the model of colonization, which finally becomes the barely veiled model subtending reproduction (and vice versa). But even this constantly morphing model never accounts for everything. Taxonomy always has a remainder, proving both its function and its lie.

Plant Sex: The Flowery Language of Heteronomy

The first subjects of Linnaeus's scientific taxonomies were botanical, although his attention to plant reproductive morphology reiterated more ancient observations of sex traits from the Greeks and the Chinese. As taxonomizing became more elaborate and sophisticated, the range of kingdom through genus incorporated more than the heterosexed, reproductive model Linnaeus used on plants. Modes of reproduction remain, however, a very significant determinant of genus, even in the classification of animals. Taxonimizing plants according to their reproductive mode accompanied the domestication and breeding of exotic plants, whose discovery, classification, and crossbreeding became the playground for wealthy European industrialists. Hybridizing such plants as orchids also meant naming the new hybrids. Plants became property, their reproduction a hobby, their offspring curious objects to be enjoyed, specifically by men.

Susan Orlean reports that "Victorian women were forbidden from owning orchids because the shapes of the flowers were considered too sexually suggestive for their shy constitutions, and anyway the expense and danger and independence of collecting in the tropics were beyond any Victorian woman's ken."[25]

Even so, as eminent a Victorian as Queen Victoria herself was an orchid fancier, and the rage for propagation reveals a much more perverse flair for the reproduction of others. Quoting rogue orchid hunter John LaRoche, Orlean points to the aggression involved in orchid hybridizing: "The only ones with features that have no real purpose are the hybrids, because someone put them together and came up with an unnatural thing. That's the cool thing with hybridizing. You are God. You do the plant sex. It's a man-made hobby."[26] To produce hybrids, breeders cross varieties that would never cross in nature. They also resort to tactics such as microwaving seeds to induce potentially valuable mutations. Most of the orchid plants produced, however, are clones, since it takes an orchid seven years from seed to produce its own seeds, and with hybrids, the offspring will not likely be true to type.

The reproductive control of plant breeds especially requires a husbandry that reflects almost anything but a naturalized heterosexual complementarity. Almost all plant sex involves an intermediary, so that the bees, wasps, birds, other insects, and now humans who carry pollen from plant to plant are an intrinsic third party to any plant sex, making plant sex always already a ménage à trois instead of anything like a heterosexual marriage. Crossbreeding, cloning, mutating—humans do plant sex as they try to control the breeds of other species such as dogs, cattle, vegetables, and fruit. This husbandry is ultimately about consumption, either the consumption of a desirable breed or the consumption of a tasty morsel. Controlling the product produces the illusion of some control over nature, a control practiced through breeding and reproductive methods that are anything but natural. For example, the apple breeds we enjoy today are all hybrid clones. Apple seeds never reproduce the same apples as those from which they originated. Fruits true to type result from grafting and proliferating the stock of a single tree. So, as Michael Pollan recounts, someone like Johnny Appleseed was not providing the Ohio Valley with orchards of luscious red orbs, but was instead sowing stands of cider-producing spitters.[27]

Plant breeding displays our mastery over the sex of others, but it is not unrelated to the aggression that underwrites the hetero-reproductive narrative of our own species. The "other" is othered as a preliminary to taking over its reproductive capacities and marking the product with our name. Although we currently believe that this is a mutual instinct—that both male and female participants gain the same thing—the narrative itself seems to require a very stubborn asymmetry that perpetuates aggression and assimilation as its primary acts, as if the other is not even "other" at all, but "something less" entirely. This "something less" both distances the other and enables its return as an extension of self, taken over, assimilated, and productive. Capital employs this othering to conceptualize labor. Despite discourses of instinct and fulfillment, humans do this with one another, the horror story being when women use "other" sperm donors, or use men, for their own reproductive purposes. Science fiction narratives, such as the Alien movie series, imagine the othering of humans for the reproductive purposes of another species as something horrible and abject (although we have no hesitation in doing such things ourselves). And cloning seems to have spawned a joint aversion and fascination of its own.

Apart from obvious speciesism, our godlike control of breeding reveals the aggressive assimilative impetus behind taxonomy as the sorting action that underwrites reproductive activities. We see all of this as civilization and survival, as a necessary step in becoming gardeners from being hunter/gatherers. But it also represents a turning away from nature, a taking over the other for our own use. This is not a judgment about the ethics of gardening, but rather an observation about how literal the assimilation is when we begin to manage the reproduction of other species—and maybe our own (which suggests the truly hostile impetus of laws governing females' right to manage their own reproductive activities). The sorting and naming activities of taxonomy are intrinsic to the process, since sorting and differentiating as "other" are the necessary first steps to objectification, manipulation, and, ultimately, digestion.

Only when we try to play God at home do we become queasy

about our matchmaking. Eugenics, though often a side effect of human practices such as genocide, is unpalatable as an overt social program. Sorting out the "other" among humans occurs as recognizable aggression both within the domestic sphere and as a part of rationalized national and religious programs. Soviet leader Nikita Khrushchev banging his shoe on a podium and assuring the "West" that the Soviets will "obliterate" them is no different than football teams threatening to "bury" one another, bumper stickers carrying on interstate tensions by declaring "Muck Fichigan," or the retributive erasures of gang wars.

The question is whether or how the reproductive narrative can be imagined otherwise—as other than harboring assimilative aggression. Does the very suggestion of binariness produce and also hide assimilations? Is binariness a product of aggression masked under the veneer of balanced complementarity?

Kinship and Cannibalism

The Möbius relation between the heteroreproductive narrative and binary gender taxonomies produces what structural anthropologists such as Claude Lévi-Strauss call a "kinship system."[28] This system correlates sex with familial relation (i.e., brother, sister, husband, wife, aunt, uncle) around sets of counterbalancing attitudes. In this system, the relations among family members are defined as sets of coordinated structures based on a series of sex/gender and age taxonomies. So, for example, in one patrilineal culture, if a husband and wife have cordial relations and the father and son are friendly as well, but the wife has more formal relations with her brother, then the son's relation to his maternal uncle will be formal and respectful. The friendliness of the relations between different terms correlates with or is in inverse relation to the degrees of friendliness of the relations of other terms.

This structural approach, deployed primarily in relation to preindustrial cultures, presumes the normative and binary regularity of sex/gender and the heterosexual character of all bonds as basic inclinations of sociocultural organizations. What is visible and accounted for is always clearly binary and heterosexual, which produces heterosexuality as the system that underlies itself, even if there are (as in some cultures) glaring exceptions. Assuming that the basic operation governing human relations is heterosexual marriage, participants in culture are defined in relation to sets of dialectical binary exigencies that subtend the fantasy of the purely heterosexual as both oppositional and complementary. The hetero-reproductive narrative is, thus, a tautology whose very structure reproduces itself over and over as the central product of its own telling. If, as the story goes, taxonomic "opposites" merge and produce more taxonomic opposites who meet other taxonomic opposites who merge and produce, what is reproduced ultimately is both the narrative of reproduction as ineffable truth and the taxonomic oppositions that sustain it. There is neither beginning nor end to this dynamic, but only self-perpetuation through an operation seen as always already given and natural.

The insistence of taxonomic binaries, thus, is produced and perpetuated via the heteronarrative as the cover story for heterosexual reproduction understood as the combination of opposites. It does not matter whether participants in the narrative actually are taxonomically opposite; it matters that they will schematically occupy such sites as an effect of the story. Two females, or two males, or two people of indefinite gender might have a family, but the kinship relation will still be understood within the imaginary of this heteronarrative, and that is because all notions of kinship belong to that narrative from the start. Kinship, though potentially infinitely variable (especially given the serial substitutions of present-day versions), always returns to the heteroreproductive narrative as the condition of its existence.

Lévi-Strauss suggests that kinship systems result from a taboo against incest.[29] Proximity and prohibitions between parents and children, brothers and sisters, and husband and wife radiate from the forbidden nexus of intrafamilial coupling. As a version of the heteroreproductive narrative, the "short circuit" of incest (one understood as a short circuit only in terms of oppositional differences) reveals that the proper function of taxonomic sorting is difference defined in as many ways as are relevant. Sons and daughters must therefore look beyond the family for mates, and children are presumably protected from the predations of parents and relatives. "This is really saying," Lévi-Strauss explains, "that in human society a man must obtain a woman from another man who gives him a daughter or a sister."[30]

The binary correlative systems that Lévi-Strauss discerns seem, however, to have little practical relation to an incest taboo, but rather to a taxonomized economy of exchange that does not work, as Lévi-Strauss admits, the other way around. Although he admits the "theoretical" possibility that kinship systems might be reversed (i.e., women might exchange men among themselves), he insists, "In human society, it is the men who exchange the women, and not vice versa."[31] This lack of reversibility exposes the primary dispositive role of taxonomic othering in kinship systems in which incest is only the negative Oedipal fantasy of a practice of othering produced by and sustaining the relations among males. The power to name, dispose, and use in turn produces and sustains maleness itself as the fantasmatic, asymmetrical point of the "all" in a system where exchange can only take place among equals and at the expense of the other. In essence, Lévi-Strauss's kinship system plays out socially the processes of subjective sexuation outlined by Lacan—trader subject and traded object instead of lover and beloved. Social structures produce and reinforce binary taxonomic sexes in relation to specific functions and values that reiterate and reflect the asymmetries of difference predefined as sexual and "natural." Although this all seems to depend on the visual sorting of bodies, the categories of bodies are also produced as an effect of this economy of an exchange among "sames."

Kinship works as the pragmatic support of binary sexual taxonomies, especially insofar as it perpetually reproduces a correlative, oppositional logic of relation as necessary to production and relation of any kind, both intra- and extra-familially. In the same way, binary taxonomies are produced as an effect of sorting, othering, and exchange as both cause and effect of a copular economy. Not to belabor the absolute hegemony of this narrative in our imaginary, or to be absurdly reductive, but it is almost impossible to conceive of any human relation—economic, familial, political, or religious—that does not depend on, use the terminology of, and/or overtly elicit the heteroreproductive narrative as a basic, unquestioned truth. Even our ways of questioning this narrative depend on it. It is a structural equation so pervasive that it can only reproduce everything in its own terms. So on the one hand, Michel Foucault can chafe against the tautologies of structuralism in *The Archaeology of Knowledge, and The Discourse on Language* and Anthony Wilden can decry the liberating promises of systems theory as always already structural.[32] And on the other hand, we can try to challenge its terms by re-gendering its actors—two mothers or two fathers—or extending its terms, but the narrative is always the same. Most recently American culture has reached out (albeit with great reluctance) to embrace gays and lesbians within this same structure, effectively transforming them into the same heteroreproductive relation.

Kinship per se is not primal here; the narrative is. Psychoanalysis understands the formation of the subject in terms of the kinship derivation of the "other," and feminist theory has systematically adopted familial models as ways to understand the relations among women. Kinship is so basic that it is easy to understand why Luce Irigaray[33] and Judith Butler keep returning to kinship as a site from which the binary aegis of sex/gender might be assailed. Irigaray exposes the exchange of women as revealing a "hommo-sexual" economy, one in which the binary taxonomy of gender is revealed to be really a taxonomy of one—the male as the basic condition of being human. Female, as the "other," is "not one," does not count, one whose different non-difference produces a symbolic economy of difference enabling exchange among males, but also masking the no difference that constitutes what Judith Butler points to in *Gender Trouble: Feminism and the Subversion of Identity*[34] as a foundational taboo against homosexuality. The taxonomic category of the female exists as a way to buffer unmediated relations among men that might result in exposing the open homosexuality of the male-to-male relation. This taboo against homosexuality only works, of course, in relation to the heteroreproductive narrative, which must produce oppositional difference as a precondition to any production at all. In the environment of this reproductive narrative, homosexuality works as a short circuit or deadening sameness.

Judith Butler also takes another approach to challenging the centrality of the incest taboo. Beginning with *Gender Trouble*, Butler begins an inquiry into why the incest taboo is so central a prohibition. In *Antigone's Claim: Kinship between Life and Death*[35] and *Undoing Gender*,[36] she continues to try to unravel the knot of prohibitions engendering kinship and psychic structures from the level of kinship itself, asserting a counter-taboo against homosexuality as foundational, then querying whether and to what degree kinship is necessarily heterosexual. If the target is to unravel the stubborn sites of cultural oppression, then kinship is certainly a crucial site of redress, especially if we understand the absolute hold kinship has on both the imaginary and the symbolic realms of human existence. But kinship itself, which is in practice much different than it is as a symbolic structure, is stubbornly naveled by the heteroreproductive narrative that it fronts and explains, situating it as natural, essential, foundational, and as the primal site for the imaginary configurations imagined as grounding law, order, and the positions available to the subject, especially within insistently binary and oppositional gender taxonomies.

The denial of kinship, as happened in the disposition of slaves, is a method of stripping humanity from formally othered subjects, replacing kinship systems with property rights. But removing kinship does not eliminate binary sex taxonomies. It reorganizes them within the use structures of property, which are to some degree quite similar to those of kinship. In property, as in kinship, one person always has rights and power over others, signified by naming practices, positional obligations, respect and affinity, et cetera. In property, as in kinship, names appended to objects and people produce relations where otherwise there might be none (as in the case of property) or where such relation might be in question (paternity). Ultimately at issue is the distribution of power in relation to the imaginary site of law. This power is the power to other: to name, use, apportion, delegate, assimilate, render visible or invisible, digest, obliterate, tax—and taxonomize.

Capitalist patriarchy thus distributes property rights in relation to taxonomy's sorting practices, using the asymmetries of taxonomy to justify the inequitable distribution of rights and goods. Capitalist patriarchy arguably deploys the taxonomic impetus of gender as a model subtending the asymmetries necessary to its operation. Its "all" corporations use up the "not all" powerless laborers as a part of a "natural" order of things nested nicely with what might seem to be the anti-taxonomic values of Christianity and democracy. Capitalist patriarchy's sorting proclivities define a matrix of positionings superficially organized around individual "worth" (a mixture of capital, industry, influence, kinship, and opportunity) retroactively alibied by individual degrees of success and reliant on delusions of "equality" guaranteed by documents and laws, but abrogated in practice. Capitalist patriarchy requires the maintenance of two myth systems simultaneously. One is the delusive fantasy of equality and possibility (i.e., the American Dream), the other the pseudo-Darwinian "law of the business jungle," which underwrites the definition and cannibalization of the other as a part of the "survival of the fittest." This second myth justifies poverty, exploitation, and socially damaging corporate practices with inequitable effects. The first myth must be sustained in order for the majority of subjects to withstand the second myth without too much complaint. Poised as a sort of natural selective process, capitalist patriarchy is actually a cannibalistic taxonomy that chews up the other and spits it out.

Eating Out

Though we find it abhorrent, cannibalism is the final, almost naïve literalization of the sorting and othering impetus. We can and do account for cannibalism in humans in many ways, but in the end it is the literal assimilation of the other. Although starving plane crash survivors may need to consume a dead comrade to survive, only life-or-death situations can rationalize the nutritional use of other human beings. In other situations, we regard cannibalism as either primitive or criminal—as a version of tribal magic or psychopathology.

Sigmund Freud understood cannibalism as a mode of magical control, seeing it as a way to govern or assimilate the other. "By incorporating parts of a person's body through the act of eating," he notes in *Totem and Taboo*, "one at the same time acquires the qualities possessed by him."[37] Cannibalism is a part of mourning and war rituals, practices observed by anthropologists who have formulated several different theories to account for various kinds of cannibalistic practices. Peggy Reeves Sanday sees the phenomenon of cannibalism as ontological, but not unified, meaning that cannibalistic practices fulfill different functions within different ontological systems. In the context of war, cannibalism can be a form of aggression, a version of dominance over and integration of the other understood as an enemy. As a religious ritual, cannibalism is practiced to feed the gods (the Other) as a way of perpetuating the life of the culture. As a part of mourning rituals, cannibalism is often a way of preserving the virtues and strengths of the dead within a kinship group, contributing to its successful self-reproduction. Sanday's theory for these various practices is that "rituals of cannibalism summarize and express an ontology, provide a model for individuation, and control violent emotions. . . . The basic psychological mechanism that seems to be involved . . . is individuating by physically differentiating oneself from primordial, inchoate energy."[38]

A literalization of the taxonomic, cannibalism is the final reification of othering, of the process of sorting the individual from chaos. By ingesting the outside and other, cannibalism assimilates and incorporates traits and being-ness within what is often, according to Sanday, an ontology of binary sortings between good and bad, them and us, life and death, monstrous and sacred, male and female. As Sanday also points out, attitudes around the position and function of cannibalism are sometimes linked to gender binaries. "It is also true," she notes, "that in more complex societies there is a significant relationship between male aggression against women and cannibalism."[39]

For cannibals such as Jeffrey Dahmer or the fictional Hannibal Lecter, there is great confusion (at least among website pundits) about how to understand the cannibalistic part of their activities. Dahmer, for example, is linked to a chain of figures beginning with Adolf Hitler and ranging through Charles Manson. What Dahmer and Hitler have in common is the popular perception of their "pure" evil, which translates into the way these figures each incarnate the unapologetic obliteration of others. Like the fictional Borg from *Star Trek: The Next Generation*, who assure everyone that "resistance is futile, you will be assimilated," Hitler set out to obliterate all kinds of "others," from Jews, Gypsies, and homosexuals, to entire nations. Hitler is the image of our taxonomic aggression come back to haunt us in the frighteningly literal form we associate with the uncanny evil of vampires and zombies (who also eat and assimilate their victims). Disturbed serial killers such as Dahmer make more evident the ways that all aggression is, at heart, both digestive and cannibalistic, especially insofar as such violence has a ritual aspect. Analysts of Dahmer's dietary practices speculate that his cannibalism was the literalization of his wanting to keep his lovers with him, an extreme psychopathic version of loving without boundaries.

Cannibalism seems, thus, to be a "worst-case scenario," the face of our own aggression looking back in the most basic terms within which othering occurs. Cannibalism is the return of the other—a return to a oneness, a reincorporation as the ultimate goal of taxonomy's otherings. Finally, the relation between taxonomy's otherings, the heteroreproductive narrative, and a taxonomic gender regime lies in the realm of the subject itself. What seems like social organization reiterates the scene of subjective sexuation, separation, and castration trauma perpetually projected onto others. Any subject forced to accept the limits of sexuation (and doing so is intrinsic to becoming a subject in the first place) has fullness cut off, experiences violence or a threat of violence as a part of the traumatic moment of accepting a sex. This drama relates to the sortings of negation—of "I" and "not I"—that form the ego.[40] As constitutive of subjective boundaries, this process of sorting is ultimately aggressive. It secures the sexuated self by containing the other through the repeated replay of differentiation and negation extended outward. At the same time it secures the psychic slippage rehearsed to account for the disturbing remainder that can never fit.

The Gender of Clones

Against or in relation to (at varying moments and in varying degrees) the heteroreproductive narrative persists in a model of cloning in which an individual (re)produces a selfsame version. Our rough popular cultural idea of cloning does not require oppositional binaries, nor does it rest on taxonomies, though cloning is often imagined (in science fiction) as the end product of the crazed imperialism of dictatorships. Cloning completely bypasses the heteroreproductive narrative, evading, in the process, both sex and gender. Because cloning is so far from the heteroreproductive narrative, it both threatens and settles into a non-gendered dynamic of repetition. For the most part, we do not think of cloning as a mode of reproduction at all, but rather as something more like mass production, a species of biological Fordism linked to robotic industrial culture, impersonality, and extensive sterility. One of the few places cloning emerges as a potential mode of human reproduction is in relation to lesbians and gay men who, if they are true to their sexual types, could not reproduce according to typical heterosexual reproductive modes without outside help.

Human culture has been cloning plants for a long time and human cells for at least half a century. Dolly, the cloned sheep, born in 1997, made prosaically material science fiction and fantasy versions of (typically) cloned and expendable minions such as J. R. R. Tolkien's Orcs (at least as Saruman produces them), or *Star Wars'* vengeful millions. In its overpopulated and monstrous forms, this version of the clone as mass-produced, identical, and robotic expresses fears of cloning in terms of an overwhelming sameness, mechanistic dehumanization, and the threatening triumph of the automatonic, uncanny other. Cloning produces an other to the heteroreproductive itself. It is the odd remainder of a heteroreproductive process that has been abrogated, mined, and perverted into the route taken by single-celled organisms and lower forms of life, which, in the divisions of cellular fission, clone themselves.[41]

Significantly, most of these robotic versions of the clone have no gender, or their gender is the gender "clone," such as developed by post-Stonewall gay men. Reacting against old stereotypes of gay men as effeminate, limp-wristed queens, gay male culture of the '70s developed a taut, muscled, mustachioed masculine version of a gay man called a "clone" because all clones looked alike and had a lot of anonymous sex with multiple partners. As Martin P. Levine describes it, gay clones aped "blue-collar workers, they butched it up and acted like macho men. Accepting me-generation values, they searched for self-fulfillment in anonymous sex, recreational drugs, and hard partying. Much to the activists' chagrin, liberation turned the 'Boys in the Band' into doped-up, sexed-out Marlboro men."[42]

In the context of gay male culture, the term "clone" would seem to refer only to the clone's connotation of multiple identicality, but it does carry with it a link between the idea of the clone and the abrogation of the heteroreproductive narrative. When individuals are disconnected in some way from this narrative, binary gender disappears. The lack of a subtending narrative results in a vista of apparent sameness, and in the case of gay male clones, all masculine without a difference. Their sexuality, then, belongs to a narrative of selfsame (i.e., cloning), and what they seem to produce is themselves. If gay male clones have the gender of gay male clone, gay male reproduction becomes a matter of style, sometimes understood in more hysterical discourses as contagion rather than (re)production. This is not to say that gay male clones are neither male nor masculine, but instead that any sense of their regime as gender moves from the realm of the taxonomic to a regime of sameness against which binaries define themselves as difference. Clones become the regime against which gender as difference might be understood as such.

A more extreme example makes even clearer the necessary link between the heteroreproductive narrative, gender as difference, and the ways cloning as an imaginary version of sameness is linked to destruction. In *Star Wars: Episode II—Attack of the Clones*, clone soldiers are deployed as a supernumerary force against the goodness of the democratic empire. Skeletal and functional, the clone forces resemble the hoards of awakened dead in *The Lord of the Rings: The Return of the King*, the Terminator at the end of *The Terminator*, or slicker versions of the zombie craze of the first decades of the twenty-first century. Relentless, conscienceless, and almost unstoppable, clone forces are overwhelming in the paralyzing quantity of their sameness. Because they are outside of any reproductive narrative and because they are all the same and hence fungible, they have nothing to lose. What their massed appearance suggests is the way death itself becomes appended to sameness (instead of chaos) as the background against which difference operates. In the films above, difference is embodied by the film's main characters who defeat the clones against the odds. But the odd circularity of sameness, difference, reproduction, death, and fullness suggests an economy of shifting and ambivalent terms at the heart of human consciousness.

Sexuation represents an interpretation of difference that arrives as a traumatic cut from the plenitude and fullness of existence as part of becoming a subject. As sexual difference, this difference is ambivalent. On the one hand, it promises a return to fullness in the drives' quest for satisfaction, and on the other, it is a warning that any return to fullness is death. As Georges Bataille suggests, reproduction is itself ambivalent, signaling both fulfillment and the inevitable death of the parent.[43] Gender, as one indirect manifestation of sexuation, maps imaginary differences as a mode of subjective suture with the socius. At the same time, its organization of differences hides the inchoate heterogeneous mass that persists anyway to return, not as difference, but as a threatening sameness covering our inability really to organize any differences in other than symbolic or imaginary fashion. Thus the chaos underlying the uncanny, taxonomy, or difference itself is interpreted as a sameness that is deadly.

In their shifting systematic interrelation, gender regimes fend off sameness and distract us from the full deadliness lurking beneath and within our projects. The remainder of taxonomy is not that which does not fit, but rather death.

7 Gender Is as Gender Does

On the Rebound

Gender is an action, a doing. It regulates, locates, and signals desires in complex ways. Sometimes gender appears as the effect of someone's behavior. Subjects who offer persistent care and generosity enact an "ethical" gendering, produced as a feature of the ways subjects regard their obligations and attitudes toward others. Ethical actions undertaken by subjects rebound back to those subjects as genders that are constituted as an effect of this metastatic, cybernetic dynamic. Some lesbians, for example, manifest an ethical gendering of chivalric care as do some nurturing males. This ethical regime accounts for how children understand mother as the gender "mother." Ethical actions do not originate in a fixed gender identity, since perceiving oneself as either courtly or nurturing cancels out the courtly or nurturing effect (it is not courtly to think oneself courtly, nor particularly generous to think oneself nurturing). Nor are these genderings performative in even the extended Butlerian sense that one takes on what one repeats. An ethical gender regime is cybernetic in that actions define the regime that then characterizes the gender of the subject. The nature of a subject's ethical actions may derive from the process of sexuation as subjects adopt positions in relation to lover or beloved, all or not all, especially in the register of the perverse that sees itself as that which can fill the lack in others.

Unconscious sexuations do not, however, necessarily define individual performances of ethical imperatives, which are also influenced by social expectations and cultural models. Even in relation to cultural mores, however, ethical regimes tend to define themselves as counter-normative, even as individuals may seem to embody behaviors valorized culturally (e.g., mothers, the nurturing male). Ethical genders derive from attitudes toward the other that are neither negative, aggressive, nor assimilative, but are, instead, generous, acknowledging, and self-sacrificing. The ethical regime reflects a desire to be necessary to the other as well as to be the object of its desire. No matter how cynically we may understand versions of generosity as self-serving, ethical actions are to some degree always about the other.

Lacan's account of female homosexuality (though not in itself a gender regime) offers one analysis of the relation among genderings, sexuation, and desire. Female homosexuals may, as Lacan notes, take on "the airs of courtly love. In that such a love prides itself more than any other on being the love which gives what it does not have, so it is precisely in this that the homosexual woman excels in relation to what is lacking in her."[1] In this 1958 essay, Lacan hypothesizes that female homosexuality is produced by a demand for love thwarted in the real. In other words, a kind of incestuous impossibility produces an attitude of sacrifice that grounds an ethical behavior. It does not matter whether Lacan has correctly characterized the unconscious formations of lesbian desire; what does matter is the ethic of giving that results—an ethic that Lacan comments makes up for the "absence of the sexual relation by pretending that it is we who put an obstacle to it."[2] Because Lacan suggests there is actually no such thing as sexual rapport insofar as each individual's desire is for a desired object or aspect of self in the other (sexual rapport is self with self), all sexual rapport is feigned in one way or another. Courtliness is the dynamic of feigning feigning, which perhaps paradoxically produces some rapport in generosity itself. Lacan produces his formulation of courtly love in relation to males, for whom courtliness is "the only way to elegantly pull off the absence of the sexual relationship."[3] But, he comments, "it is truly the most staggering thing that has ever been tried. But how can we expose its fraud?"[4] How can one, in other words, show up the feigning of an absence?

Lacan links the courtly to what he calls "the discourse of fealty, of fidelity to the person," which he says refers ultimately to "the discourse of the master."[5] The courtly is an ethics and practice of consistent, principled behavior such as fidelity. Fidelity means being true and loyal to the person, understood on one level to be faithfulness to the object of desire, but on another, to be an ethic of generosity and sacrifice, itself feigned by master discourses, usually in the guise of religion, but also by philanthropy. Fidelity radiates in both directions, producing a gendering rebound formed both by a sense of virtue and by any acknowledgment of fidelity from the recipient other. With fidelity, both parties may get what they want based on never getting what they want. If a subject's desire is for desire (as lesbian desire has been theorized to be), then courtliness is one mode of perpetuating desire through a gender regime.[6]

As a gender regime, ethical behaviors produce a reverse metastasis. Typically, a metastasis occurs when someone repels a characterization back to its originator: "You're a pig." "No, you're a pig." Fidelity produces a gender regime when a call, originating with the one behaving in a courtly fashion, returns to the originating subject as the gender this subject becomes: "I swear fealty to you my lady," says the subject. "You are faithful and courtly," says the object of desire, whereby the subject, engaged in fidelity, becomes faithful as a rebound. In this way, we might understand as ethical (among other regimes) the gendering of some butch lesbians; this is not because such figures are masculine, but because they have been recognized as courtly. This is different in systemic function, but may be associated with such formulations as Judith Halberstam's "female masculinity," itself a swirl of regimes misidentified as binary, especially insofar as such apparently oxymoronic phrases appear to shake up binary systems (while of course substantiating them).[7] We may also link courtliness to male subjects, but the regime is an ethical rather than a social regime, organized around acts rather than a reductive compulsion, or as an attribute of taxonomic interpretations of masculinity and femininity.

Rebound

The forms and vestiges of ethical behaviors that rebound back to subjects as genderings change through time and in differing contexts and circumstances. What might have been read as courtly at the time of Radclyffe Hall, for example, no longer looks the same—is no longer, for example, so etched by class and sex signifiers. Such genderings may still be marked by such signifiers, but the signifiers have changed. It is also possible for such genderings to manifest only as behaviors. This is often the case with the "mother" as a gendering. The ethical gendering attributed to and as mothering accompanies multiple other regimes, which may themselves belong to other ethical dynamics—"wife," for example, or caretaker. And we always know when mother is "mother" and not something else. Not all mothers are "mother," and few mothers are "mother" all the time.

In some subcultures, these ethical genderings are overtly ritualized—signified by appearance, manner, linguistic practices, and modes of social conduct. The styles of these rituals change, so that, for example, butch/femme culture of the late 1950 and 1960s in the United States might interpret the butch figure as chivalrous, but also as masochistic and suffering. Versions in the first decades of the twenty-first century are less overtly "butch" (which has shifted its signification into modes of "transgender") but may take on other gendering signifiers including behaviors, speech, dress, et cetera.

Body languages may be the most dispositive of all cues to ethical genderings. These differ from context to context, depending on social class, race, age, ethnic origin, location, sex, and other attributes. A nurturing male, for example, may avoid aggressive body postures, an absence noticed only after a period of association. Chivalrous females may stay in the background until they perceive they are needed, while mother figures may persistently hover.

One other aspect of this ethical rebound is that it is almost always anachronistic—out of time and out of sync. Ethical behaviors tend to present as old-fashioned—as yet another kind of "rebound" to a previous time. In this sense they are both far more intelligible in retrospect than they might have originally been, and nostalgic insofar as this intelligibility seems to point toward a simpler mode of interaction.

Re-*Bound*

The Wachowskis' 1996 film *Bound* relies on the operations of an ethical gender regime, anatomizing the relation between behavior and gendering as well as the anachronistic quality of the chivalrous "butch." The film also reveals one other aspect of the ethical gendering process: the necessity of a decoy or distraction that enables and perpetuates the rebound's metastasis as an accruing and reverberating field. The film is already stylized and nostalgic, set within the domain of the mob, a group for which fealty is one of the most highly valued requirements. As a mode of organization among men, the omertà enforced by fidelity as well as by the idealized hierarchical, patriarchal economy of all organized crime ventures exists in the landscape of idealized father/son relations. It is also a formalized chivalric practice.

In *Bound*, Caesar (Joe Pantoliano), money launderer and cousin of mob boss Gino Marzzone, is given the task of tracing how another mob member managed to embezzle $2 million before being caught, tortured, and killed. Caesar's conventionally fashionable girlfriend, Violet (Jennifer Tilly), an apparently dutiful and loyal mistress, becomes attracted to the recently released convict Corky (Gina Gershon), who is remodeling the apartment next door. Corky somewhat unrealistically bears the marks of butchness in her exaggerated walk, her labyris necklace and prison tattoos, her pickup truck, clothes, tidy-whitey men's underwear, job as a laborer, et cetera. Working for the mobster who owns the apartment building, Corky already knows the fealty drill. As Violet and Corky begin their flirtation and are nearly discovered by Caesar, he tries to buy Corky's loyalties by offering her a bundle of cash so he does not have to "worry" about her.

Although schematically the two women form what looks like a heterosexual couple, the film's plot depends on their being overlooked—Violet being feminine and invisible and Corky being asymptotic and even more invisible. The two women deliberately play on the issue of loyalty among the men, depending on the fear and internecine battles generated by the mob's fealty model to sway Caesar and his associates into making assumptions about what has happened when Corky replaces the embezzled money with stacks of newspaper. Deploying layered interlocking lures, each of which consists of providing a plausible malefactor for the mob to blame, Violet and Corky steal the money while making certain the mob does not suspect them.

The entire plot depends on Violet shifting her loyalty from Caesar to Corky. Corky, who has been in prison because her last partner in crime ratted her out, advises Violet that the success of the scheme depends on trust, although what she does not yet understand is that the success of the entire scheme will depend even more on the ethical relation between the women. And not just on Corky's courtliness. Violet does not merely occupy the aloof position of the lady object of courtly attentions, she also practices a courtly ethics of her own. In the course of the film, Violet's gender morphs from the primarily social to the ethical. In switching her loyalty from Caesar to Corky, Violet, the almost perfectly feminine mistress, has shifted from her slightly vertiginous masquerade of social femininity to a reciprocal fealty with Corky. Her social gender operates as a decoy enabling her schematic regime shift to hero, collaborator, and ethically reciprocal partner. When Caesar catches her phoning Corky in the next apartment, Violet tries to protect Corky, even as Caesar tortures Violet. In the end, as Caesar closes in on Corky, Violet shoots him point blank, a step Caesar did not believe she could take. Mistaking Violet's relation with Corky as merely a substitute for her relation with him, Caesar has no reason to understand the shift in the quality of her loyalty.

Corky behaves in the expected chivalrous fashion. Heedless of danger to herself, she goes to Violet's rescue when Caesar discovers Violet's infidelity. She plots the entire heist, not only out of greed, but also to rescue Violet from her mob moll life. At the end of the film, mob fortune in hand, Caesar disposed of, and the mob fooled into looking where Caesar stashed the money, Corky and Violet, identical in obscuring sunglasses, drive off in Corky's new pickup truck. Before they drive off, Corky takes off her glasses, looks at Violet, and asks, "Do you know the difference between you and me?" When Violet says "No," Corky finishes, "Me neither." This final appeal to the protagonists' sameness appears to be an open and ironic acknowledgment of the schematic disposition of lesbian figures as a version of short-circuiting sameness. In terms of the gender morphing that enables the scheme, however, the comment also suggests that Violet's gendering regimes have altered as an effect of an ethical rebound.

Muscle Mom; or, The Sudden Dimensionality of Masculine Nurture

An example of the same rebounding dynamic occurs in the case of certain nurturing males. It is difficult to find examples of nurturing males who are not also homosexualized, such as Albert Goldman (Nathan Lane) in *The Birdcage* (1996), Robert Preston as Toddy in *Victor Victoria* (1982), or the gay male caretaker characters in such films as *Love! Valour! Compassion!* (1997). The genre of daddy turned mommy or strong man turned babysitter films—such as *Mr. Mom* (1983), *Kindergarten Cop* (1990), and more recently *The Pacifier* (2005)—present males as accidentally, and only reluctantly, nurturing. Forced, usually by highly macho professional circumstances into child care, figures such as Arnold Schwarzenegger and Vin Diesel are burnished with a patina of generosity and sacrifice typically reserved either for gay males or for male nurses. Like butch lesbians, ethical care rebounds to he-men with a vague suggestion of the feminine, but unlike butches, these heterosexual macho males resist their roles until the regard of their charges rebounds back to them. Their gendering shifts to participate in the regime of the ethical where they are not feminized, but dimensionalized.

In Western culture, daddy figures are not incapable of kindness, but their kindness is shy, unwilling, and clumsy. Since, in the regime of the social, masculinity is poised on the edge of a risk of emasculation, participating happily in child care or housework constitutes a sign of slippage. This has nothing to do with the fact that we have high regard for men who can nurture, but it rather suggests the occasional incommensurability of regimes, especially insofar as some regimes—such as the social—tend to be one-dimensional and superficial by definition. Evincing both willingness and innate kindness toward charges has a tendency to rebound to male figures as depth, when they are forced by circumstances into functions taxonomically assigned to females, such as nurturing,

Before the appearance of sympathetic muscle-bound heroes in the 1980s and '90s, figures such as Cary Grant and James Garner occasionally played masculine figures manifesting this soft side. In both *Houseboat* (1958) and *Father Goose* (1964), Grant played men forced into child care. The effect was to produce the illusion that Grant's masculinity had depth. The rebound from nurturing produced a more complex and multifaceted figure who became all the more masculine by virtue of the fact that child care did not threaten him. The same is true for Garner, whose forays into child care in *The Thrill of It All* (1963) and the appearance of homosexual courtship in *Victor Victoria* exposed his tender side while making his masculinity unassailable.

When the muscled rather than the suave become nurturing, the effect is often comic, but no less effective in providing the illusion of dimensionality to he-men probably more in need of another side than the charismatic Grant or Garner. Schwarzenegger even evinces this tenderness in *Terminator 2: Judgment Day* when John Connors's mother (Linda Hamilton) comments that the cyborg Terminator is a better father for John than a human would be. In *Kindergarten Cop*, Schwarzenegger plays an undercover police officer forced to take over a kindergarten class to protect a child in danger of being kidnaped by his criminal father. Schwarzenegger's militaristic child discipline soon bends to the humane as the character reveals his intrinsic sense of fun and kindness as an effect of the rebound of his care for the children.

Men nurturing other men also produces a rebound of ethical gender. This nurturing goes beyond simple male bonding and soldiers' duty to an ethical behavior of care, a species of "daddyness" extending beyond paternity. Fatherhood and motherhood may also rebound as a gender, which is why children often understand their parents' genders first as a behavior and role, and only later as social or taxonomic ("Is Daddy a boy?" "Was Mommy ever a little girl?"). Daddyness is mentoring and care that go beyond the familial and beyond friendship, not that daddyness is deeper or more intense than friendship, but in that the attention and care are ethical in addition to emotional (and often the ethical comes first). New submarine sailors have "daddies," more experienced sailors who show them the ropes. War movies have a long tradition of soldiers whose homosocial bonding is ethical—that is, it plays out the care and responsibility of one for the other. In *Top Gun* (1986), for example, the older Goose (Anthony Edwards) and the unit commander Metcalf (Tom Skerritt) both evince an ethical care for Maverick (Tom

Cruise): Goose as a contemporary who loses his life and Metcalf as a father substitute. In more gritty ground combat or claustrophobic ship films, there are always a couple of soldiers bound by an ethical relation. In *Mister Roberts* (1955), for example, Mr. Roberts (Henry Fonda) operates almost entirely as a hermetic daddy, caring deeply and on principle for his crew in the face of the despotic ship's captain. John Wayne is the universal daddy of gritty combat films.

In films, documentaries, and plays about the AIDS epidemic, gay men often exhibit this species of nurturing toward one another. In combat films, such nurturing often becomes literal when one soldier is injured; in AIDS films, the interrelations among the characters are almost always ethical, in addition to friendships, romance, and desire. The ethical character of these relationships extending beyond or in addition to sexual or romantic interest makes gay male characters heroes. Their willingness to fight for the rights and wishes of partners and friends against the heterophilic, familial aegis of law and culture casts these characters as honorable, faithful, and chivalric. These behaviors rebound onto the gay male characters as an intrinsic part of some gay male genders as in, for example, *Longtime Companion* (1989) or *Love! Valour! Compassion!*

In relation to extrafamilial ethical genders, family roles and relations can take on the rebound of an ethical care not necessarily as an extension of parental roles, but as the rebounding effects of ethical and caring behaviors. Not all fathers and mothers participate in this regime, nor do the roles themselves necessarily bespeak an ethic. Fathers and mothers can be cruel, selfish, removed, and/or abusive; in short, they can be completely unethical. Although we like to associate ethical behavior with parental roles and pretend to be shocked when parents fail expectations (which they often do), as a gender regime the rebounding ethics associated with parental care attach only to the ideal and the unusual, the culturally romanticized, and those individuals who privilege ethics above selfishness. The feminist deployment of maternity or even sorority as models for relations among females is inspired by an idealistic and ethical model of motherhood and sisterly care, which, of course, rarely works because very few individuals persist within this ethical gender regime. Maternity shares in other, less laudable behaviors such as cannibalism. Sisters compete.

Because ethical behavior in itself has neither gender nor taxonomy even though we associate certain behaviors with certain societal roles, sexes, and genders (caretaking and maternity with female, for example), and because ethical gender occurs through a bounceback dynamic, ethical behavior offers a particularly clear example of the way in which all genders are dynamics instead of roles, identities, ontologies, or simple stylistic choices. One is never, for example, chivalric because one is butch. Rather, certain versions of butchness are the effect of chivalric behavior. No one is ever nurturing because he is a daddy; nurturers can become daddies. Ethical behaviors produce a feedback loop that contributes to other gender regimes in the production of particular gender complexes. For example, younger "baby" butches often evince a naïve chivalry that combines with signifiers of masculine social gender, vertiginous gender expressions (drag kingness), the metamorphic, the asymptotic, and social femininity to produce the phenomenon of the "soft butch." Manifestations of social femininity, vertiginous gender, and nurturing produce a recognizable version of the gay male queen. The already physically enhanced masculinity of muscled nurturers is multiplied into hypermasculinity by the dimensional effects of their hidden tenderness.

Black Holes and Women Who Have It

If generosity, caring, and sacrifice rebound as a gender regime, then does a similar effect occur with less culturally laudable behaviors? Does the ethical rebound as well from evil or from the abuse of power? The dynamic of the ethical manifests itself by dimensionalizing genders—expanding and complicating regimes. As the opposite of ethical behavior, evil reappears as a narrowing and simplifying rebound. Instead of dimensionalizing subjects, malevolent behavior reduces subjects to a single (sometimes phallic) point—a devil's horn, a pointed tail, the black half-swastika of a mustache, a black helmet, clawlike fingernails, Cruella De Vil's (of the famed Disney movie *101 Dalmatians* [1961]) cigarette holder. The intense singularity of this point is a signifier of its potency: all desire collapsed into itself, a black hole from which nothing escapes, swallowing all gestures.

This evil aspect of an ethical regime tends to appear as cartoonish—as the hyperbolic reversal of any serious ennoblement. Just as generosity rebounds to the nurturing male as depth of character, evil behaviors make him shrink. Body language, for example, is hunched and crabbed, as in the travestied version of Dr. Evil in the Austin Powers films. Despotic power rebounds as singularity at the expense of others. The unfortunate choice of the term "blackness" as a way to understand this evil is itself an effect of the way this short-circuited rebound pulls into itself and never lets anything escape—like a black hole. Its cartoon figures are most often garbed in black veiling costumes—caped vampires, Darth Vader–like attire from *Star Wars*, SS Blackshirts—or in hidden lairs under volcanoes, in caves, sewers, or shrunk to the point of invisibility—every villain, ranging from Lex Luthor of DC Comics' *Superman*, to James Bond's nemesis Blofeld, to Sauron of J. R. R. Tolkien's *Lord of the Rings*, or the villain of J. K. Rowling's wizarding world in the Harry Potter series, Lord Voldemort.

As power usurped beyond the ethical this evil is phallic, either as a species of incredible overcompensation, or as a hijacking, or both. It sequesters the Phallus for the self in a taxonomy arranged around a single point of having. Any rebound exists within a nonradiant closed circuit. The primary dynamic of this black hole is the usurpation of the gaze, the occupation of the all-seeing panopticon, verging on the uncanny. The most obvious example of this purely evil, unseeable, but all-seeing eye is Sauron in *The Lord of the Rings*. Sauron has distributed his power in ten rings whose ownership by others binds them reciprocally to him as long as he wields the single ring by which the other nine are brought together. The figure of the ring is the emblem of this mode of rebound, especially as it demonstrates the circular and self-contained economy of evil. Evil has no outside to itself.

The confusion between evil and power is, in the regime of the ethical, a matter of degree and disposition. Female characters can occupy a similar site of evil internal rebound as males, but their operation of power is more broadly circuitous. Though much rarer than male evildoers, females occupying a veiled site of singularity, such as Lady Macbeth of William Shakespeare's *Macbeth*, are horrors indeed, as such females become a fearsomely veiled phallus off-limits to everyone. Unless females "soften" their use of power with large doses of camouflaging generosity, the rebound of their exercise is an attribution of phallic usurpation or "castrating bitch," which females often try to redress through masquerade, or the overcompensations of social femininity. Because females always threaten lack, they are always evil to some degree (i.e., the "castrating bitch" as any female who stands up to a male at all), but they are rarely evil because in the cultural imaginary they rarely have the power to be evil. Female evil is always minor and parasitic, indirect, sneaky, and betraying, practiced through their mates whom they dupe (again see *Macbeth*; also, consider the variety of female serial killers on several "evil women" websites).[8] Medusa may best figure this series of phallic contradictions with her head full of snakes and her glance (or a glance at her) turning people into stone.

Evil in women most often comes down to mere bitchiness manifested as narcissism, self-centeredness, and pettiness. Such behaviors rebound only as intrinsically feminine, as proof of the truth of misogyny in a patriarchal imaginary. Unethical behaviors, in other words, never dimensionalize, but only narrow and intensify as the bad essence of a gender presumed to align with the essential characteristics of a sex—a sex assumed to have such characteristics in the first place. We never really get rid of the essentialism linked to sexual difference; we only layer and disburse it. Evil males overreach their phallic powers. Evil women's power is petty.

Negative versions of ethical rebounding tend to be imaginary, archetypal, and projected onto a figure one fears. They manifest as projections onto characters removed from the interpersonal into the realm of the mythical. Although there are truly evil people, the sequestering dynamic of the negatively ethical accrues into fiction instead of rebounding as a mode of gendering based on behavior. The reduction to an evil archetype operates as the limit of gender, where genderings ossify as essence. As a declension of the phallus into the Phallus and as the closing down of further systemic exchange, evil archetypes are extremes to be avoided. Their possibility provides the terminal points of the system—the imaginary beyond which gender cannot go—but within those extremes, gender systems circulate in endless permutation.

8 Spurious Displays

Spurious gender displays continually emerge, morph, and disappear as an effect of unresolvable contradictions, cultural pressures, commodity attacks, and/or large-scale anxieties. Sometimes these displays repeat earlier manifestations of phenomena—as in the case of vampires, zombies, goths, nerds, hippies, and dandies. Occasionally, spurious displays seem to emerge anew, as in gay male clones or the recent "girl" phenomenon. These displays are versions of existing gender regimes in that they still respond to basic relations to the gaze, the voice, and narrative positions, but they tend to be organized around thematic styles that appear to push back against social and taxonomic gender regimes by organizing themselves around otherworldly activities, fixations on style, contemporary cultural narratives, and/or the signifiers of a particular social attitude. These regimes also quickly align with identity fictions understood as individual positionings within groups of like-styled others as well as in contradistinction to mainstream culture. These spurious regimes also seem far more agenic than other regimes, the apparent choice of wielders who deploy these regimes (and deploying a regime may itself be a gender regime like the vertiginous) as a way to signal social position, attitude, and perhaps, finally, desire. But even the "choice" of these is up to a plethora of other factors ranging from unconscious positionings and subjective motivations to peer pressure. Such spurious displays also expose the ways gender regimes shift historically and contextually.

The eighteenth-century male fop, for example, may well have been a spurious gender regime organized in relation to a hyperbolized set of class affectations, perhaps answering an anxiety about status, while the nineteenth-century American Southern belle manifests a hyperbolized social feminine ideal in relation to the presence of slave women. Certainly, both of these phenomena have multiple determinants and work to signify both class and gender extremes. But they are gender regimes sharing in the social and the vertiginous insofar as they each organize a self-presentation specifically through an appeal to hyperbolized versions of social gender as something to be seen. Their hyperbole, exceptionality, and ideality appear to remove such subjects from all but an exclusive circulation, while also situating them as parodies of an ideal and as perverse counter-reflections of the gender system's contradictory valorization of impossible and wooden perfection.

When these spurious displays organize around new, unfamiliar, or opportunistic dynamics such as the recent zombie craze, they tend to over-deploy commodity signifiers of class or identity, using display as a means of rejecting or burlesquing decorum, and they formulate self-conscious and cynical philosophies about the difference between appearance and reality, which they perform through their mode of self-presentation. Because spurious displays respond to and reflect contemporaneous impasses primarily in the social regime, they morph and reorganize quickly. Although they may seem to have some staying power as character "types," their meaning shifts from context to context, often providing a referent and platform for the formation of a similar but different spurious display. So the "girl," for example, takes up parodically the signifiers of a previous generation of successful young female actresses (the women on the television show *Friends*, for example), organizing them around a cynical reflection of "girl" possibility and empowerment.

Fops

Spurious genders are temporary phenomena, reminding us of the historical changeability of gender regimes and demonstrating the ways gender regimes respond to, reflect, and are produced within sets of larger material and cultural factors. Impasses in culture provoke the formulation of spurious displays, which align with existing regimes in different ways and provide alternative answers to particular enigmas. The fop, for example, manifests an almost feminizing excess of display as a way to assure both class and aesthetic ascendency in an emerging industrial and commoditized culture in which old, landed privilege is expanding to include the nouveaux riches. Who is a gentleman in a culture in which both the integrity of labor and the privilege of inherited wealth have been displaced by a class of wealthy entrepreneurs? If bourgeois values of virtuous industry openly begin to replace the prerogatives of leisure as intrinsically masculine, how do men of leisure understand their masculinity? In his hyperbolic display of display, the fop draws attention to his decorativeness as a cynical assertion of class ascendancy and highly stylized crass excessiveness. The self-involvement of dress signifies both disdain for bourgeois values and the performance of intrinsic individual value magnified by sartorial extremes and social affectation. In its layering of signifiers, foppishness is a vague feminization that challenges the presumptive link between business and masculinity by displacing busyness onto the body itself.

The fop morphs into the nineteenth century's decadent dandy, who, still interested in clothing and appearance, deploys style less as a sign of wealth and class than as a signifier of individuality and exceptionalism in relation to the enlarging practices of mass production and the increasingly smug category of the bourgeoisie.[1] In the nineteenth century, the dandy's sartorial splendor responded increasingly to crises of individuality provoked by the democratization of the aesthetic. The dandy takes up an aestheticism that separates his sensibilities from those of the philistines, linking good taste with masculinity as simultaneously a hallmark and a burlesque of civilization. The dandy is the display of presumed vantage by which the bad taste of other regimes can be appreciated. The most notorious dandy, Oscar Wilde, used dress and behavior as spectacle designed to set himself off as unusual as well as to enact a mode of cultural critique characterized by its forking ambivalence. Dandies organize around irony; they are and say what they mean by brazenly being and saying the opposite of what they mean. In this sense, while the fop plays on anxieties about the feminized uselessness of wealthy men of leisure by appropriating a feminized display, the dandy produces a complex set of double entendres that locate the display as partially anamorphic—as in need of constant decoding.

Belles

The feminine version of the dandy is the Southern belle that secures femininity as a pure form of other in relation to obvious other versions of female—the slave woman, the cracker—as a way to certify the other woman's de-feminization. Like the dandy, the belle is hyperbolic; like the dandy, the belle must be decoded, her excessive politeness an indication that she indeed is never saying what she means or says it by saying it otherwise. "The main characteristic of the Southern Belle," claims the *Dixie Belle* website, "is inner strength and control hidden by exaggerated femininity."[2] "The non-Southerner," the site continues, "may see only the appearance of the Belle and think her shallow and vain, but she appears helpless and demure when actually she's independent, stubborn, and a survivor." If the dandy is about securing individuality, the belle is about taking control, about operating the system that would otherwise make wealthy women mere objects. Both are excessive; both must be decoded; both combine a sophisticated and complex combination of sartorial and mannered style that represents a fascinating duplicity in relation to the very gender stereotypes that would seem, in one way or another, to limit them. Hyperbolizing ideality turns its appearance into a means of control.

Some believe the Southern belle persists as a type, but her function as a gender display is long past.[3] What remains is a character type, parasitic on the regime's dynamic of anamorphic control; but in the contemporary environment, it becomes a mode of flirtation and travesty rather than the negotiation of class differences among women. The Southern belle of nineteenth-century plantation culture—or even of Scarlett O'Hara of *Gone with the Wind*—has become a regional identity signifier and variant of social femininity.

Goths

Currently, the commodity-object-of-desire systems of late capitalism produce what might seem to be a mode of identity clarity. As commodities come to signify particular subject positions, the problem of determining one's identity is taken over by pre-thematized accessories associated with leisure practices, attitudes, and aspirations—all still organized through the dynamics of existing gender regimes. Typically, commodity themes produce stylized versions of existing gender regimes. Male athletes and beauty queens continue their exemplification of the ideals of the social regime, while geeks are understood as asymptotic, occasionally anamorphic and/or ethical. The stereotype of the gang member, persisting in American popular culture since the 1950s, offers its version of the social mingled with the vertiginous, the asymptotic, and the ethical. All are still taxonomized; all still make sense within the swirl of coexistent regimes.

Commodity culture, however, also produces its discontents, who cynically seeing commercialized manipulation produce spurious identity themes as protest, paralysis, or ineffable difference. The 1960s witnessed a protest response in the form of hippies, whose subject manifestation was less a matter of gender than of lifestyle. The '70s produced punk, and the '90s produced goth, as arguably the former morphs into the latter. Scholars of goth trace its inspiration to late-'70s and early-'80s punk bands such as Bauhaus and Siouxsie and the Banshees.[4] Fans, a denomination itself produced through certain identity processes of social location and disaffection, picked up the bands' predilection for black clothing as well as the dark introspection of their lyrics.

As a subcultural denomination, however, goth cybernetically produced itself as even more followers associated the term with gothic revival and gothic horror and imported signifiers associated with vampires, horror in general (spiders), and exaggerated religious iconography. With black clothing, dyed black hair, black fingernails, piercings, and the cultivation of a wan "undead" look, goth followers also affected clothing styles that seemed to cross the lines of gender taxonomy. One goth commentator observes that "three words sum up what the stereotypical goth is all about: death, pretension, and angst."[5] Their "pretension," however, is precisely about a negotiation of cultural exhaustion. Their predilection for the vampiric presents metaphorically an understanding of the production of sex/gender regimes and identity as depleting and parasitic. Like the dandy and the belle embracing hyperbolically the gender and identitarian enigmas they cannot solve, the goth solves them by incorporating an almost pop version of death as style. Goth is post-outrage, deflecting feared meaninglessness into a fascination with the occult. Their cross-gender affectation, mainly exhibited by males, is the performance of a brave impersonation and defiance of being subject to death, to imprisoning and meaningless normative identity categories, to the emptiness of commodity culture. The androgynous character goth can sometimes take exists in relation to both a dramatization of the site of the "beloved" of death and the irrelevance of social gender categorizations in the face of more dire and dramatic concerns. Eschewing and counter-deploying social gender signifiers, such as skirts, corsets, and makeup, also provide the subject with a sense of universal management in an arena in which binary gender seems less relevant.

Although goth would seem most likely a subcultural social formation, it is also spurious display insofar as the enigma it cannot solve is the problem of binary gender itself in relation to an apocalyptic worldview that defends against death by seeming to embrace it. Goth gender indeterminability is linked to vampiristic evocations of death-in-life and life-in-death, the ambivalence of their status and participation in other cultural institutions, and their resigned rejection of the mainstream. Androgyny produces a kind of stylized leveling linked to the ascendency of death over (re)production. As specifically a gender display, goth locates subjects as metaphors—as in an arrested process of metamorphosis—represented by evocations of exhaustion, vampirism, leather culture, piercings, tattoos, and the performance of outrage (much like biker culture—another spurious display). This performance is finally a defiance of other gender and commodity regimes by enacting the parasitic quality of their operation.

Even as I write this, goth continues to alter, becoming itself a commodity alternative, a style without substance, a shorthand of faded critique, and finally passé. At this moment in 2014, zombies and transgender dominate a rebellious gender scene, both pretending to cross the lines they reassert as they cross them.

Conclusion

I exercise my faculty of synthesis here because again I must
proceed with precision among sounds, bodies and institutions.

—Nicole Brossard, *Picture Theory*

This is neither an extended list of categories nor a more complex taxonomy. Genderings play dynamically among four registers: time, attitude, sexuation, and desire. The combinations producing genderings are infinite and perpetually changing. There is no way to trace these multifarious possibilities back to any original theme or desire in subjects, nor do subjects necessarily retain any completely stable formations, even unconsciously. Nothing undergirds this process; it comprises an extended field from the subjective unconscious to cultural display, from social interactions to desires and fantasies, from available material in the symbolic to the foundations of subjective drives. Accounting for such a holistic system is impossible, as it is an open system on which there can be no perspective, only the imaginary of a chimeric vantage. Instead of a structural (i.e., binary), linear (i.e., existing within a unidirectional, developmental, cause/effect logic), and compulsive mimesis, gender is a systemic, machinic process—networked, inter-inflective, responsive to any number of catalysts from any number of registers, perpetually changeable. The ideal representation of gender would be a moving hologram in which the various dynamics and attitudes shift, veer, alter, and recombine to produce a flickering, multi-dimensional, animated, ultimately synthetic display. Imagine people surrounded by such holograms that both do and do not represent some desire, by some psychical track that can never be traced back—that is scribed but not transcribed, that shifts the moment that it is "read" or apprehended.

But we already know this. We already know that people change gender regimes, displays, varieties, versions . . . whatever, from one context to another, from one age, one context, one person to another. We already know how to "read" these genders, even if they can never be read. So what? As Judith Butler notes in her critique of the work of Monique Wittig in *Gender Trouble*, "If the multiplication of gender possibilities expose and disrupt the binary reifications of gender, what is the nature of such a subversive enactment? How can such an enactment constitute a subversion?"[1] What advantage does seeing gender in this complex fashion give us? What does it enable us to do?

It enables us finally, perhaps, to untangle gender from sexual difference—a "sex" that as Joan Copjec insists, "does not budge." "For it is," she continues, "by making it conform to the signifier that you oblige sex to conform to social dictates, to take on social content."[2] Being able to see gender and identities as not conforming "to the signifier"—as not reflecting individual sexuation in any traceable way—enables us perhaps, finally, to displace gender from sexual difference. And insofar as sexuation precedes any notion of subjective identity—a subject must be sexed to engage in the orthopedics of identity (that consistently mutable fiction)—we might be able to displace identity and its ever-expanding categories from the center of political/cultural attention, where they have accomplished only minimal advantage for anyone on the disadvantaged side of symbolic asymmetries (patriarchy, colonialism, racism, capitalism). Engaging with the asymmetrical politics of sexual difference itself, and especially with their fictional underpinning that begins precisely with the "signifier" (the Phallus) that exceeds any possibility of signification and yet stands in the place of a very vulnerable signified, might enable a focus on the pervasive dynamics by which groups of carelessly categorized people (people conformed "to social dictates") are demeaned, put at a disadvantage, oppressed, their capacities wasted in the name of a violent "signifier"-based othering that continues no matter how liberated, proliferative, or varietal we might be about either gender or identity. As Luce Irigaray declares, "Women's exploitation is based upon sexual difference; its solution will come only through sexual difference."[3] The unjustified, irrational asymmetries of broad structural binaries premised on that belief in an "all" somewhere—patriarchy, capitalism, racism—and their adherent oppressions are the real problem. And that signifier "all, phallus" poses a real problem insofar as its operations inveigle all registers of existence from the unconscious to the institutional, from interpersonal relations to broadly Foucauldian dispositions of power.[4]

Gender is a lure that distracts us from the very problem it seems to represent.

Lost in Translation

Luce Irigaray in *je, tu, nous*: "L'espèce humaine est divisée en *deux genres* qui en assurent la production et la reproduction." Translated: "The human species is divided into *two genders* which ensure its production and reproduction." In a book that insists that the site of any sociopolitical activism can only occur in a direct encounter with sexual difference and its essential, mythical, increasingly under-rationalizable asymmetries (though none of this has anything to do with reason), it is highly symptomatic to find a mistranslation of the very terms at issue at the very moment of its trenchantly direct statement. "Deux genres" does not translate to *two genders*, but instead to "two kinds or types." In the French, "genre" does not mean gender, but "kind." This "genre" clearly refers to sexual difference. This mistranslation enacts the ways "gender" occludes, misdirects, and diverts the matter at hand from sexual difference to the subjective and social fictions of identity. That this mistranslation happens as a matter of course in the United States is not simply an effect of a belief in inclusive enfranchisement, or that social identities are the basis for rights activism, or even a touchy distaste for the word "sex." The mistranslation is the effect of a hoaxic confusion by which fictions (both gender and identity) stand in the place of, obscure, and misdirect sociopolitical action in such a way that sexual difference itself not only persists, but becomes even more insistent. Although we might understand the erosion of women's rights in the United States as the necessary compensations on behalf of a crumbling patriarchy, those compensations in themselves produce even more disadvantage premised on a sexual difference that makes even less sense than it might have, say, in biblical times.

Any political action on behalf of "gender" in the United States is hamstrung by confusion from the start. Gender fronts and actually endorses a variety of very different and much more basic structures while simultaneously diverting any energy away from the actual structural causes of inequities. Confusing gender for sexual difference, for example, enables the easy alignment of desire for "opposites" with "normative" sexual desire with reproduction with family with the asymmetrical and delusory power distributions of patriarchy premised on sexual difference. Binary gender guarantees the entire imaginary tidiness of this structure, as it seems to repeat itself on every level, from individual desire to social order. At the same time, it enables a confusion between gender and sexual orientation, which, if we subscribe to the more complex understandings of sexuation, has very little to do with gender as an incitement to desire and everything to do with how individuals unconsciously situate themselves in relation to ascriptions of power and possibility. Sexuations cannot be distilled into binaries that accord tidily with the patriarchal asymmetries of contemporary American culture. In fact, sexual orientation (or preference or identity) has very little to do with sexual difference even if we seem to define orientations according to sets of binary oppositions. Conflating sexual orientation with gender on various fronts (and especially in the interminable list of GLBTAI . . .) is the primary symptom of a deliberate confusion that perpetuates the delusions of complementarity (that itself stands in for and hides the asymmetry at its core), instead of liberating subjects from a way of thinking that has subordinated one sex in favor of the other (with no good reason) for millennia. Tying everything up in neat alignment continues to occlude the specificities that might enable a gradual shift from the inherent asymmetries of binarism to a field of differences that cannot be contained within or support the dying patriarchal alibi.

Nonetheless, comingling binary categories premised on very

different formations seems to provide some current advantage in terms of civil rights in the United States. Interpretations of both the Fourteenth Amendment and the Civil Rights Act of 1964 set out very specific categories for rights' protection. The Equal Employment Opportunity Commission (EEOC) defines these categories on its website as "race, color, religion, sex (including pregnancy), national origin, age (40 or older), disability or genetic information." The EEOC website also has a page devoted specifically to "Enforcement Protections for LGBT Workers."[5] Already the confusions among sex, sexual orientation, and gender proliferate, requiring incredible intellectual gymnastics and elastic mental stretchings to arrive at EEOC protections, where sexual difference, gender, and sexual preference are all squeezed under the category "sex." The commission confuses sex and gender in finding a rationale for protecting transgendered workers under the "sex" provisions, while it also determines "that discrimination against lesbian, gay, and bisexual individuals based on sex-stereotypes, such as the belief that men should only date women or that women should only marry men, is discrimination on the basis of sex under Title VII," as the commission reads sexual orientation as "sex role stereotyping."

The EEOC conflates sexual difference with sexual orientation with gender when it comes to non-normative (or, let us read non-male, non-heterosexual) possibilities. Given the fact that male subjects also have rights and protections, the "sex" this seems concerned with is female. Should a government agency equate "female" with "sex"? This confusion seems to reiterate the conflations that already produce patriarchal asymmetries. Although federal anti-discrimination statutes seem to serve various groups by providing transient protections, the conflation of sexual difference, sexual desire, and gender is only a matter of interpretation by the EEOC and does not provide any constitutional protection for any of these activities, identities, positions, or desires, especially insofar as sex is not a constitutionally protected category. The EEOC's evident confusion, used here to extend rights, is always subject to the EEOC changing its mind.

In overseeing the civil protections offered by the Civil Rights Act of 1964, the EEOC by necessity shepherds an "identity" politics, which at first glance would seem to defy this perpetuated binarizing: "Race, color, religion, sex (including pregnancy), national origin, age (40 or older), disability or genetic information." The list continues to annex additional "identity categories" as they emerge, and it never wants to exclude an identity category that becomes a pressure group, amending the list as Congress conceives of additional categories that might need protection. But protection against what? The very process of defining these categories produces certain "identities" as identities insofar as they are categories that push against majoritarian and primarily patriarchal assumptions. That, of course, is not what the EEOC is saying in its list. The list produces identity categories that become significant because they are conceived of as needing protections, but these categories may just as easily protect citizens whose "identities" are completely mainstream. The idea is that no one should be put at a disadvantage because of traits, choices, and behaviors that fall within the listed categories. This extends rights to those for whom the Constitution provides no specific protections (females, citizens with disabilities, older citizens) while also providing protections against disparate treatments for those who already have constitutional protections (males, people of various races and religious faiths). The list is actually a list of identity categories instead of a list of categories in dire need of protection, a tendency that is masked both by the conflation of multiple, disparate, and sometimes conflicting interests within one "category" (i.e., "sex") and by the commingling of categories that enjoy constitutional protection (white males) alongside those that do not.

These "identity" categories are, of course, artificial, seeming to make meaningful only certain aspects of a subject's "identity," while completely ignoring others. It would be fair to say that there is no agreement between these categories as "identity" and any individual's "identity." Identity categories and the politics based on them, as inclusive as they might try to be, never represent any subject at all, but instead seem to urge individuals toward a reductive self-sorting in a fiction of community—or even "intersectional" communities, based not on subjective affinities, but on situationally defined sites of mainstream oppression that perpetuate division and oppression based on the very categories deployed for legislative liberation. Gender and identity as treated by federal law offer delusively liberating screens that obscure the driving disposition behind any "extension" of rights: the need to perpetuate the asymmetries of sexual difference as the underlying and immutable truth. Why else would we need to cautiously extend "rights and protections" to people who should already and without special provision enjoy them?

Younger "queer" advocates of whatever ilk optimistically decry identity categories as limiting and oppressive in themselves. And they are right. They favor differences instead of difference, are reluctant to locate themselves in more "traditional" binaries such as sex, and want very badly to see gender as an operational choice that pushes back against such traditional binaries as sexual difference, sexual orientation, and race. They desire, perhaps, to shock ingrained structures out of existence by simply appearing to fly in the face of the surface signifiers by which they believe such structures persist. The problem is that they are barely aware of the intransigency of these structures, or even what might constitute them as they also, in a continuation of the confusion of gender and sexual difference, want to deny the operational asymmetries of sexual difference itself. Denying that there are "women" and "men" or that they enjoy very different privileges and positions precisely because they have been tricked by gender variety and identity positions means that they cannot even conceive of patriarchy and its adherent sexism, colonialism, and racism, or its model for capitalism. Instead, they see these foundational asymmetries as merely alternative (and voluntary) organizations in the broad range of differences. The tactic of displaying confusing gender signifiers or refusing to comply with categories, apparently, is simply to wish away difference by substituting an inmixture of differences. But because there is no recognition of the sources of oppression and their foundations in precisely the binarized categories to which their mixed gender play ultimately subscribes, all remain on the surface as a set of wishes—as a fantasy of whisking away the symptoms of the binaries of which they seem oddly unaware. They do not generally know, for example, that women are accorded no constitutional protections by the Fourteenth Amendment, for example. And as a recent *New York Times* editorial reminds us, sexism is as alive and thriving as always.[6] What has happened instead is the production of a larger binary—queer versus normative—that can never be politically efficacious because it ignores the cultural regimes and binary compensatory structurations that have produced the oppression in the first place, mistaking surface performance for deep structure, or mere symptoms for persistent discursive formations. In so doing, paradoxically, gender play supports the very thing it wishes were not there—oppression based on difference.

Focusing on gender and identity causes other problems as well. While there is an illusion of political power offered as incitement to align with one category (or more) or another, there is also loss—not only the loss of infinite variety (seen paradoxically as politically inefficacious) and the loss of individuality and infinite subjective difference, but also the loss of any clear insight into the assumptions that produced the ever-expanding series in the first place. Focusing on identity categories distracts from the many ways in which patriarchy, property, financial systems, religions, racism, colonialisms, et cetera, continue to produce and depend on the inequalities and asymmetries represented by identity categories as necessary to their perpetuation as these modes also perpetuate one another.

As a set of assumptions based on available notions of significant "difference" (i.e., oppression), identity categories have lost sight at the very least of the basic discriminations premised on sexual differences. It may be the case that if sexual difference only becomes one of a number of elements that define genders, then categories themselves can no longer be either clearly delineated or so easily binarized. But one cannot ignore the very real disparities that still exist culturally on the basis of sexual difference. And the material and psychical disparities of sexual difference reside primarily in patriarchy's asymmetrical valuation of the sexes.

For example, the asymmetries produced by and necessary to patriarchy are asymmetries premised on sexual difference. Patriarchy is a compensatory structure that doubles the workings of law as that which produces relations where there otherwise may not be any. Just as a deed links an owner with property, paternity (until the late 1980s) linked a child with its unknowable father. Patriarchy is the asymmetrical operation of a binary sexual difference that centers itself by othering the other sex. It produces a relation where no relation may exist (father–child), compensates for emptiness by projecting value where there is none, and then enforces sets of delusional disparities in worth premised on those fictions. Patriarchy fosters the myths that men are intrinsically better and worth more than women, that fathers mean more than mothers do, and that women should serve men, all designed to overcompensate for the fact that no one ever used to know for sure who Daddy was, that men are less central than women in terms of gestation and genetic donation, that males are not intrinsically better, smarter, or stronger than females, especially not in a world where physical strength and hunting skills no longer matter. Given the fact that we no longer need the name of the father, we might also understand the current craze for guns as yet another version of panicked overcompensation. The disparities based on sexual difference then provide the model for other disparate unequal practices in religions, in economic systems (women are still paid less than men for the very same work), in access to privileges, and in the very operations of such other "othering" binaries such as race, colonial appropriation, et cetera. Now that we can know who Daddy is, patriarchy itself is a structure that has outlived its usefulness. But how to displace that formation? How to refashion a sexual difference that is no longer asymmetrical—that no longer needs to assimilate the "other" to prop itself up?

This is the dilemma from which our attention to gender and identity distracts us. Serving as commodity categories, compensatory fantasies of address and belonging, the entire gender identity endeavor is like a shell game. We think liberation is there, but because we think it is there—at the site of gender—we never even consider the formations that deploy gender as a cover. And these are far more crucial, but hopefully not unassailable.

Notes

Introduction

1. Stories and images of sexual reproduction circulate as reproduction's "truth," but they are really imaginary in the sense that all sexual reproduction is more complex than a mere yin/yang of complementary opposites. The history of reproductive accounts shows the ways this imaginary is still slanted toward the paternal contribution initially as reassurance about what one could not know (who Daddy is) and now as a compensation for the more minor role paternity plays in reproduction and gestation, especially as we now know that all children inherit more genetic material from the mother than from the father. This reproductive imaginary is the engine and result of many cultural processes that instate an uncertain patriarchy as a significant cultural term. For the history of concepts of reproduction, see Roy Porter, *The Greatest Benefit to Mankind: A Medical History of Humanity* (New York: Norton, 1998).

2. "Symbolic," in this context, refers to the given sets of laws and operations by which meaning accrues. This means everything from language, to religion, to jurisprudence. This sense of the symbolic is more broadly Lacanian. See, for example, the entire section on the "symbolic" in Richard Feldstein, Bruce Fink, and Maire Jaanus, eds., *Reading Seminars I and II: Lacan's Return to Freud* (Albany: State University of New York Press, 1996).

3. "Objective" in this context refers to making others into objects.

4. Thinking of genders as systems raises the question of the point from which such a gender system might be apprehended. If we think of genders as a first-order system to which there is no outside—and as a system that is perpetually open—then there is no position from whence genders can be seen as a system in toto. See Cary Wolfe, *What Is Posthumanism?* (Minneapolis: University of Minnesota Press, 2009), 108–13.

5. In *The Second Sex*, ed. and trans. H. M. Parshley (New York: Knopf, 1953), Simone de Beauvoir outlines many of these. In *Alice Doesn't: Feminism, Semiotics, Cinema* (Bloomington: Indiana University Press, 1984), Teresa de Lauretis demonstrates the gendering politics of narrative. And in *Gender Trouble: Feminism and the Subversion of Identity* (New York:

Routledge, 1990), Judith Butler develops theories of both the "performative" quality of gender and its possible foundations in melancholia.

6. In its most basic biological sense, "autopoiesis," according to the Humberto R. Maturana and Francisco Varela in *The Tree of Knowledge*, trans. Robert Paolucci (Boston: Shambhala, 1987), refers to an "autonomous system" that specifies "its own laws, what is proper to it" (48). Such a system persistently produces itself.

7. In their different ways, transgender and transsexuality take literally some relation between bodily presentation and self-conceptualization, aligning body and identity within a binary matrix. Insofar as many transgendered and transsexual individuals are not completely one sex/gender or the other, both might be seen playing with that alignment as well or fashioning its signifiers to enact something other than conventional sex/gender. But the basic elements exist within a normative binary gender perceived as working with sex, even if some regard "trans" permutations of those conventions as "queer." In the end, both display other gender regimes in addition, even if the gender regime is one wherein one takes on a gender (the "metamorphic" and/or the "chimeric"). There are a number of critical approaches to both transgender and transsexuality, including the psychoanalytic readings of Catherine Millot in *Horsexe: Essay on Transsexuality*, trans. Kenneth Hylton (New York: Autonomedia, 1990); the collection of essays edited by Joan Nestle, Clare Howell, and Riki Wilchins, *GenderQueer: Voices from beyond the Sexual Binary* (Los Angeles: Alyson Books, 2002); Kate Bornstein's *Gender Outlaw: On Men, Women, and the Rest of Us* (New York: Routledge, 1994); and Beatriz Preciado's *Testo Junkie: Sex, Drugs, and Biopolitics in the Pharmacopornographic Era* (New York: Feminist Press, 2013).

8. Anne Fausto-Sterling defines multiple sexes in her thoughtful questioning of the constructions of gender and sexuality in *Myths of Gender: Biological Theories about Women and Men* (New York: Basic Books, 1985) and *Sexing the Body: Gender Politics and the Construction of Sexuality* (New York: Basic Books, 2000).

9. See, generally, Jacques Lacan's *The Seminar of Jacques Lacan: On Feminine Sexuality, the Limits of Love, and Knowledge, 1972–1973 (Encore: Vol. Book XX)*, ed. Jacques-Alain Miller, trans. Bruce Fink (New York: Norton, 1998). See also Ellie Ragland's *The Logic of Sexuation: From Aristotle to Lacan* (Albany: State University of New York Press, 2004).

10. See Havelock Ellis's *Studies in the Psychology of Sex, Volume 2: Sexual Inversions* (TheClassics.us, 2013); as well as Lillian Faderman's *Odd Girls and Twilight Lovers: A History of Lesbian Life in Twentieth-Century America* (New York: Columbia University Press, 1991).

11. Studies of narrative have observed this pattern as basic to narrative structure. See, for example, Robert Scholes, *Fabulation and Metafiction* (Urbana: University of Illinois Press, 1979); de Lauretis, *Alice Doesn't*; and

Judith Roof, *Come as You Are: Narrative and Sexuality* (New York: Columbia University Press, 1996).

12. As a part of their call to the "heteroclite," Deleuze and Guattari point out the function of language itself as providing a "whole" for that which has no unity. Categories function this way as well, they argue. Gender is thus a species of category that functions like language to label and unify that which has no intrinsic unity. See Brian Massumi, *A User's Guide to Capitalism and Schizophrenia* (Cambridge, Mass.: MIT Press, 1992), 90.

13. In "The Mirror Stage as Formative of the Function of the I," Lacan theorizes that at a certain point in infant development, subjects perceive themselves as suddenly separable from the world around them. They anticipate a mastery that is not yet theirs, but they are simultaneously cast into a history in which the sameness of the world and their place within it is now in the past. *Ecrits: A Selection*, trans. Alan Sheridan (New York: Norton, 1977), 1–7.

14. This is Massumi's interpretation of Deleuze and Guattari's take on gender as a "form of imprisonment" (*User's Guide*, 87).

15. Ragland, *Logic of Sexuation*, 12. Ragland's book admirably summarizes the complexities of Lacan's concept of sexuation: there is no sexual relation, and a subject's positionings stretch across a quadrated set of beliefs about whether anyone can or cannot have it all.

16. As Ragland glosses it, "by which both sexes interpret their sexuality as lacking (or not) in reference to the mother's unconscious desire regarding her own sexual difference" (ibid., 10).

17. Ragland explains the phallic signifier as that which "masks the real of sexuality and trauma by linking language to the law of difference—not only in so far as one sound or one meaning always differs from another—but also in so far as phallic 'law,' by delineating this from that, the masculine from the feminine, for example, orients desire" (ibid., 11).

18. Ibid., 22.

19. Ibid., 15.

20. As Ragland suggests, sexuation "fixes one's language, enjoyment, and lack-in-being along four possible axes for the development of desire as it commands language and sexuality from a point halfway between language and repetition" (ibid., 21).

21. Ibid., 175.

22. Ibid., 145.

23. Ibid., 124–25. Summarizing this aspect of Lacan's axes, Ragland points out that lover and beloved cannot be reduced to gender, even if "*all* is a masculine logic and the *not all* a feminine one" (125).

24. Ibid., 97.

25. These correlations are summarized by Ragland, ibid., 96–97.

26. Marie Hélène Brousse, "The Drive (II)," in *Reading Seminar XI:*

Lacan's Four Fundamental Concepts of Psychoanalysis: The Paris Seminars in English, ed. Richard Feldstein, Bruce Fink, and Maire Jaanus (Albany: State University of New York Press, 1995), 113. In addition, both Lee Edelman in *No Future: Queer Theory and the Death Drive* (Durham, N.C.: Duke University Press, 2004) and Teresa de Lauretis in *Freud's Drive: Psychoanalysis, Literature, and Film* (London: Palgrave Macmillan, 2010) consider the importance of the drive as a dynamic different from, but operating alongside, desire.

27. Brousse, "The Drive (II)," 111–12.

28. Ibid., 112.

29. Ibid.

30. Ragland, *Logic of Sexuation*, 25.

31. Gilles Deleuze and Félix Guattari, *A Thousand Plateaus: Capitalism and Schizophrenia*, trans. Brian Massumi (Minneapolis: University of Minnesota Press, 1987), 111.

32. Ibid.

33. These are definitions from the *Oxford English Dictionary*.

34. Deleuze and Guattari, *Thousand Plateaus*, 88.

35. Ibid.

36. Ibid.

37. Ibid., 86.

38. Ludwig von Bertalanffy, *General System Theory: Foundations, Developments, Applications*, rev. ed. (New York: George Braziller, 1969), 55.

39. This is a distillation of Humberto R. Maturana and Francisco Varela's rendition of systems in *Tree of Knowledge*.

40. In so far as the paternal function operates through its symbolic capacity—that is, its putting a name where no relation exists—the paternal function is over. Now that we are capable of discerning via DNA who Daddy is, the name of the father has become literal. The father's name, therefore, can no longer serve as a symbolic suture or as the energetic center of a culture bent on proving its superiority.

41. Butler, *Gender Trouble*, 137.

42. In discussing how gender performativity both constructs an identity and reveals its own contingency, Butler says in *Gender Trouble*, "Such acts, gestures, enactments, generally construed, are *performative* in the sense that the essence of identity that they otherwise purport to express are *fabrications* manufactured and sustained through corporeal signs and other discursive means" (136).

43. J. L. Austin, *How To Do Things with Words*, 2nd ed. (Cambridge, Mass.: Harvard University Press, 1975).

44. Butler, *Gender Trouble*, 125.

45. Joan Copjec, *Read My Desire: Lacan against the Historicists* (Cambridge, Mass.: MIT Press, 1994), 201–2.

46. Ibid., 204.

47. The popularization of gender performativity in academe occurred as a result of the publication of Butler's *Gender Trouble* in 1990. By the late 1980s, feminist critical impact had waned, while "queer" had emerged as an effect of political action in response to AIDS. Eighties feminist (and especially lesbian) concerns about visibility, essentialism (i.e., one's sexed body determined one's gender, which determined an individual's intellectual and social roles and capabilities), and the differences among women of divergent races, ethnic origins, classes, and sexualities had shifted feminism's questions from the arena of ideo-mythology addressed by earlier thinkers such as Simone de Beauvoir to questions of social inequity and a focus on identity categories.

48. As a political tactic, visibility assumed that were disadvantaged groups seen, their inequitable treatment would be addressed. This in turn assumes that visibility produces knowledge and recognition, which would motivate cultural changes. ACT UP's tactics were all about making AIDS and gayness visible. This same logic underwrites the concept of the role model and now the ever-expanding list of sex/gender/sexual preference initials. Although ACT UP was anything but conservative, feminist appeals to visibility were more interested in gaining social acceptance and hence favored the visibility of normative types.

49. Sigmund Freud, *Three Essays on the Theory of Sexuality*, trans. James Strachey (New York: Basic Books, 1962). Freud's structural rendition of the dynamics of sexual desire in *Three Essays* splits the object of desire from what one desires to do with that object, producing separable taxonomies of sexual desire and sex/gender. Dividing object from aim produces the elements of a sexual identikit in which various forms of sexuality can be taxonomized as heterosexual (aim: intercourse, object: the opposite sex), homosexual (aim: intercourse, object: the same sex), voyeur (aim: to look, object: the opposite sex), et cetera. Thus, categorizing desire in relation to the taxonomic gender of the object as well as the taxonomic imagination of proper genital merging, Freud gestures both toward the interrelation of desire and gender (subtended by its imagined link to biology) and toward their taxonomic separability.

1. Making Over

1. "Nia Vardalos," *AskMen*, n.d., http://www.askmen.com/celebs/women/actress_150/198_nia_vardalos.html.

2. Roger Ebert and Richard Roeper's review is no longer available.

3. Craig Roush, "Review of *My Big Fat Greek Wedding*," *Rotten Tomatoes: Kinnopio's Movie Reviews*, January 7, 2003, http://www.rottentomatoes.com/m/my_big_fat_greek_wedding/.

4. Sigmund Freud, *The Uncanny*, trans. David McLintock (New York: Penguin, 2003), 123. Freud's first hypothesis is that "the uncanny is that

species of the frightening that goes back to what was once well known and had long been familiar" (124).

5. Henri Bergson, *Laughter*, in *Comedy*, ed. Wylie Sypher (New York: Doubleday, 1956), 59–190.

6. This goes back to Peter Brooks's description of the function of the narrative middle in "Freud's Masterplot," in *Literature and Psychoanalysis: The Question of Reading: Otherwise*, ed. Shoshana Felman (Baltimore: Johns Hopkins University Press, 1982), 280–300.

2. Prosopopeias

1. Jacques Lacan, *The Seminar of Jacques Lacan: The Four Fundamental Concepts of Psychoanalysis (Vol. Book XI)*, ed. Jacques-Alain Miller, trans. Alan Sheridan (New York: Norton, 1981).

2. Antonio Quinet, "The Gaze as an Object," in *Reading Seminar XI: Lacan's Four Fundamental Concepts of Psychoanalysis: The Paris Seminars in English*, ed. Richard Feldstein, Bruce Fink, and Maire Jaanus (Albany: State University of New York Press, 1995), 139.

3. "Let us schematize," Lacan says in *Seminar XI*, "at once what we mean. From the moment that this gaze appears, the subject tries to adapt himself to it, he becomes that punctiform object, that point of vanishing being with which the subject confuses his own failure. Furthermore, of all the objects in which the subject may recognize his dependence in the register of desire, the gaze is specified as unapprehensible. That is why it is, more than any other object, misunderstood (*méconnu*), and it is perhaps for this reason, too, that the subject manages, fortunately, to symbolize his own vanishing and punctiform bar (*trait*) in the illusion of the consciousness of *seeing oneself see oneself*, in which the gaze is elided" (83).

4. Ibid., 74.

5. Ibid.

6. Robert Samuels, "Art and the Position of the Analyst," in *Reading Seminar XI*, ed. Feldstein, Fink, and Jaanus, 184.

7. Joan Rivière, "Femininity as Masquerade," in *Formations of Fantasy*, ed. Victor Burgin, James Donald, and Cora Kaplan (London: Methuen, 1986), 35–44. See also Leila Rupp and Verta Taylor, *Drag Queens at the 801 Cabaret* (Chicago: University of Chicago Press, 2003); and Judith "Jack" Halberstam and Del LaGrace Volcano, *The Drag King Book* (London: Serpent's Tail, 1999).

8. De Beauvoir, *The Second Sex*, xxvi.

9. Ibid., xxvii.

10. Ibid.

11. Michel Foucault, "Introduction," in *Herculine Barbin (Being the Recently Discovered Memoirs of a Nineteenth-Century French Hermaphrodite)*, trans. Richard McDougall (New York: Pantheon, 1980).

12. Ibid., x.

13. Ibid., 99.

14. Catherine Millot, *Horsexe: Essay on Transsexuality*, trans. Kenneth Hylton (New York: Autonomedia, 1990).

15. Ibid., 134.

16. Ibid., 135.

17. Qtd. in Morris, *Conundrum*, 65.

18. Ibid.

19. In "Fragment of an Analysis of a Case of Hysteria," in *Standard Edition of the Complete Psychological Works*, vol. 7, ed. and trans. James Strachey (London: Hogarth Press, 1953–74), 1–122, Sigmund Freud traces Dora's distaste at being kissed to a hysterical "reversal of affect" whereby what should be pleasurable is unpleasurable. He elaborates this phenomenon in discussions of voyeurism and exhibitionism, and sadism and masochism. See ibid., 44.

20. For example, Laura Mulvey's famous essay "Visual Pleasure in Narrative Cinema," *Screen* 16 (1975): 6–18, reads the relation between film spectator and film as one that must negotiate sexual differences and which also locates female spectators in a self-contradictory position. Sigmund Freud's theory of fetishism from "On Fetishism," in *Standard Edition of the Complete Psychological Works*, vol. 21, hypothesizes that fetishism arises from a male child's inability to acknowledge the sexual difference of his mother.

21. Georges Bataille, *Story of the Eye*, translated by Joachim Neugroschel (San Francisco: City Lights Books, 1987).

22. Djuna Barnes, *Nightwood* (New York: New Directions, 1937).

3. Temporality Still

1. Teresa de Lauretis notably establishes the feminine ground of narrative in *Alice Doesn't: Feminism, Semiotics, Cinema* (Bloomington: Indiana University Press, 1984).

2. In his essay "Freud's Masterplot," Peter Brooks maps narrative dynamics in relation to Freud's categories in *Beyond the Pleasure Principle*. See Brooks, "Freud's Masterplot," in *Literature and Psychoanalysis: The Question of Reading: Otherwise*, ed. Shoshana Felman (Baltimore: Johns Hopkins University Press, 1982), 280–300. On the narrative functions of secondary female characters, see Judith Roof, *All about Thelma and Eve: Sidekicks and Third Wheels* (Champaign: University of Illinois Press, 2002).

3. Portions of this argument appeared in a different version in Judith Roof's "Working Gender/Fading Taxonomy" *Genders* 44 (2006): 1–33.

4. Lacan defines these knotted registers in in many of his *Seminars*, but see particularly "Seminar XXII, R.S.I.: 1974–1975: From 19th November 1974: Jacques Lacan," *Lacanian Works*, n.d., http://www.lacanianworks .net/?p=45.

4. Social Algebras

1. This is the simplest description of the two-axes problems of algebra. See "What Is a Quadratic Equation? Definition and Examples," *Education Portal*, n.d., http://education-portal.com/academy/lesson/what-is-a -quadratic-equation-definition-examples.html#lesson.

2. Gould's "full house" refers to the oft-ignored fact that in any statistical measure, there are just as many possibilities that fall outside of the norm as occupy its center. Statistics are mappings of probabilities, not actual positionings.

3. See Luce Irigaray, "The Mechanics of Fluids," in *This Sex Which Is Not One*, trans. Catherine Porter (Ithaca, N.Y.: Cornell University Press, 1985), 106–19.

4. See Irigaray, "This Sex Which Is Not One," in ibid., 33.

5. In "Womanliness as Masquerade," in *Formations of Fantasy*, ed. Victor Burgin, James Donald, and Cora Kaplan (London: Methuen, 1986), 35–44, Joan Rivière hypothesizes that the woman who presents herself of hyperbolically feminine is in fact covering over a suspected masculinity.

6. See Roland Barthes, *The Pleasure of the Text*, trans. Richard Miller (New York: Hill and Wang, 1975), 7.

7. In "This Sex Which Is Not One," Irigaray analogies genitals and their imaginary apprehension to the relation of males as "one" or singular to females as "not one"—"as neither one nor two" (26).

8. In his speech in Plato's *Symposium*, Aristophanes recounts this origin story of doubled beings. See Plato, *The Collected Works of Plato*, 4th ed., trans. Benjamin Jowett (London: Oxford University Press, 1953), 520–25.

9. Both the Oedipus story and the myth of the priests of Nemi envision the relations among males as competitive replacement, the younger man vanquishing the elder. See, for example, Sir James George Frazer, *The Golden Bough: A Study of Magic and Religion* (New York: Simon and Brown, 2013).

10. See my reading of bodybuilding as massive overcompensation in Judith Roof, *Reproductions of Reproduction: Imaging Symbolic Change* (New York: Routledge, 1996), 60–80.

5. Scopic Folding, Layered Economies

1. A hologram is produced by the interplay of two laser beams, one focused on a recording medium, the other on an object. Light scattered by the object also reaches the recording medium. The beams of light from the two sources intersect and interfere with one another: the result of these processes constitutes the hologrammatic image. The image itself is an encoded version of the scene insofar as the hologram represents only the fallout from the interference of the two beams. To be reconstituted, a beam identical to the original shines on the surface of the developed image. As an

analogy to gendering, the hologram offers a tripartite model: (1) a directed beam (much like the Symbolic possibilities available culturally); (2) a scattered beam in reference to an object (subject) that reflects light idiosyncratically; and (3) a process of decoding the resulting mix (interference/intersection) by recourse to the original light source (Symbolic).

2. Luce Irigaray, "The Mechanics of Fluids," in *The Sex Which Is Not One*, trans. Catherine Porter (Ithaca, N.Y.: Cornell University Press, 1985), 117.

3. Judith Butler, *Gender Trouble: Feminism and the Subversion of Identity* (New York: Routledge, 1990).

4. J. L. Austin, *How to Do Things with Words*, 2nd ed. (Cambridge, Mass.: Harvard University Press, 1975) lays out his theory of the linguistic performative.

5. See Jennie Livingston's documentary *Paris Is Burning* (1990) for its presentation of voguing culture.

6. This characterization of the stain's operation is from Jaime Hovey's *A Thousand Words: Portraiture, Style, and Queer Modernism* (Columbus: Ohio State University Press, 2006), 131.

7. Joan Nestle, Clare Howell, and Riki Wilchins, eds., *GenderQueer: Voices from Beyond the Sexual Binary* (Los Angeles: Alyson Books, 2002), 24.

8. Ibid., 25.

9. Dennis Allen, "A Queer 'I' for the Straight Guy," *Genders* 44 (2006): par. 22 (http://www.genders.org/g44/g44_allen.txt).

10. Ibid., par. 23.

11. Ibid.

12. MilDRED's website was unavailable in 2013. All quotations are from the website as it existed in 2006. See, however, http://www.dredking.com/.

13. This photo, "The San Diego Drag Kings Club," is still available at https://www.pinterest.com/pin/207236020323061917/. Checking Google Images under the search words "drag kings" will provide several additional group drag king portraits.

14. Or very rarely. Lily Tomlin plays a male lounge singer character, "Tommy Velour," working-class "Rick," and black R&B singer "Pervis Hawkins." A video of "Tommy" is available on Tomlin's website, http://www.lilytomlin.com/characters. Tomlin's "Tommy" makes visible a showbiz version of masculinity that is already for show.

15. "I know but all the same" is Octave Mannoni's formula for Freud's reading of fetishism in *Clefs pour l'imaginaire; ou, L'autre scène* (Paris: Editions du Seuil, 1969), 9.

16. David Hwang, *M. Butterfly* (New York: Plume, 1986).

17. There are rumors of celebrities (Eddie Murphy, Matt Lauer) caught with transvestite sex workers. These are unsubstantiated for the most part, but even the public fantasy of these encounters plays into the

combination of understanding homophobia as over-compensatory and illicit sex as an open secret. See, for example, Kyle Smith, "Double Trouble: A Pickup Turns into a Drag for Eddie Murphy," *People*, May 19, 1997, http://www.people.com/people/archive/article/0,,20122170,00.html.

6. The Fixer

1. Carl Linnaeus, 1729. Quoted in "Carl Linnaeus," n.d., http://www.ucmp.berkeley.edu/history/linnaeus.html.

2. Ibid.

3. Ibid.

4. This is the definition as paraphrased by Alexander Hellemans and Bryan Bunch in *The Timetables of Science: A Chronology of the Most Important People and Events in the History of Science* (New York: Simon and Schuster, 1988), 204.

5. Simone de Beauvoir, *The Second Sex*, ed. and trans. H. M. Parshley (New York: Knopf, 1953), 2.

6. Ibid., 3.

7. Ibid.

8. Ibid.

9. Ibid.

10. For an account of the history and treatment of intersexed individuals, see Elizabeth Reis, *Bodies in Doubt: An American History of Intersex* (Baltimore: Johns Hopkins University Press, 2012).

11. See "The Intersex Spectrum" from *Nova* (October 30, 2001) at http://www.pbs.org/wgbh/nova/body/intersex-spectrum.html for the wide range of rates of different kinds of intersex presentation.

12. See, for example, the first chapter of Donna Haraway's *Simians, Cyborgs, and Women: The Reinvention of Nature* (New York: Routledge, 1991); Anne Fausto-Sterling's *Myths of Gender: Biological Theories about Women and Men* (New York: Basic Books, 1985); and Simone de Beauvoir's *The Second Sex*, ed. and trans. H. M. Parshley (New York: Knopf, 1953).

13. Jeffrey Eugenides, *Middlesex* (New York: Picador, 2007).

14. Counting the mitochondrial DNA passed on only by mothers as well as the larger number of genes on the X chromosome, mothers do contribute a greater quantity of their DNA to children.

15. Georg Hegel, *Philosophy of Nature*, qtd. in de Beauvoir, *The Second Sex*, 4.

16. Ibid.

17. Ibid.

18. Hegel, *Philosophy of Nature*, §288, available at https://www.marxists.org/reference/archive/hegel/works/na/naconten.htm: "Through the process with external nature the animal achieves self-certainty and its

subjective concept, truth and objectivity as a single individual. And it is the production of itself just as much as its self-preservation, or reproduction as production of its first concept. Thus the concept joins together with itself and is, as concrete generality, genus. The disjunction of the individual finding itself in the genus is the sexual difference, the relation of the subject to an object which is itself such a subject."

19. Ibid., §290.

20. This myth can be found in Plato, *Collected Works of Plato*, 4th ed., trans. Benjamin Jowett (London: Oxford University Press, 1953).

21. Sigmund Freud, *Beyond the Pleasure Principle*, ed. and trans. James Strachey (New York: Norton, 1961), 51.

22. Ibid., 52.

23. Ibid., 53.

24. Hegel, *Philosophy of Nature*, §288.

25. Susan Orlean, *The Orchid Thief: A True Story of Beauty and Obsession* (New York: Ballantine, 2000), 75.

26. Ibid., 94.

27. Michael Pollan, *The Botany of Desire: A Plant's-Eye View of the World* (New York: Random House, 2001).

28. See Claude Lévi-Strauss, *Structural Anthropology*, trans. Claire Jacobson and Brooke Schoepf (New York: Basic Books, 1963).

29. For example, in the chapter "Linguistics and Anthropology" in *Structural Anthropology*, Lévi-Strauss remarks, "We reduce the kinship structure to the simplest conceivable element, the atom of kinship, if I may say so, when we have a group consisting of a husband, a woman, a representative of the group which has given the woman to the man—since incest prohibitions make it impossible in all societies for the unit of kinship to consist of one family" (72).

30. Ibid., 46.

31. Ibid., 47.

32. In *The Archaeology of Knowledge, and The Discourse on Language*, trans. A. M. Sheridan Smith (New York: Pantheon, 1972), 15, Foucault states he is specifically "not" trying to deploy anthropology's structuralist method with history. See also Anthony Wilden's *System and Structure: Essays in Communication and Exchange*, 2nd ed. (New York: Tavistock, 1980).

33. In chapter 9, "Commodities among Themselves," in *This Sex Which Is Not One*, trans Catherine Porter (Ithaca, N.Y.: Cornell University Press, 1985), 192–97, Luce Irigaray demonstrates the collision of systems of family, sex/gender, and capital.

34. Judith Butler, *Gender Trouble: Feminism and the Subversion of Identity* (New York: Routledge, 1990).

35. Judith Butler, *Antigone's Claim: Kinship between Life and Death* (New York: Columbia University Press, 2002).

36. Judith Butler, *Undoing Gender* (New York: Routledge, 2004).

37. Sigmund Freud, *Totem and Taboo*, trans. James Strachey (New York: Norton, 1950), 82.

38. Peggy Reeves Sanday, *Divine Hunger: Cannibalism as a Cultural System* (Cambridge, U.K.: Cambridge University Press, 1986), xii.

39. Ibid., 12.

40. For an exploration of the psychic function of negation, see Jacques Lacan, *The Seminar of Jacques Lacan: Book I, Freud's Papers on Technique, 1954–1954*, ed. Jacques-Alain Miller, trans. John Forrester (New York: Norton, 1988), 173–74.

41. It is worth pointing out that DNA essentially clones itself when cells reproduce. Although gametes offer half of a full genotype, thereby producing a new individual with a genotype that is different from either parent, mitochondrial DNA, supplied only by the mother, is perpetually self-cloned as a function of cellular existence. Humans thus are a combination of a joint product and cloned cellular biology.

42. Martin P. Levine, *Gay Macho: The Life and Death of the Homosexual Clone* (New York: New York University Press, 1998), xv.

43. For the link between reproduction and death, see chapter 9 of Georges Bataille's *Erotism: Death and Sensuality*, trans. Mary Dalwood (San Francisco: City Lights Books, 1986), 94.

7. Gender Is as Gender Does

1. "Guiding Remarks for a Congress on Feminine Sexuality," in *Feminine Sexuality: Jacques Lacan and the Ecole Freudienne*, ed. Juliet Mitchell and Jacqueline Rose, trans. Jacqueline Rose (New York: Norton, 1985), 96.

2. Jacques Lacan, "God and the *Jouissance* of Woman: A Love Letter," in *Encore: The Seminar of Jacques Lacan, Book XX*, ed. Jacques-Alain Miller, trans. Bruce Fink (New York: Norton, 1998), 69.

3. Ibid., 141.

4. Ibid.

5. Ibid.

6. See Judith Roof, *A Lure of Knowledge: Lesbian Sexuality and Theory* (New York: Columbia University Press, 1991). I argued that lesbian desire is desire for desire. In Teresa de Lauretis's *The Practice of Love: Lesbian Sexuality and Perverse Desire* (Bloomington: Indiana University Press, 1994), she also makes a case for lesbian desire as desire for desire.

7. See Judith Halberstam, *Female Masculinity* (Durham, N.C.: Duke University Press, 1998).

8. In the several years between drafts of this book, most web references to the most evil women in history have shifted from the vampiric Elizabeth Báthory, to Nazi prison camp guards, serial child murderers,

and political criminals (i.e., Queen Mary of England). There are any number of such sites to be found under "evil women."

8. Spurious Displays

1. For a thorough examination of the dandy figure, see Susan Fillin-Yeh, ed., *Dandies: Fashion and Finesse in Art and Culture* (New York: New York University Press, 2001).

2. The website in question, http://www.uptowncity.com/Dixie/Belles.htm, is unfortunately now defunct, although the belles live on in beauty pageants, especially among the toddler beauty pageants (e.g., those featured in TLC's hit television show *Toddlers and Tiaras*). The term has also become a regional identifier for bands, majorette groups, and other group performance endeavors.

3. See Candace Thompson, "21 Differences between a Southern Belle and a Modern Woman," *Thought Catalog*, February 18, 2014, http://thoughtcatalog.com/candace-thompson/2014/02/21-differences-between-a-southern-belle-and-a-modern-woman/.

4. See, for example, the elaborate definitions and explanations of goth from "What Is Goth?" Goth.net, n.d., http://www.goth.net/goth.html; or "Origins of Gothic," *A Study of Gothic Subculture*, n.d., http://www.gothicsubculture.com/origin.php. These goth sites disappear as the styles change, which is the point of their spurious position.

5. See "Goth Stereotype," *A Study of Gothic Subculture*, n.d., http://www.gothicsubculture.com/archetype.php.

Conclusion

1. Judith Butler, *Gender Trouble: Feminism and the Subversion of Identity* (New York: Routledge, 1990), 125.

2. Joan Copjec, *Read My Desire: Lacan against the Historicists* (Cambridge, Mass.: MIT Press, 1994), 211.

3. Luce Irigaray, *je, tu, nous: Toward a Culture of Difference*, trans. Alison Martin (New York: Routledge, 1993), 12.

4. "Sexual difference" is a concept and/or term both Judith Butler and Rosi Braidotti address. In Butler's essay "The End of Sexual Difference," in *Undoing Gender* (New York: Routledge, 2004), 174–203, she notes the persistent confusions among sexual difference, gender, and sexual orientation, but tends only to trace this confusion through its occurrence (or not) in various international venues, and she has a somewhat vague notion of how it might operate. Rosi Braidotti envisions sexual difference as "perfectly suitable to a nomadic vision of subjectivity" that has a potential for social change in *Metamorphosis: Towards a Materialist Theory of Becoming*

(Cambridge, U.K.: Polity, 2002), 28. As illustrated by these different approaches, sexual difference is still very much at issue. The problem may be the impasses feminism has reached in the past decades precisely over essentialism, materialism, exclusion, et cetera, that have somehow blunted the structural character of asymmetry as an operative, material fact.

5. See the U.S. Equal Employment Opportunity Commission's statement at http://www.eeoc.gov/eeoc/newsroom/wysk/enforcement_protections_lgbt_workers.cfm. The EEOC oversees federal employment discrimination laws and has a commission that makes rulings interpreting these federal statutes. It does not include other kinds of rights or discrimination generally.

6. "When Talking about Bias Backfires," *New York Times*, December 6, 2014.

Filmography

Absolutely Fabulous. Television program. Performed by Jennifer Saunders and Joanna Lumley. 1992–2012. London: BBC One.

Alien. Directed by Ridley Scott. Performed by Sigourney Weaver and Tom Skerritt. 1979. Los Angeles: Twentieth Century Fox Film Corporation.

Aliens. Directed by James Cameron. Performed by Sigourney Weaver. 1986. Los Angeles: Twentieth Century Fox Film Corporation.

*Alien*³. Directed by David Fincher. Performed by Sigourney Weaver. 1992. Los Angeles: Twentieth Century Fox Film Corporation.

Alien: Resurrection. Directed by Jeanne-Pierre Jeunet. Performed by Sigourney Weaver and Winona Ryder. 1997. Los Angeles: Twentieth Century Fox Film Corporation.

All in the Family. Performed by Carroll O'Connor, Jean Stapleton, Rob Reiner, Sally Struthers, and Danielle Brisebois. 1971–79. Los Angeles: CBS.

Ally McBeal. Television program. Performed by Calista Flockhart and Portia de Rossi. 1997–2002. Los Angeles: Fox.

America's Next Top Model. Television program. Performed by Tyra Banks. 2003–present. Burbank, Calif.: The CW.

The Andy Griffith Show. Television program. Performed by Andy Griffith and Don Knotts. 1960–68. Los Angeles: CBS.

Austin Powers: International Man of Mystery. Directed by Jay Roach. Performed by Mike Myers and Michael York. 1997. New York: New Line Cinema.

The Big Bang Theory. Television program. Performed by Johnny Galecki and Jim Parsons. 2007–present. Los Angeles: CBS.

The Big Lebowski. Directed by Joel and Ethan Coen. Performed by Jeff Bridges, John Goodman, Julianne Moore, and Steve Buscemi. 1998. Los Angeles: Working Title Films.

The Biggest Loser. Television program. Performed by Allison Sweeney and Bob Harper. 2004–present. New York: NBC.

The Birdcage. Directed by Mike Nichols. Performed by Robin Williams and Nathan Lane. 1996. Beverly Hills, Calif.: United Artists Media Group.

Bound. Directed by Andy and Lana Wachowski. Performed by Gina

Gershon and Jennifer Tilley. 1996. Universal City, Calif.: Dino De Laurentiis Company.

Boys Don't Cry. Directed by Kimberly Peirce. Performed by Hilary Swank and Chloë Sevigny. 1999. Los Angeles: Fox Searchlight Pictures.

Bridesmaids. Directed by Paul Feig. Performed by Kristen Wiig and Melissa McCarthy. 2011. Universal City, Calif.: Universal Pictures.

Bridget Jones's Diary. Directed by Sharon Maguire. Performed by Renée Zellweger and Colin Firth. 2001. Burbank, Calif.: Miramax.

Bridget Jones: The Edge of Reason. Directed by Beeban Kidron. Performed by Renée Zellweger and Colin Firth. 2004. Universal City, Calif.: Universal Pictures.

Chopped. Television program. Performed by Ted Allen. 2009–present. New York: Food Network.

Cinderella. Directed by Clyde Geronimi. 1950. Burbank, Calif.: Walt Disney Pictures. Animation.

Cinderella. Directed by Kenneth Branagh. Performed by Helena Bonham Carter and Cate Blanchett. 2015. Burbank, Calif.: Walt Disney Pictures.

Desert Hearts. Directed by Donna Deitch. Performed by Helen Shaver and Patricia Charbonneau. 1985. New York: Samuel Goldwyn Company.

Die Hard. Directed by John McTiernan. Performed by Bruce Willis. 1988. Los Angeles: Twentieth Century Fox Film Corporation.

Die Hard 2. Directed by Renny Harlin. Performed by Bruce Willis. 1990. Los Angeles: Twentieth Century Fox Film Corporation.

Die Hard with a Vengeance. Directed by John McTiernan. Performed by Bruce Willis. 1995. Los Angeles: Twentieth Century Fox Film Corporation.

Die Hard 4.0: Live Free or Die Hard. Directed by Len Wiseman. Performed by Bruce Willis. 2007. Los Angeles: Twentieth Century Fox Film Corporation.

Eraser. Directed by Charles Russell. Performed by Arnold Schwarzenegger and Vanessa Williams. 1996. Los Angeles: Twentieth Century Fox Film Corporation.

Extreme Makeover. Television program. Performed by Sam Saboura. 2002–7. Burbank, Calif.: ABC.

Father Goose. Directed by Ralph Nelson. Performed by Cary Grant and Leslie Caron. 1964. n.p., Granox Company.

Food Network Challenge. Television program. Performed by Claire Robinson. 2005–present. New York: Food Network.

Friends. Television program. Performed by Jennifer Aniston, Courteney Cox, Lisa Kudrow, Matt LeBlanc, Matthew Perry, and David Schwimmer. 1994–2004. Los Angeles: NBC.

From Russia with Love. Directed by Terence Young. Performed by Sean Connery and Robert Shaw. 1963. London: Eon Productions.

Gilmore Girls. Television program. Performed by Lauren Graham and Alexis Bledel. 2000–2007. Burbank, Calif.: ABC Family.

The Girl with the Dragon Tattoo. Directed by David Fincher. Performed by Daniel Craig and Rooney Mara. 2011. Culver City, Calif.: Columbia Pictures.

Girls. Television program. Performed by Lena Dunham. 2012–present. New York: HBO.

The Godfather. Directed by Francis Ford Coppola. Performed by Marlon Brando and Al Pacino. 1972. Los Angeles: Paramount Pictures.

Goldfinger. Directed by Guy Hamilton. Performed by Sean Connery. 1964. London: Eon Productions.

Gossip Girl. Television program. Performed by Blake Lively. 2007–12. Burbank, Calif.: The CW.

The Hangover. Directed by Todd Phillips. Performed by Bradley Cooper and Zach Galifianakis. 2009. Burbank, Calif.: Warner Brothers.

Heathers. Directed by Michael Lehmann. Performed by Winona Ryder and Christian Slater. 1988. Atlanta: New World Pictures.

Hercules Returns. Directed by David Parker. Performed by David Argue and Mary Coustas. 1993. Los Angeles: Philm Productions.

Hoarders. Television program. 2009–13. New York: A&E Network.

Houseboat. Directed by Melville Shavelson. Performed by Cary Grant and Sophia Loren. 1958. Los Angeles: Paramount Pictures.

How I Met Your Mother. Television program. Performed by Josh Radnor, Neil Patrick Harris, Jason Segel, Cobie Smulders, and Alyson Hannigan. 2005–14. Los Angeles: CBS.

I Love You, Man. Directed by John Hamburg. Performed by Paul Rudd and Jason Segel. 2009. Universal City, Calif.: DreamWorks Studios.

Intervention. Television program. Performed by Jeff VanVonderen and Candy Finnigan. 2005–13. New York: A&E Network.

Iron Chef. Television program. Performed by Bobby Flay, Cat Cora, Wolfgang Puck, et al. 2005–present. New York: Food Network.

The Joy of Painting. Television program. Performed by Bob Ross. 1983–2015. Muncie, Ind.: BRI Productions.

Kindergarten Cop. Directed by Ivan Reitman. Performed by Arnold Schwarzenegger and Penelope Ann Miller. 1990. Beverly Hills, Calif.: Imagine Entertainment.

Kitchen Nightmares. Television program. Performed by Gordon Ramsay. 2007–14. Los Angeles: Fox.

Knocked Up. Directed by Judd Apatow. Performed by Seth Rogen and Katherine Heigl. 2007. Universal City, Calif.: Universal Pictures.

The L Word. Television program. Performed by Jennifer Beals and Laurel Holloman. 2004–9. New York: Showtime.

Lethal Weapon. Directed by Richard Donner. Performed by Mel Gibson and Danny Glover. 1987. Burbank, Calif.: Warner Brothers.

Lethal Weapon 2. Directed by Richard Donner. Performed by Mel Gibson and Danny Glover. 1989. Burbank, Calif.: Warner Brothers.

Lethal Weapon 3. Directed by Richard Donner. Performed by Mel Gibson and Danny Glover. 1992. Burbank, Calif.: Warner Brothers.

Lethal Weapon 4. Directed by Richard Donner. Performed by Mel Gibson and Danny Glover. 1998. Burbank, Calif.: Warner Brothers.

Longtime Companion. Directed by Norman René. Performed by Stephen Caffrey and Patrick Cassidy. 1989. n.p., American Playhouse.

The Lord of the Rings: The Return of the King. Directed by Peter Jackson. Performed by Orlando Bloom and Ian McKellan. 2003. New York: New Line Cinema.

Love! Valour! Compassion! Directed by Joe Mantella. Performed by Jason Alexander and Stephen Spinella. 1997. Beverly Hills, Calif.: Krost/Chapin Productions.

M*A*S*H. Television program. Performed by Alan Alda and Loretta Swit. 1972–83. Los Angeles: CBS.

The Matrix. Directed by Andy and Lana Wachowski. Performed by Keanu Reeves, Laurence Fishburne, and Carrie-Anne Moss. 1999. Burbank, Calif.: Warner Brothers.

The Matrix Reloaded. Directed by Andy and Lana Wachowski. Performed by Keanu Reeves, Laurence Fishburne, and Carrie-Anne Moss. 2003. Burbank, Calif.: Warner Brothers.

The Matrix Revolutions. Directed by Andy and Lana Wachowski. Performed by Keanu Reeves, Laurence Fishburne, and Carrie-Anne Moss. 2003. Burbank, Calif.: Warner Brothers.

Mean Girls. Directed by Mark Waters. Performed by Lindsay Lohan. 2004. Los Angeles: Paramount Pictures.

Miss Congeniality. Directed by Donald Petrie. Performed by Sandra Bullock and Benjamin Bratt. 2000. Hollywood, Calif.: Castle Rock Entertainment.

Mister Roberts. Directed by John Ford and Mervyn LeRoy. Performed by Henry Fonda and James Cagney. 1955. Burbank, Calif.: Warner Brothers.

Modern Family. Performed by Ed O'Neill, Sofía Vergara, Julie Bowen, Ty Burrell, Jesse Tyler Ferguson, Eric Stonestreet, Sarah Hyland, Ariel Winter, Nolan Gould, Rico Rodriguez, and Aubrey Anderson-Emmons. 2009–present. Burbank, Calif.: ABC.

Move Over Darling. Directed by Michael Gordon. Performed by Doris Day and James Garner. 1963. n.p., Arcola Pictures.

Mr. Mom. Directed by Stan Dragoti. Performed Michael Keaton and Teri Garr. 1983. Culver City, Calif.: Metro Goldwyn Mayer.

My Big Fat Greek Wedding. Directed by Joel Zwick. Performed by Nia Vardalos and John Corbett. 2002. Beverly Hills, Calif.: Gold Circle Films.

My Fair Lady. Directed by George Cukor. Performed by Audrey Hepburn and Rex Harrison. 1964. Burbank, Calif.: Warner Brothers.

My Favorite Wife. Directed by Garson Kanin. Performed by Irene Dunn and Cary Grant. 1940. Los Angeles: RKO.

New Girl. Television program. Performed by Zooey Deschanel. 2011–present. Los Angeles: Fox.

The Next Food Network Star. Television program. Performed by Marc Summers. 2005–present. New York: Food Network.

The Next Iron Chef. Television program. Performed by Alton Brown and Mark Dacascos. 2007–12. New York: Food Network.

The Nutty Professor. Directed by Jerry Lewis. Performed by Jerry Lewis and Stella Stevens. 1963. Los Angeles: Paramount Pictures.

The Nutty Professor. Directed by Tom Shadyac. Performed by Eddie Murphy and Jada Pinkett Smith. 1996. Beverly Hills, Calif.: Imagine Entertainment.

Ocean's Eleven. Directed by Lewis Milestone. Performed by Frank Sinatra, Dean Martin, and Sammy Davis Jr. 1960. Burbank, Calif.: Warner Brothers.

Ocean's Eleven. Directed by Steven Soderbergh. Performed by George Clooney, Brad Pitt, and Matt Damon. 2001. Burbank, Calif.: Warner Brothers.

Ocean's Twelve. Directed by Steven Soderbergh. Performed by George Clooney, Brad Pitt, and Matt Damon. 2004. Burbank, Calif.: Warner Brothers.

Ocean's Thirteen. Directed by Steven Soderbergh. Performed by George Clooney, Brad Pitt, and Matt Damon. 2007. Burbank, Calif.: Warner Brothers.

101 Dalmations. Directed by Clyde Geronomi and Hamilton Luske. Performed by Rod Taylor, Betty Lou Gerson. 1961. Burbank, Calif.: Walt Disney Pictures.

The Pacifier. Directed by Adam Shankman. Performed by Vin Diesel and Lauren Graham. 2005. Burbank, Calif.: Walt Disney Pictures.

Pimp My Ride. Television program. Performed by Mad Mike. 2004–7. New York: MTV.

Project Runway. Television program. Performed by Heidi Klum and Tim Gunn. 2004–present. 2004–8, New York: Bravo; 2009–present, New York: Lifetime.

Pygmalion. Directed by Anthony Asquith. Performed by Leslie Howard and Wendy Hiller. 1938. n.p., Gabriel Pascal Productions.

Queer Eye for the Straight Guy. Television program. Performed by Ted Allen and Carson Kressley. 2003–7. New York: Bravo.

Paris Is Burning. Directed by Jennie Livingston. Performed by Carmen and Brooke. 1990. New York: Art Matters.

Ramsay's Kitchen Nightmares. Television program. Performed by Gordon Ramsay. 2004–14. London: BBC Channel 4.

Restaurant: Impossible. Television program. Performed by Robert Irvine. 2011–present. New York: Food Network.

Sex and the City. Television program. Performed by Sarah Jessica Parker, Kim Cattrall, Kristin Davis, and Cynthia Nixon. 1998–2004. New York: HBO.

Shallow Hal. Directed by Bobby and Peter Farrelly. Performed by Jack Black and Gwyneth Paltrow. 2001. Los Angeles: Twentieth Century Fox Film Corporation.

Shrek. Directed by Andrew Adamson and Vicki Jenson. Performed by Mike Myers and Eddie Murphy. 2001. Universal City, Calif.: DreamWorks Studios.

Shrek 2. Directed by Andrew Adamson and Kelly Asbury. Performed by Mike Myers and Eddie Murphy. 2004. Universal City, Calif.: Dream-Works Studios.

Shrek the Third. Directed by Raman Hui and Chris Miller. Performed by Mike Myers and Eddie Murphy. 2007. Universal City, Calif.: Dream-Works Studios.

Shrek Forever After. Directed by Mike Mitchell. Performed by Mike Myers and Eddie Murphy. 2010. Universal City, Calif.: DreamWorks Studios.

Skyfall. Directed by Sam Mendes. Performed by Daniel Craig. 2012. London: Eon Productions.

Some Like It Hot. Directed by Billy Wilder. Performed by Jack Lemmon and Tony Curtis. 1959. Los Angeles: Ashton Productions.

The Sopranos. Television program. Performed by James Gandolfini. 1999–2007. New York: HBO.

Spider-Man. Directed by Sam Raimi. Performed by Tobey Maguire and Kirsten Dunst. 2002. Culver City, Calif.: Columbia Pictures.

Spider-Man 2. Directed by Sam Raimi. Performed by Tobey Maguire and Kirsten Dunst. 2004. Culver City, Calif.: Columbia Pictures.

Spider-Man 3. Directed by Sam Raimi. Performed by Tobey Maguire and Kirsten Dunst. 2007. Culver City, Calif.: Columbia Pictures.

Star Wars: Episode II—Attack of the Clones. Directed by George Lucas. Performed by Ewan McGregor and Natalie Portman. 2002. San Francisco: Lucasfilm.

The Swan. Television program. Performed by Amanda Byram. 2004–5. Los Angeles: Fox.

S.W.A.T. Directed by Clark Johnson. Performed by Samuel L. Jackson and Colin Farrell. 2003. Los Angeles: Sony Pictures.

Tabatha's Salon Takeover. Television program. Performed by Tabatha Coffey. 2008–present. New York: Bravo.

The Terminator. Directed by James Cameron. Performed by Arnold Schwarzenegger and Linda Hamilton. 1984. Los Angeles: Hemdale Film Corporation.

Terminator 2: Judgment Day. Directed by James Cameron. Performed by Arnold Schwarzenegger and Linda Hamilton. 1991. Beverly Hills, Calif.: Carolco Pictures.

The Thrill of It All. Directed by Norman Jewison. Performed by Doris Day and James Garner. 1963. Universal City, Calif.: Universal International Pictures.

This Old House. Television program. 1979–present. Performed by Norm Abram and Tom Silva. Arlington, Va.: PBS.

Toddlers and Tiaras. Television program. 2009–present. Silver Spring, Md.: TLC.

Top Chef. Television program. Performed by Padma Lakshmi and Tom Colicchio. 2006–present. New York: Bravo.

Top Gun. Directed by Tony Scott. Performed by Tom Cruise and Anthony Edwards. 1986. Los Angeles: Paramount Pictures.

Training Day. Directed by Antoine Fuqua. Performed by Denzel Washington and Ethan Hawke. 2001. Los Angeles: Warner Brothers.

True Lies. Directed by James Cameron. Performed by Arnold Schwarzenegger and Jamie Lee Curtis. 1994. Los Angeles: Twentieth Century Fox Film Corporation.

Two and a Half Men. Television program. Performed by Jon Cryer, Charlie Sheen, and Ashton Kutcher. 2003–15. Los Angeles: CBS.

2 Broke Girls. Television program. Performed by Kat Dennings and Beth Behrs. 2011–present. Los Angeles: CBS.

Venus Boyz. Directed by Gabrielle Baur. Performed by Diane Torr and Dréd Gerestant. 2002. Riverdale, Md.: Clockwise Productions.

Victor Victoria. Directed by Blake Edwards. Performed by James Garner and Julie Andrews. 1982. Culver City, Calif.: Metro Goldwyn Mayer.

What Not to Wear. Television program. Performed by Stacy London and Clinton Kelly. 2003–present. Silver Spring, Md.: TLC.

Will & Grace. Television program. Performed by Eric McCormack and Debra Messing. 1998–2006. New York: NBC.

Index

Judith Roof is William Shakespeare Chair in English at Rice University. She has authored books on feminist, narrative, and lesbian theory, including *A Lure of Knowledge: Lesbian Sexuality and Theory; Come as You Are: Sexuality and Narrative*, recipient of Narrative's Perkins Prize; and *All about Thelma and Eve: Sidekicks and Third Wheels*. She has also written about contemporary culture in *Reproductions of Reproduction* and *The Poetics of DNA* (Minnesota, 2007).